Our Friend Mona

Our Friend Mona

by
Azadeh Rohanian Perry

with
Mark Perry

CIRCLE OF SPIRIT
Chapel Hill, North Carolina

Circle of Spirit Publications
 c/o Drama Circle
P.O. Box 3844
Chapel Hill, NC 27515 USA

Email: info@dramacircle.org
Website: www.circleofspirit.org

Cover art by Parisa Nourani Rinaldi

Our Friend Mona

17 18 19 20 21 22   10 9 8 7 6 5 4 3 2

To the Youth of the World

And were anyone to say unto them on their way,
"Whither go ye?"
they would say,
"Unto God, the All-Possessing,
the Help in Peril, the Self-Subsisting!"

Bahá'u'lláh

Table of Contents

Preface & Acknowledgments

This book is about the life of the young martyr, Mona Mahmudnizhad. Mona had many, many friends. I was one among probably hundreds of them, and we all have memories of her. Some knew her better than I did, and they could fill a book with just their memories.

My husband Mark and I decided to put this book together because there is no single volume available on Mona's life. There are several important books that share the stories of the persecution of the Bahá'ís of Iran, and some of them provided important source material for this work. We could see that Mona's life, although brief, would easily fill a book of its own. We especially felt moved to share the story in a manner understandable to youth and junior youth.

Some people may wonder about putting so much focus on just one of the many Bahá'í heroes and heroines from the years just after Iran's Revolution. One special value in Mona's story is the light that it sheds on the stories around her. My family was also blessed to be linked with the Mahmudnizhad family. So it seemed like the right path to take, and we have felt confirmed in our effort.

While Mark and I have put this book together, we must credit a third contributor. That is Mona's mother, Mrs. Farkhundih Mahmudnizhad, who told the stories of her famous daughter and saintly husband tirelessly for 28 years until her passing in 2011. Her writings about Mona and her father, both published and unpublished, have provided a large amount of the material in this book. This book is a continuation of her attempt to share with the world the stories of their unbelievable heroism and love.

Many Bahá'í friends have taken time to record her words and those of her older daughter, Taraneh. We are grateful to them and to Taraneh for her assistance. There are so many friends, inside and outside Iran, whose ongoing sacrifice and example have contributed directly and indirectly to this effort. This includes the sharing of precious photographs, some of which are included in this volume and others of which are available online via the website www.circleofspirit.org.

We received generous support from Wildacres Retreat and the UNC Institute of Arts and Humanities, and thanks go to Tim Marr and Adam Versenyi for opening up these opportunities. We are grateful for the assistance of Phyllis Ring with editing and Vahid Nourani with translation. With the help of many, we have tried to check all the facts to make sure we give you the story as faithful as possible to the real events. Still, if you have any corrections or clarifications, please feel free to share them with the publisher to be considered for any future printings.

—Azi (and Mark)

Mona

Introduction

Mona was a sixteen-year-old girl who gave her life for unity and peace for all humanity. Her life was taken because of hate and ignorance. The people who killed her thought they could use force and terror to break her religious faith and make her obey them instead. They thought by putting her to death, they could inspire fear in others like her. They failed. Instead, Mona's story has become a source of courage, hope and inspiration not only to people in her own country but to millions around the world. As you read her story, you will see how Mona was not just a victim. She was a hero.

Mona was my friend, and I'd like to share her story with you. My name is Azadeh, which means "freedom." My family and friends call me Azi. (It's pronounced AH-zee). I am from a country called Iran, where we speak the Persian language. Iran is a very old country with a wonderful culture and a rich history, and I encourage you to learn about it. In recent years though, Iran has faced a lot of trouble. The story I'm going to tell you took place mostly in the years 1979 to 1983 when I was between the ages of 12 and 16.

In 1979, the government of Iran was taken over by men with extreme religious beliefs. They did not believe that religion is meant to promote love and unity and create ties of friendship and fellowship among different people. Instead, they think everyone else should believe just as they do or else they will use force including violence, torture and death. Many Iranians have suffered terribly because of this government, including my friends and family. I, along with some of my brothers and sisters, escaped the country a number of years ago. We found refuge in countries that allow freedom of religion, places where we could have our beliefs and practice our religion openly and peacefully. While I miss my family members who still live in Iran, I am grateful for this freedom.

I am from a city called Shiraz. It is famous in Iran for a number of things, including poetry, flowers and gardens, and, apparently, pretty girls! It is also famous because it is where my religion began. My religion is called the Bahá'í Faith, and it started in 1844 when a young man called "The Báb" (or "The Gate") declared that a New Age was dawning for all humanity. He said this was a time when the promises of all religions would come true and the world would be united like one country and one people.

Mona was also from Shiraz. She and her family had moved there when she was about seven years old. I didn't meet her until many years later, however, because we lived in different areas of the city. In fact, I met her father first. What a wonderful man! I loved him very much and I remember clearly the first time I met him.

I'm from a big family and we lived in a big house. It was always full of children and youth, and our door was always open to everyone. I am actually the youngest of nine children, and so I would spend a lot of my time with my nephews and nieces that are my same age. Some of my older brothers and sisters had started attending classes for Bahá'í youth that were being held at our house. They spoke about the teacher, how gentle and knowledgeable he was. I was 12 years old and not old enough to join them. School was out, but I and the other children would go to one of my older sisters' homes for the day while the classes were going on. Whenever we came back home, the teacher and the class would be gone. I was curious about this man that had impressed my family so much.

So one day I decided to stay home, and I waited in the hallway for 3 o'clock, when the teacher would come and the class would start.

I was a little short for 12, but I had very long black hair and an independent spirit. I was usually more interested in the adventures and pranks my nephews were getting into than the activities girls were supposed to do, such as helping in the kitchen.

The door opened. My sister, Monir (*Muní r*)*, came in with some other youth. Monir was 22 and had volunteered to be the teacher's assistant, to help organize schedules and take notes. She was followed by a man in his forties with a kind, smiling face. This was certainly their teacher. This was Mr. Mahmudnizhad (*Mahmúdni<u>zh</u>ád*).

"Alláh-u-abhá," I said, standing up. This is an expression Bahá'ís use to greet one another. It means "God is most glorious."

"Alláh-u-abhá," replied the teacher, his loving eyes fixing themselves on me. I was a little anxious.

"What's your name, my dear?"

"Azadeh."

"Azadeh … Very good, very good. 'Freedom.' Your sister, Monir, has told me about you."

He hugged me, not worrying about it being the first time we'd met. He had a loving embrace that came from deep inside, as if he found God in everyone he met. That meant no one was a stranger to him. The youth had continued on their way into the house while their teacher continued to talk with me.

"How precious you are." He bent down a little to look me in the eye, and stroked my hair like a loving father would.

---

* When a new Persian name is mentioned, I will generally follow it with its proper transliteration in parentheses. After that, a simpler version of the name will be used. Transliteration helps people know how the name is written in the original language. The transliteration for Mona would be Muná, and Azadeh would be Ázádih.

"Azadeh, my dear, look at your beautiful, shining hair."

He then pointed out the window and said, "I wish I could take down a bright star from the sky out there and put it in your shining hair."

A thrill raced through me. The depth and sincerity of his love melted away any anxiety I felt. I don't remember if I said anything else.

"Call me Amu," he said. In Persian, Amu (*'Amú*) means uncle. And then he waved goodbye and went to his class.

He had taken only a few moments with me, but that is one of my most precious memories even to this day. It makes me wonder at the power of when we first meet people. Most other people would have said hello and walked away, but he took time to be with me and share his love, and it made such a difference.

And this was the example he set for others. It was this bright light inside him that would help guide his daughter Mona so far down her own spiritual path, so that, at such a young age, she would cause the whole world to marvel.

Amu became part of our household. My parents even gave him his own room so that he could rest, since he lived quite far away. He used our home regularly to teach classes for those Bahá'í youth who were college age. This was 1980, and the previous year, my country had experienced a Revolution. All the Bahá'í students had been kicked out of the universities just because of their religion. They were understandably upset and not sure what to do. This was a time of large demonstrations in the streets. Young people were joining different political groups, some with extreme points of view. The Bahá'í youth wondered whether they should also protest publicly, like many of their friends.

One night, Amu had a dream of Bahá'u'lláh, who is the Prophet who founded the Bahá'í Faith and whose coming had been announced by the Báb. Bahá'u'lláh suffered difficulty, imprisonment and exile throughout His life for teachings that called for the unity and oneness of all people. In the dream, Bahá'u'lláh took a red apple and cut it into four pieces. He then handed Amu the pieces as if he should do something with them. Thinking about this dream, Amu decided that the apple symbolized the youth and especially the university students. Now that their schooling had been interrupted, their sense of purpose and direction had been divided like the pieces of an apple. He believed it was his job to make them whole again and he could do this by sacrificing his time and teaching them what he knew.

Amu was not a university professor, but he had a lot to teach. First, he was very knowledgeable about the Bahá'í Faith and its teachings. He was trained professionally in radio engineering, and he had worked for a large international company before the Revolution, selling and repairing TVs and radios. When the Revolution came, he lost that job not because he was a bad worker, but because he was a Bahá'í. Teaching these youth would now become his full-time job, sharing his understanding and opening them up to the power of love that he himself embodied.

He made everyone in our family feel special. Sometimes during his lunch break, he would take the time to drive me back to school and he would talk to me about my life. Other times, he would take my young niece to the park. She had started showing signs of a learning disability, but he was always encouraging, telling the family not to worry about her and that she would one day go to university herself. Like the rest of us, she developed a deep attachment to him.

"54 ... 55 ... 56"

I was making my way up the five flights of stairs to the Mahmudnizhads' apartment. At 12 years old, counting steps is a natural way of dealing with them. There was no elevator, and counting gave you something to do. It's a way to measure your progress, like moving prayer beads on a string.

"66 ... 67 ..."

I looked up, knowing I was almost there. I was surprised to see a beautiful girl standing there at the top looking down at me. She had long brown hair, green eyes, and a beautiful smile. I stopped in my tracks and forgot my counting.

"Hi," the girl said. She wore a dark blue coat and seemed to be on her way out.

I knew this must be Amu's daughter. She had his same smile, his same radiance, and his same openness of spirit. She didn't have that thing that many adolescents have of being self-conscious.

"I'm Mona."

I introduced myself. While I was just a year younger, the difference in our ages seemed greater because Mona was beginning to mature physically. Still she was eager to befriend me and make me feel welcome.

"Please don't leave. I'll be back soon, and then we can get to know each other better." She was on her way out on an errand.

"Hello, Mona."

My sisters, Monir and Shahin (_Shahin_), had caught up to me on the stairs and exchanged greetings with Mona, too. We then went down the hall to the apartment, while Mona went on her errand.

The three of us had come to visit Amu's wife, Mona's mother. Her name was Farkhundih (_Farkhundih_), and she had been sick. In Iran, the custom is to visit people when they are sick (unlike in some countries in the West).

The apartment was small, but nicely decorated. It had two bedrooms, one for Mona and one for her parents. Mona's older sister, Taraneh (*Taránih*), had recently gotten married and moved out. When we were inside, Mrs. Mahmudnizhad thanked Monir for helping her a few days earlier. She had been so sick that she had needed to go to the doctor, but the authorities had closed down all the streets except to authorized vehicles. Monir is a resourceful person. She had contacted a neighbor of ours who worked for the Mayor of Shiraz. Monir had met this man when she was a newspaper reporter and had interviewed the Mayor. That was before the Revolution, when Bahá'ís could still work for the newspapers. Monir had called this influential man to get permission for a car to drive Mrs. Mahmudnizhad to a doctor, and he had arranged it.

I peeked into Mona's room. I could see the light from her window coming through the bright blue curtains.

My sisters talked with Mrs. Mahmudnizhad about her health and about the conditions in the country. Things were getting worse, with different political and religious groups fighting and killing each other. None of these groups were friendly towards the Bahá'ís, even though the Bahá'ís are peaceful and welcoming of others. The main group that had come to power after the Revolution was the Islamic clergy, the Mullas, and they hated the Bahá'í Faith. They wanted to rip it up by the roots the way you would tear out a tree, so no sign of it would remain. We knew their coming to power was bad news for us, but times were still uncertain. We had no idea how bad it would get.

Mona came back like she had told me she would. She made us feel very welcome and showed us hospitality, offering us something to drink. Afterwards, she invited me into her room. It was neat and inviting, with lots of blue in it. Blue was her favorite color. Her curtains, her bedspread and many other items were made of this bright, blue- and-white checkered fabric. She loved to do arts and crafts. She had made drawings, posters and flower arrangements, and even though she was only 13, she had sewn or embroidered many of the decorations in her room herself.

Much of her artwork was inspired in some way by the Bahá'í teachings. For example, she had made a number of cushions. Most had flowers decorating them. On one of the cushions, though, she had embroidered a doll. The doll had eyes, but no ears and no mouth. Mona said she had made the doll this way because sometimes her friends would come over and start to backbite. She wanted to teach them to hear no evil and speak no evil. Speaking about other people's faults is strongly forbidden in the Bahá'í teachings, because it damages trust and unity. Bahá'u'lláh said:

> Hear no evil, and see no evil, abase not thyself, neither sigh and weep. Speak no evil, that thou mayest not hear it spoken unto thee, and magnify not the faults of others that thine own faults may not appear great ... [1]

You see how creative Mona was, to come up with this gentle way to teach a lesson to her friends. I was very impressed with her many good qualities. From that day, my friendship with Mona began. It's a friendship I still value to this day.

One of the qualities I really admired in her was her openness. She was not shy in the least. If she wanted to cry, she would cry. If she wanted to dance, she would dance. She didn't worry too much about what people would think or say.

Some months later, we were together during a holiday called Naw Rúz. This is the Iranian New Year, and we celebrate it on the first day of spring. Naw Rúz is also a holy day for Bahá'ís around the world. In Iran, there are about two weeks of celebrations that go on at Naw Rúz time. People celebrate by offering hospitality and visiting their families and friends. The Mahmudnizhads had come over to visit our home at this time, and we all had lunch together. My mother had made *Sabzí Polo Máhí*, a traditional holiday dish of Herb Rice with Fish. We enjoyed the delicious food and each other's company. Mona was very intrigued with my mother's carefully prepared *Sofreh*—that is, the traditional display of Naw Rúz decorations, also known as *Haft-Sín*. My sister promised to help Mona with her own *Haft-Sín* display the following year.

Soon it was time to go visiting other family and friends. So ten of us—my parents, me, and four of my siblings, plus Mona and her parents, all piled into Amu's car, everyone on another's lap. We must have been quite a sight going down the road in the silver Paykán car, laughing and bursting the seams!

My sister asked Mona to chant. Mona had a lovely voice for chanting prayers. This is something that Bahá'ís in Iran do regularly. We don't just speak a prayer or whisper it to ourselves. We like to set the words to a melody and sing it. This is called chanting, and chanted prayers can be so beautiful that they take you into another world. Mona had recently memorized a new prayer. When my sister asked her to chant it, she wasn't shy or nervous. She folded her arms, closed her eyes, and began the prayer. Everyone else was quiet while the car continued down the road filled with Mona's sweet voice.

Amu pulled the car up to my aunt's house. My parents, my brother Daniel (*Dányál*) and I got out—the rest were all going to the home of another Bahá'í friend. I was really mad, because I wanted to be with Mona and the others, but my mom told me I needed to go with her. As the car drove away, everyone in it waved and laughed, and I complained in my mother's ear all the way to my aunt's door.

A few days later, I was able to see Mona again. It was still Naw Rúz time, and our family friend, Mahvash Vahdat (*Mahvash Vahdat*), invited some youth, including me and my siblings, to lunch. She was showing the town to some visiting friends and wanted us to join.

Mahvash was in her late 20s, and she was funny, bold, and outspoken. Her family would suffer enormously in the next couple of years. Today, however, Mahvash was taking us to eat at the fancy Kúrosh hotel, a well-known spot for tourists. I was excited to go. Here I was 12 and Mona was 13, and we were going out with all these older youth. We took some pictures together inside the elegant hotel while we waited for Mahvash's friends. We enjoyed a good lunch with lots of laughs. Mahvash then invited us all to go to the Eram garden. It was a beautiful spring day in Shiraz, perfect to walk around, do some sight-seeing and enjoy the holiday atmosphere. Unfortunately, right after lunch, Mona had to go. My sister had to take her back. This time I was staying where the fun was, and it was Mona who had to go. We all waved goodbye.

I remember one very special night. It started with a conversation. Amu had stayed for dinner with us after his classes and after the youth had gone home. He and my family were sitting in the living room after dinner talking about the situation in Iran. What were we Bahá'ís supposed to do? we wondered. None of us had ever lived in such a time as this, and things were changing so fast around us.

Things were not great for the Bahá'ís before the Revolution, when the Sháh, the King of Iran, was still in power. There were times when his government would look the other way while the Islamic religious leaders told their followers to mistreat the Bahá'ís. The people would then go abuse some unfortunate families, vandalize their property or drive them out of a village, and they believed this was their religious duty and what God wanted them to do.

I listened as the adults talked. Before 1979, the government was not run by the religious leaders. The Sháh, and his father, who was king before him, both wanted to bring to Iran the material benefits, the technology and some of the liberal ideas of the western world. I grew up watching western television programs like *Little House on the Prairie* and *Star Trek*. (I was terrified of Mr. Spock and his pointed ears!) We listened to western music, we wore western clothes. We felt part of the greater world. The airports were open and we could fly to any country. The TV and newspapers shared stories from all different countries. We could read books that opened our minds to new ideas. I had dreams of growing up to be a child psychologist.

Now, that life seemed to be going up in smoke. Now that the clergy was in power, they were turning the country in another direction, an old direction. The conversation was animated as my older siblings added their points of view. We girls now had to wear head scarves to cover up our hair in school and in public. A female couldn't be seen with a man in public if he was not a family member, even if you were just friends. Guards were everywhere forcing us to follow new rules. Many books were banned. Western music, television and movies were forbidden. On the TV, they had people chanting the Qur'án, the holy book of Islam, and they broadcast heavily-censored news. We only heard the stories the clergy wanted us to hear. In school, we were pushed to curse America and Israel.

And for Bahá'ís, things looked even worse. All who worked as public employees—teachers, social workers, and other civil servants—lost their jobs. All other employers were pressured by the clergy to fire the Bahá'ís. Universities no longer admitted Bahá'í students, and we could even be expelled from primary and secondary schools. The damage was represented in the lives of those talking together in this living room: My older siblings had been fired from jobs, expelled from schools, or prohibited from attending. Our family was able to stay fed and housed only because of my father's pension from his career in the military. He was retired, and my mother worked hard raising a large family and serving her community. She did not, however, work outside the home, like most

Iranian women of her generation. My mother and father were wonderful role models of faith and selfless service. I cannot express how grateful I am to them for all they have done for me.

Amu had lost his job too, of course. He was able to get a little work helping some friends in business with their accounting, but he basically threw himself into full-time service. His wife made some money with her sewing, and so the family kept going.

The discussion turned to what should be the next steps for the Bahá'ís: How should we live our lives now that we were a target of discrimination and persecution? Should we hide? Should we leave Shiraz? We discussed the idea of sacrifice and the idea of wisdom. With sacrifice, you choose to give up something to achieve a greater purpose. With wisdom, you don't sacrifice randomly, but you choose which course of action will be most effective. Maybe we should stop or reduce our teaching, which is to say, openly sharing information about the Bahá'í Faith?

Here Amu was crystal clear in his word and in his deed: Teaching others about Bahá'u'lláh's message is essential for humanity to grow and move past the very dark days of ignorance and violence that now threaten our country and the planet. If we stop promoting unity and stay quiet about overcoming prejudices— religious, racial, national, ethnic and gender, humanity will die as a result of its ignorance. In despair, it will commit suicide. We work to bring hope and spirit and love back into the world. We know we are not the only ones who believe this way, and that is why we search out other people who want to join us in our mission. Bahá'u'lláh's teachings are a rich source of hope and spiritual promise for this country and the planet. It can transform this war-torn world into a reflection of the kingdom of heaven. How can we keep from sharing it? Even if that means that we suffer because we do so.

Amu always seemed to be able to see the spiritual way, even in the darkest of times. I know he was not perfect, and he had struggles like everyone else. But he was one of the most perfect men I've ever known.

We asked: What should we do? Should we leave the city? Should we wait and see? My father was getting older and he had a number of young, unmarried daughters to look after. He didn't say this in so many words, but how could he protect us if the guards or a mob came to the house and wanted to take us?

The spirit in that room was strong. When people speak the truth out loud, it seems to change the air in the room. We didn't have all the answers, but the questions helped us reflect on our deepest purpose in life.

The subject changed to how my parents became Bahá'ís. Most Iranians can trace their religion back several generations, many even to the 1800s, to the time of the Báb and Bahá'u'lláh. My mother, father and Amu were unusual, however, in that they had each learned of the Bahá'í Faith on their own, each when they were youth.

My parents' stories were familiar to me. My father and mother had each been raised Shí'ih Muslim. Shí'ih is the branch of Islam that most people in Iran follow. Both my parents lost their fathers when they were young. My dad was taken away from his mother as a toddler to live with his father's family, even though he didn't know them. This was very painful for him, but it was the accepted practice of the time. My parents married young—when my father was in his early 20s and my mother was 13—in an arranged marriage. They didn't even know each other. Again, this was the accepted practice for Muslims in that time. And my mother was relatively old, since Muslim girls could be married as young as 9!

It turned out, fortunately, that my parents were both spiritual people and they learned to love each other deeply. They both heard of the Bahá'í Faith in their teens or twenties.* My father accepted first, but he placed no pressure on my mother. She had a series of dreams that helped her see the truth in the Bahá'í Faith. (Those dreams are for another story.) The bad part was that when they became Bahá'ís, their families either rejected them or treated them poorly.

Amu remarked on the similarity of his story to theirs. I really wanted to hear Amu's story. Hearing Bahá'ís tell the stories of how they found the Faith is like hearing the story of how a couple fell in love. I noticed, however, my eyelids were starting to get heavy. It was 9 o'clock already. I went and got another cup of tea to help me stay awake.

Finally, it was Amu's turn to tell his story. I waited, but he hesitated. You see he didn't often share this story. It was a long story with a lot of pain associated with it. And so much of the time he listened to others' stories. In fact, he had not even told his daughter Mona the complete story of how he came to find the Faith. So he was hesitating because he didn't want to share his story and not have Mona there to hear it. It was her story, too. They had a very special connection, Mona and her father.

"I'm sorry," he said, "I want to tell you the story, but I want Mona to hear it, too. Would it be okay with you if I went home and picked up Mona and came back?"

They lived 25 minutes away, so it would be 10pm before he'd be back.

My parents agreed that that would be fine. We all loved Amu and wanted to do whatever he asked.

It's okay?

---

* My father later discovered that, coincidentally, his father had become a Baha'i himself, only a year or two before he died.

It's okay.

No taarof?

No taarof.

This *taarof* is when Persian people are being polite but don't necessarily mean what they say. So saying, "No taarof?" is like saying, "You really mean it?"

He quickly left with a promise to be back.

This was going to be tough for me, because I have always been trained to wake up early and go to bed early. This was a special night though—not only did I want to hear the story, but now I really wanted to see Mona. I needed to be awake. But maybe, I thought to myself, if I just closed my eyes and took a little nap until he came back …

I awoke to someone crying loudly, a girl. It wasn't my sisters. I knew what their cries sounded like. I looked and Mona was there, but she wasn't the happy Mona I had always known. She was sobbing uncontrollably. Her father had been telling his story. He was now at the tail end of it. I had missed almost the whole thing!

Still, I was happy to be there with my family and with Amu and Mona. I just hoped that they wouldn't leave now that I was awake. These were souls I loved to be with, even if I was tired. Do you know what that feels like, to be with someone that you love and don't want to be separated from?

So I heard only the last part of the story. Mona kept crying. I think she was both sad for her father's pain and difficulty and grateful for the journey he had taken and the faith that he had found. His discovery was indeed her treasure.

When he finished, it was very late and Mona was still filled with such heavy emotions. Amu said, "I can't take her home like this." So he agreed to let her sleep over. I was very happy, and still a little bit awake, so I got a chance to talk to my friend. After her father left, we talked about school and how it was odd that both of us were still able to go to school when so many of the Bahá'í children had been expelled. We laughed because some children were happy not to go to school. Not us, though. We both wanted to learn. After such an emotional night, our hearts felt quite close.

I had a sleepover that night with a 13-year-old girl who, within three years, would become one of the greatest spiritual lights of our generation. But that night, she was just my friend Mona. And I fought to stay awake just a little longer, to push up my drooping eyelids, to make that special moment last.

The next morning my mother had made breakfast for everyone and we all ate together. That day, they told me the story I had missed the night before, about how Amu discovered the Bahá'í Faith.

Mona (left), Azi (center), with Rohanian
siblings and Mahvash Vahdat

PART ONE

Amu's Story

"I have something for you,
but you can't open it just yet."

Amu was born in June 1932 into a Shí'ih Muslim family. His parents called him Jamshid (*Jam<u>sh</u>íd*), which is an old Persian name. He had two older sisters, and the family lived in Tabriz, a city in the north of Iran. Sadly, both his parents died when he was young—his mother when he was 7, his father when he was 11. So the orphaned boy went to live with an uncle.

This uncle was quite old, but very wealthy. Almost fifty years earlier, he had held a position in the court of Násiri'd-Dín Sháh. (This was the same king who had allowed the Báb to be executed, Bahá'u'lláh to suffer terrible imprisonment and exile, and tens of thousands of their followers to be slaughtered.) The uncle had always been very involved in politics. The 1940s were a time of great political unrest and activity. World War II was raging, and Iran was invaded by the Allies for its close ties to Germany.

Now this uncle was quite fond of his nephew, whom he called Yadu'llah (*Yadu'lláh*). This is an Arabic name meaning "The Hand of God." It was actually the name on his birth certificate, and it was the name that Amu used from then on. It was only his wife who later on called him Jamshid.

Unfortunately for young Yadu'llah, his uncle was also a serious alcoholic. He did not look after the boy well and would often behave strangely. He would give him unreasonable tasks to do. For example, he asked him to change the pool water by himself in the high heat of summer. He woke the boy up in the middle of the night in the cold wintertime and demanded he go out and walk to buy milk for the cat. Yadu'llah obeyed his uncle and he went, but he didn't have proper shoes or clothing. As a result, he suffered pain in his legs for the rest of his life.

His older sister heard he was having difficulty living with his uncle. She was married and lived a long way away, south of Tabriz, in a town called Andímeshk. It is in the Khuzestan province, not far from the Iraqi border. She invited him to come stay with her. It was a long trip, but he didn't have very many things to carry. The only school that he could go to was in a town called Dezfúl, quite far from his sister's home. So she bought him a bicycle, which he would ride every day.

As a youth, Yadu'llah had a love of truth and a deep desire to see a better world around him. At the same time, he didn't see religion as helping the world. It seemed to have a lot of superstition, or beliefs that are not practical or reasonable. Also, religious people seemed mainly interested in pushing other people to follow their way. So he didn't give it much attention. What he found appealing was politics. He was attracted for a time to the revolutionary attitude of a political group called the "Tudeh."

One day, Yadu'llah was in his Grade 9 history class, and the subject of the Bahá'í Faith came up. The teacher spoke about the life of the Báb. In 1844, the Báb had begun teaching His new Faith in Shiraz, and many people followed him. This included people who were educated and well-known. It even included prominent religious leaders. The Báb traveled to the city of Isfahan, and the same thing happened. More people followed him, including some well-known mullas and powerful rulers. The teacher was saying all this, but he was mocking the people of that time—how could they be so stupid as to follow the Báb?! He had the whole class laughing about this. Well, almost the whole class.

A boy who was sitting next to Yadu'llah leaned over and whispered to him: "If there was no truth to what the Báb said, then why would all these well-known, well-educated and faithful people follow him?" This got Yadu'llah thinking.

A short time later, the same boy came to visit Yadu'llah at his sister's home. He invited him to come stay at his home, because all his family was gone. They had gotten ill with jaundice and had left town to get treatment. Yadu'llah liked the boy, so the next morning he went.

When he arrived at the house, there seemed to be no one home. He went in and noticed two huge bookshelves in the living room. He didn't see anyone around, so he approached the bookshelves. They were full of books he didn't know. He chose two. One was called Borhán-i-Vázeh, or "The Clear Proof", and the other was called Kitáb-i-Íqán, or "The Book of Certitude." Certitude means certainty or strong faith. This second book is one of Bahá'u'lláh's most famous books.

Yadu'llah began to read, lost track of the time, and forgot about going to school that day. He was captivated by what he was reading. Today, these books would be his teachers.

In the afternoon, he looked up to see his friend. He was just returning home for the noon break. His friend saw that something had changed in Yadu'llah, in his face. They started talking. Yadu'llah had a lot of questions to be answered.

Yes, these were Bahá'í books. Yes, his friend was a Bahá'í. What was this Bahá'í Faith all about? The conversation continued for four hours. Yadu'llah drank it all in. Again, school and its style of education had been forgotten.

Over the next couple of months, his friend, whose last name was Haqqjú, invited some well-known Bahá'ís to come and speak to Yadu'llah about the Bahá'í Faith. Then, Yadu'llah's sister heard about this. She was very upset and confronted him:

What was he thinking? He had no business making crazy decisions like this on his own. He needed to go right back there and tell them he wasn't interested anymore.

He argued back. Up until now, he had been interested in politics and in radical movements. Now that he had found faith, now that he believed in God, she should be happy for him.

No, she said, if he had any interest in continuing to stay with her, he needed to go back and tell them he had no interest in this Bahai-Mahai stuff.

He stood his ground.

So his sister began to invite some local mullas, the Islamic clergy, to come to speak against these dangerous ideas and to persuade him back to the "straight path." One by one, they came, and the discussions would overheat and turn into arguments. The mullas would start to use bad language, which would make Yadu'llah upset and he would end the discussion. Finally, he told his sister he'd listen to no more of their arguments.

His sister had one last hope. There was a man in town who was well-respected by everyone for his piety, or spiritual devotion. He was known as a dervish, a member of the Sufi branch of Islam. Sufis focus on finding a close, mystical connection with God. They try to detach themselves from the everyday world and its concerns. This man was called Darvish Badi (*Darvísh Badî*); Badi means "wonderful." For Yadu'llah's sister, he was her last resort. Certainly, this spiritual man would not lose his temper, and he would be able to speak reasonably against this Bahá'í thing.

Yadu'llah resisted this.   He had heard the arguments of the mullas, and he saw no good reason to stop investigating this Bahá'í Faith. This new religion had so many helpful answers to his many religious questions and concerns.

She insisted. He told her "No." She insisted more. Finally, out of respect, he agreed to this one last time. He expected this would be no different than the previous encounters. So the meeting was arranged.

Darvish Badi smiled. Yadu'llah was respectful, while the sister served tea, and looked on. Darvish Badi began.

"Don't you think that the purpose of religion is to unite people?"

"Of course."

"And that all the religions come from one single Source, which is God, who created the pea and the pod, the sun and the speck, the universe outside us and the spiritual worlds within?"

"Most certainly."

The sister was pleased as she watched the discussion unfold. Darvish Badi seemed to be removing the youth's resistance with words like these.

Yadu'llah was warming up to the visitor. This man wasn't just repeating the same old closed-minded ideas like the others. He also wasn't using his age and experience to bully the young man into his way of thinking. He spoke words that rang true.

Darvish Badi then took Yadu'llah by the hand and stood up. He led him outside, where it is always easier to find the glories of God. The sister saw how well this was going and went back to her daily affairs. She was sure her brother was back on track.

"I have something for you," Darvish Badi said, his eyes gleaming. "But you can't open it just yet. Everything has its time and its place, you understand. We must learn to be patient in this life. So tomorrow morning, go to the top of that hill over there and sit under that tree. Then and there you should open this."

He handed Yadu'llah a package that he had brought with him. Yadu'llah went to take it, but Darvish Badi didn't let go.

"You promise to wait until tomorrow?"

Yadu'llah promised and took the package. With that, their meeting was ended.

That night the youth couldn't sleep. What could be in that package? It felt sort of like a book, but then what book was it? It could be about anything. Would it really change his mind about the Bahá'í Faith? What kind of book—if that's what it was—could possibly put that genie back in the bottle? Then again, Darvish Badi had not even mentioned the word "Bahá'í." He had spoken in a general manner that did not even try to argue against the Bahá'í position.

He started to think about his own thinking and behavior. Was he just being stubborn because of the attitudes of the clergy? Was there some basic flaw in the Bahá'í Faith he had not noticed? Darvish Badi seemed to have that spark of faith and understanding he had only found in the Bahá'ís up to this point.

At daybreak, he took the package and rode his bike to the top of the hill. He sat beneath the same tree pointed out by the dervish. As the sun came up, he opened the package.

It was a book. It was called "The Hidden Words." He opened it up and began to read. It didn't take long to figure out that this was a Bahá'í book, written by Bahá'u'lláh Himself. That meant Darvish Badi must be a Bahá'í! He was using the dervish costume or exterior as a cover to teach the Bahá'í Faith. He was hiding in plain sight.

Thrilled that he had this confirmation of his belief, Yadu'llah jumped on his bike and raced down the hill. He headed straight for town to find Darvish Badi. He found him in the middle of a Sufi ceremony with other worshipers around him. Darvish Badi welcomed him in. He invited the youth to sit in the seat on his right. This was a spot kept for well-known and respected people.

"You have found the Truth. This is your seat now."

After that, the youth and the dervish-with-a-secret became dear friends. Together they would read and discuss the Bahá'í writings. Together they were diving into the Sea of Truth. As Bahá'u'lláh says, *"Immerse yourselves in the ocean of my words, that ye may unravel its secrets, and discover all the pearls of wisdom that lie hid in its depths."*[2]

Yadu'lláh soon learned that the Bahá'í Faith was more than the truth in these books. He was meeting more Bahá'ís, and he came to understand that each individual Bahá'í was part of a worldwide movement. There were Bahá'ís in many different countries around the world, from different races and backgrounds. The center of the Bahá'í world was not even in Iran, where the Báb and Bahá'u'lláh were born. It was on the coast of Palestine (or Israel) in the cities of Haifa and Akka. This was where Bahá'u'lláh had been exiled and imprisoned and where He had died in 1892.

So the Bahá'ís around the world were now leaving their own homes to go and bring the Bahá'í teachings to new countries and peoples who had not yet heard of it. They called this 'pioneering.' They were going to places such as South America, the Pacific Islands and Africa. This pioneering effort was being organized from Haifa by Shoghi Effendi, who was the great grandson of Bahá'u'lláh. He was the leader of the Bahá'í Faith from 1921 to 1957. The Bahá'ís loved Shoghi Effendi very much and they called him the Guardian.

Learning about the Guardian's call for people to pioneer, the youth was ready to move.

"Wait, wait," the dervish counseled. "You aren't even finished with school yet. You will need that education before you go out into the world. The world needs you, but it needs you more with a well-trained mind."

Yadu'llah learned that each day has a new requirement. At one time, the Bahá'ís had been terribly persecuted by the Iranian government and the Muslim clergy. At that time, they needed to be steadfast, that is, to stand strong even if they were tortured or killed. Now, the Bahá'ís enjoyed more freedom so their challenge was to leave their homes and move to a foreign land. But the job of a 15- or 16-year-old was to be patient and dedicate himself to learning, so he could use that understanding to help himself and others.

Darvish Badi was wise. He suggested that the young man keep his religion secret until he finished high school. Then he could declare openly his Bahá'í belief and move where he wanted.

Yadu'llah agreed, but all that while, he was building his understanding not only of this world through his schooling, but of the spiritual world through his careful study of the Bahá'í teachings.

Pioneering

"The avowed, the primary aim of this Spiritual Crusade is none other than the conquest of the citadels of men's hearts. The theater of its operations is the entire planet. Its duration a whole decade ... " [3]

With words such as these, the Guardian called the Bahá'ís of the world to arise and join the "Ten Year Crusade." The year was 1953, and the goal was to take the message of Bahá'u'lláh to every country in the world. This had never been done before. The Bahá'ís were to spread out into every nation and to make a foreign land their new home. They were to make friends, get jobs, enter schools, learn the local languages and customs, and to share the precious teachings. They were to live and embody Bahá'u'lláh's central teaching that *"The earth is but one country, and mankind its citizens."*

Of course not every Bahá'í was able to pick up and go, but hundreds of heroic women and men did, and in the first several months. Some were youth, some were elderly; some had families, some were single; some were wealthy, some were poor; some went to large cities; some went to remote villages where outsiders had never visited; some chose places where they knew the language; others went where they did not know a single word.

Yadu'lláh was 20 years old when he heard about the Ten Year Crusade, and he decided he would pioneer. He had finished high school in 1949 and had openly declared himself a Bahá'í. This upset his older sister, at first, but she eventually came to accept his decision. One big question now was which country should he move to?

His first language had been Azerbaijani, which the people spoke in his home city of Tabriz. He learned Persian at school, and then when he moved to his sister's home in Khuzestan province. For a number of years he had been studying the Bahá'í writings, which are partly in Persian but mostly in Arabic. He had a head start, therefore, on a language spoken in more than 20 countries in the Middle East and in Northern Africa. He did not know much conversational Arabic, but he did know many of the same beautiful passages that he was hoping to share with others.

Yadu'llah said goodbye to his family, his friends and his homeland and headed west for the Arabian Peninsula. He believed the Bahá'í teachings would be like an oasis for spiritual seekers in those desert lands. He did not know when or whether he would return to Iran.

The first place he went was just across the Persian Gulf from Iran—a city called Dubai. Today Dubai is a huge, wealthy city. At that time, it was not much more than a small fishing and trading port. He did not have much success setting himself up as a pioneer there, so he and a few other Bahá'ís decided to move to Saudi Arabia. This is the country where the Prophet Muhammad came from and where Muslims travel each year for pilgrimage. Yadu'llah and the other men set out on the long boat ride from nearby Bahrain around the Arabian Peninsula to Saudi Arabia. That was about 2,800 miles or 4,500 kilometers, which is almost like crossing the Atlantic Ocean. So they had time to talk about their plans. When they arrived, Yadu'llah was quickly taken to a place where other Bahá'ís had gathered. They were all sick with diarrhea. After several days of uncertainty and no success securing a visa, Yadu'llah had no choice but to get back on a boat to sail all the way back to Bahrain!

Yadu'llah apparently took this as a sign. He set up for a time in Bahrain and later moved to a nearby country called Qatar. These are both very small countries in the Persian Gulf. In order to stay in these Arab countries as a foreigner, he needed to become an apprentice to a tradesperson. In Bahrain, he became an apprentice at a coffee shop. His purpose was not to make money, but to share the Bahá'í teachings. He decided, however, that he could do better with a trade. So he went to university to study radio engineering. This was before the time of television, when radio was very important and the main source of news and information. All the while, he was finding it hard to build relationships. He had been learning Arabic, but he was coming up against some cultural norms that excluded single men. Yadu'llah began thinking about getting married and starting a family.

Across the sea, in the Iranian city of Abadan, lived Miss Farkhundih Anvari (*Anvari*). She was 18 years old, and for years she had watched the boats docked there in the port. She would watch as they would untie, set sail and head off for Arab lands. She dreamed someday of heading off herself as a Bahá'í pioneer.

Farkhundih had been born to a Bahá'í family from Yazd on 10 May 1940. She was the second child in a large family and had lost her mother at a young age. Her family had relocated to Abadan when Farkhundih was about 10. In Abadan, her father was an assistant to the public prosecutor and eventually became the public prosecutor himself. She had learned about pioneering at the Bahá'í classes and other gatherings she attended as a youth.

One day, her aunt and uncle came to visit in Abadan. They were themselves pioneers, and they told her about a young man who was living in Qatar and seeking to get married. His name was Yadu'llah Mahmudnizhad, and he was a friend of her uncle's. So Farkhundih agreed to go visit, and she accompanied her aunt and uncle back to Qatar. On the way, they spoke to her of this young man: how kind and funny and spiritual and dedicated he was! You two will make a great match, they insisted. Evidently, the young couple agreed, and they were married on 1 October 1958.

Within a couple of years, Farkhundih gave birth to a baby girl. Yadu'llah chose for her the name "Taraneh" (*Taránih*), which means "song" or "melody." When Taraneh was still an infant, the young family decided to pioneer to another Arab country called Yemen.

They set sail for the city of Sanaa in North Yemen in early 1961. This trip was almost as long as the trip to Saudi Arabia! This time, however, they were on board a Japanese ship with passengers of various nationalities. Yadu'llah was delighted to be able to speak openly and not have the restraints against free speech that were ever present in the Arab countries. They arrived in Sanaa and met with the Imam himself, the king of North Yemen. He agreed they could stay on the condition that Yadu'llah would be an apprentice to the barber, Aqa Salmani (*Áqá Salmání*).

Yadu'llah went out and prepared a place for his young family to stay. He waited for the barber, who was supposed to come meet with him. But he didn't come. Then again, even if he did, what would he say when he learned Yadu'llah knew nothing about hairdressing? Yadu'llah worried this might be just another failed attempt at finding a pioneering post. He opened his heart in prayer to God: "I have arrived here, and the rest is in Your hand!"

There were some Iranian Bahá'ís already living in Sanaa. There was a pharmacist named Mr. Anvar (*Anvar*), who heard of the young family's situation. He went to the Imam and told him, "This man doesn't know how to cut hair. Why don't you let him come work for me?"

The Imam agreed, and just like that, the hand of God secured the family at their post. For a time.

The following year, the Imam died. His son was just being crowned when there was a coup d'etat. Rebels took over the city, cut the electricity and set fire to the Imam's house. The Mahmudnizhad family lived nearby and heard all the noise. Yadu'llah told his wife not to worry and that the gunfire and bombs were just fireworks celebrating the new king.

The rebels declared a new "Yemen Republic" and enforced a curfew, so no one could go out into the streets. At 1:30 a.m., soldiers came to their home. They accused the family of being spies and tore up the place looking for evidence. They confiscated most of their belongings and told them they had one week to get out of the country. The family escaped to South Yemen with one suitcase of clothes, a small rug and some forks, spoons and glasses.

South Yemen was a British colony. It was peaceful for a time, and the young Mahmudnizhad family was able to share their peaceful message. They settled in the city of Lahij, which already had 3 Bahá'í pioneer families living there. The men owned a shop, where Yadu'llah began to work as well at his trade of selling and repairing radios. This was a vital service, given the importance of radio. It was not very profitable, though. Many of the people who would come to the shop for repairs did not have money to pay. Also, as a matter of hospitality, they would need to offer them tea and sweets. Yadu'llah's goal, however, was always service to humanity. These interactions allowed him to get to know people and possibly to share the Bahá'í Faith. Meanwhile, Farkhundih had started her sewing practice and was able to contribute to the household income. She later remembered that time with great fondness:

"We were always poverty-stricken, but it was so beautiful. We ate our stew together lunch and dinner with the other Bahá'ís. Those were the best days, and it was our wish—once our kids were grown—to go back to Arabia and die there as pioneers."

Even in peacetime, Yemen was not an easy place to live. The living conditions were not as clean or safe as they were used to. In early 1965, the family was expecting a second child. Poor institutions with lack of hygiene and unprofessional behavior are a problem under ordinary circumstances, but they can be very dangerous when one is giving birth.

When the time came, Farkhundih went to a local hospital to have her baby. She was put in the care of a certain doctor who had a bad reputation. The doctor gave her a drug to start labor and then apparently set off for the movies! He didn't come back in time for the baby to be born, so it was strangled during the delivery.

This baby, a son they had named Omid (*Umíd*), died because of a doctor's negligence. Now such a painful experience for a mother is hard for many of us to understand. Imagine the tears, the burning pain in the heart, and the feeling of letdown after nine months of physical and emotional preparation. It would be easy to let that pain turn into anger and blame towards the doctor, the hospital, and the backward country they lived in. This family was human too, and so they might have been tempted to blame.

They were also pioneers. They were there to share teachings of love and unity. Part of love is sacrificing what you have for something greater. It actually turns out this tragedy brought some good for the people of that place. Mrs. Mahmudnizhad told the story as follows:

> "A reporter lived near our home and wrote the story in the papers. This encouraged other patients who had suffered at the doctor's negligence to come forward with their stories. As a result, the paper gained popularity and the government was forced to bring a better doctor to the hospital. The reporter later told us that he felt that our son was sacrificed for the wellbeing of the people of that city."

They had moved to Yemen out of love and the desire to serve its people. While they never would have chosen this to happen, they learned to see their son's death as a service to that community. This would not be this family's last or most difficult sacrifice for the good of humanity.

Here is a lesson that is hard to learn. Sometimes when we suffer, it feels like there is no purpose to it. All we feel is the pain. When we look at it from a different point of view or after some time has passed, we often can see some positive outcome or meaning.

Now what about the death of Omid? In this life, many people die at a young age. Many times they die in unfortunate accidents. For these young people, our grief is especially heavy. We understand the full lives they could have lived. The Mahmudnizhad family turned to God in prayer for relief. In the Bahá'í writings, they found comfort. They were assured that the soul is eternal and that child would be protected and cared for in the next world. They read that their son was like a *"fresh and tender shrub"* that *"a kind gardener"* had moved *"from a confined place to a wide open area."* That passage goes on to say:

> *This transfer is not the cause of the withering, the lessening or the destruction of that shrub; nay, on the contrary, it maketh it to grow and thrive, acquire freshness and delicacy, become green and bear fruit.*[4]

In my years on this earth, I have known many young people who died. It is always painful. This symbol of a young plant being moved always helps me think about the journey of our souls from this life to the next one. Then I pray and I understand that the death may be sad for us, but it's happy for the young soul who is now able to grow more than ever before. I think of another passage from the Bahá'í writings that gently consoled another mother who had lost her son saying that the child was addressing her from the hidden world in the following words:

O thou kind Mother, thank divine Providence that I have been freed from a small and gloomy cage and, like the birds of the meadows, have soared to the divine world ... Therefore, lament not, O Mother, and be not grieved; I am not of the lost, nor have I been obliterated and destroyed ... Following this separation is everlasting companionship. Thou shalt find me in the heaven of the Lord, immersed in an ocean of light.[5]

Mona's Early Childhood

"One day she will cause the whole world to cry out"

The family's next child was Mona. Her name meant "desire," and the name was chosen this time by her mother. Her father used to say, "Mona is our hope and desire." She was born on September 10, 1966 when the family lived in Lahij. By that time, the country of South Yemen was engulfed in war. Like many countries that Great Britain had colonized in the past, the struggle for independence resulted in war and hardship. A booklet called *The Story of Mona* recalls the family's trip to the hospital:

> Yemen was under military alert, with the roads controlled by armed guards. Since the Mahmudnizhad's lived in the countryside where there was no hospital, they had to travel to Aden, Yemen's capital, to assure that Mona was safely delivered. Although the trip itself was long and arduous because their automobile was stopped and meticulously searched at numerous roadblocks, they reached the hospital in time. [6]

So Mona had a stressful entrance into this world. Many years later, her mother would remark, "Mona was born in wartime and she sacrificed her sweet life in wartime."

And yet she had a destiny. When she was just six months old, there was a very special old gentleman, a holy man, visiting their city. His name was Mr. Samandari (*Samandarí*). This old gentleman was respected throughout the Bahá'í world. He had even met Bahá'u'lláh seventy or eighty years earlier when he was a young man. He had a deep spiritual insight that comes from a lifetime of prayer, meditation and selfless service. He had traveled to Yemen despite being almost 90 years old. He came to encourage this family and their efforts. What they were doing was hard to do without encouragement. They were living in a foreign country at war, but they were working to help change that, to promote peace and justice in the hearts of people.

So this gentleman was speaking to a group of people inside their home. Farkhundih noticed that baby Mona needed her milk. She quietly left the room and brought Mona into the kitchen. She sat on a stool and began to feed her.

When she looked up, Mr. Samandari was standing in the kitchen staring at her and at Mona. He had just stopped speaking and left the group of people in the other room who were listening to him. He spoke to the mother in a powerful manner: "Nurture this babe well with your own milk! For one day she will cause the whole world to cry out!"

Farkhundih was amazed. She had no idea what this could mean. How could this newborn child one day cause the whole world to cry out?

That same month, Mona came very close to death. The family had put poison around the house to kill off pests such as mice. One day, her mother noticed Mona crawling around the floor acting funny. She picked her up and saw only the whites of her eyes, because her eyes were rolling back in her head. The parents rushed their daughter to the hospital to learn she was poisoned. It seems she was waking up in the morning and crawling to the wall in order to eat the poison. It was sweet after all so the mice would like it too.

It took the infant girl 6 months to recover from that. But that wasn't the only close call. Mona came close to dying at least two more times when she was very young.

When she was two, she was hit by a car. She got thrown to the sidewalk. She then stood up, pointed at the driver, and said, "You are bad!" Then she fainted. Her parents grabbed her and took off for the hospital again. This time she recovered more quickly.

One time the following year, bombs were falling around their home and the family was huddling together inside the safest room they had. One bomb fell and exploded very close to the house. It made a huge crashing sound and sent dust and debris everywhere. The parents looked around. Where was Mona? The three-year-old had wandered away!

They began to search frantically and forgot about their own safety. They looked everywhere and finally found her outside. She had a broom in her hand and a frown on her face. "It's dirty, it's dirty!" she said as she tried to sweep up the mess from the bomb.

In each of these cases, Mona could've died. Was she living, as they say, on borrowed time? Was it her destiny not to be killed in an accident but to have the choice of sacrificing herself for God's infant Faith? And, in doing so, to make the world cry out?

The war got worse and life became extremely difficult for the family. There was a lack of food, water and medicine in the country. Disease was spreading. Still the Bahá'í pioneer family tried to hold on. They were fighting the deeper disease of hatred and disunity with the loving teachings of Bahá'u'lláh and service to their community.

Not long after the poisoning incident, the battle came right into Lahij. Soldiers and rebels were firing guns from the rooftops. There was no electricity and no refrigeration, and the heat and humidity were terrible. They had barely any water and had to carefully strain what they had to remove the worms. They were so miserable, Mrs.

Mahmudnizhad tried to take the children to the roof just to cool down. They were met with gunshots and had to flee back inside.

Soon after, there was an announcement that there would be bombing and that all civilians should leave. The neighbors came to their home to get them to go. Yadu'llah refused to go.

"We are soldiers of Bahá'u'lláh, and we won't give up our post."

The young family gathered around a support pillar while bombs rained all through the night. From that night, Mrs. Mahmudnizhad claimed she lost her good health for the rest of her life.

They may well have been the only family in a city full of soldiers and gunmen. A month went by. One day, Yadu'llah went out to try to buy a watermelon. There was a knock on the door. Young Taraneh was so excited to have a visitor after so long, she ran to the door. Before her mother could stop her, she opened the door to find three coarse-looking men with guns standing there. Mrs. Mahmudnizhad tried to close the door, but they forced their way in. Taraneh and Mona were standing against the wall, frightened.

"What do you want?" Mrs. Mahmudnizhad asked them.

One of them told her to go to the bedroom to get something. She knew she had to act quickly. She had a pan of oil heating on the stove. She quickly grabbed it and threatened to burn them if they didn't leave. She began screaming and yelling to attract attention from others nearby. The men got spooked and left. Before going, they told her the family had one week to leave or they'd come back.

Soon afterward, Yadu'llah came home and heard the frightening story. Things had gone too far. It was time to go. The family moved to Al-Mansoora, a densely-packed neighborhood in Aden. The situation there was unbearable for the family. Mrs. Mahmudnizhad wrote,

"I became so ill I entered a coma, and the doctors advised us to leave. Mr. Mahmudnizhad also became sick with a stomach ulcer, and finally the government expelled us from the country. Despite all these, we tried our best to stay there, but our destiny was decreed otherwise. When I came out of my coma, I was in Abadan, one of the cities in Iran."

It was 1969, and Amu had spent a decade and a half living away from Iran. He was now coming back knowing he had given all he could to help the Arabian Peninsula. Only God knows what impact they had. We can't see the results of spiritual work immediately. We plant seeds in the heart and it takes time for them to grow. You can't judge their success because their country was at war and the leaders didn't listen. What about the regular people who listened? Did they live their lives differently? Some of them went on and they themselves began to share the Bahá'í message with others.

They say a butterfly flapping its wings in South America could cause a typhoon in the China Sea. The idea is that a small action can trigger a string of larger actions until the final effect is enormous. But how can we ever see all those connections? We can't calculate it. We might call that God's math.

Actually we have a good, easy-to-understand example of this "butterfly effect" right in front of us: Mona. In a dark field in the middle of the night, a teenage girl kisses a rope before she is hanged with it. This is a small action, like the beating of butterfly's wings. It was a pure, powerful and heroic action, so it spread and stirred other people. Only a few men witnessed this, but one of them was so moved, he had to tell the story. The people he told recorded what he said and they spread the news. Soon the picture of Mona appears in newspapers around the world. Later on, more of her remarkable story comes out. People know her story around the world. You are now reading a book about her.

Mona was a butterfly of the spirit and the typhoon is the actions that we all take in her memory. What if the people who read this book offered a prayer and some hours of service in Mona's name? Would that not eventually be the equivalent of a great spiritual storm?

So the first thing Yadu'llah needed to do was to stabilize his family. His wife needed medical treatment. His children, now 9 and 3, needed a routine and schooling. He needed to have steady work. He needed to create a home. This was not easy. Looking over his life, this had never been easy.

While in Yemen, he had begun working for an international electronics company. This company was now seeking to expand into more cities in Iran, and it needed employees to move there. So Yadu'llah decided to follow the work and accept each new assignment he was offered. In this way, he could create stability for his family. Mrs. Mahmudnizhad continues her story,

> "[From Abadan], I was transferred to Tehran and hospitalized in the Russian hospital for 19 days—until I got better. We then moved to Isfahan, where Mr. Mahmudnizhad started working … in his professional field of repairing radios and television sets. After two years*, we were transferred to Kirmanshah and a few months after that to Tabriz."

---

* In Persian culture, the counting of years is a little different than in the West. A common way of speaking is to round up to the next number even if it's less than half a year. For example, one year and four months might be referred to as two years. This also applies to people's ages. In Iran, when you are born you are one, and when you hit your birthday one year later,

Remember, Tabriz is the same city in the North of Iran where Yadu'llah came from. His children did not like it at all. The people there didn't even speak Persian, but a language closer to Turkish. Taraneh and Mona also didn't like Tabriz because it was the city in which the Báb was executed. The girls were sensitive to this history. More than a hundred and twenty years earlier, the Báb had been tied and dangled from a rope in a public square and shot by 750 government soldiers. He had never hurt a single soul.

At the young age of 5 or 6, Mona was already paying attention to spiritual things. There was a special connection already appearing between her and her father. While they were living in Tabriz, one of Yadu'llah's sisters died. He traveled to attend the funeral in Tehran, which is the capital city of Iran and a long way from Tabriz. Farkhundih stayed home with Mona because her arm was broken and in a cast. She continues the story:

"One day, I woke up to find Mona sick with the mumps. Her throat was badly swollen and she was in great pain. The weather in Tabriz was very cold and stormy, and there was lots of snow on the ground. We did not even have a telephone for me to try to call for help. So I was worried as to what to do, when suddenly the doorbell rang and Mr. Mahmudnizhad rushed in through the door with a look of worry in his eyes. He immediately asked about Mona and ran to her. When he looked at her, he started to shed tears saying, 'I had a vision of her in this state when I was in Tehran. She was begging me to come to her aid. Therefore, I arranged to come back immediately, and am here with you now.' I said, 'But she wasn't feeling like this yesterday afternoon; she was fine then.' He responded, 'The world of the spirit is free of time and place [as we know it].' "

---

you become two! Therefore in translating the Persian language, you have to be aware of this cultural element, or else, the math does not make any sense.

The girls wished and begged to live in another city: not the city where the Báb was killed, but the city where He was born. They cried and prayed so much that their prayers were answered. The parents agreed. Yadu'llah even resigned his job, although the company eventually found a position for him in his new home. So, in 1973, the family moved to the blessed city of Shiraz.

Now in all this moving, the family had developed a certain pattern. Yadu'llah would go ahead of the rest of the family to the city where they were moving. He would find a place to live, arrange the furnishings, and when it was ready, he would dress up in a nice suit and welcome his wife and daughters into their new home.

When they arrived in Shiraz, the family was very happy. Mona's first day in Shiraz was quite eventful. She made a friend, and she took a bike ride that became a kind of pilgrimage. They went to visit a small mountain called TV Hill. It's called that because the city's television station is broadcast from there. Her mother tells the story:

> "On the first day of our arrival, she became friends with a girl her own age, who was the daughter of one of our neighbors. Mona realized that her friend had two bicycles. Since her own bicycle was still unpacked and she was anxious to see the city, she asked her friend if she could borrow one of her bicycles so that they could go for a ride together and see the city. When her friend agreed to her request, she came to me and asked permission to go and buy bread and yogurt and at the same time take a ride around with her friend. I gave her permission and she went on her way. She came back a while later with the bread and yogurt, but was very sad with teary eyes. I thought that perhaps someone had bothered her or that she had fallen, so I ran to her and inquired about the problem.

> "She started sobbing and said, 'Mother, I went on the TV Hill, and from there I was able to see the whole city. I saw a pregnant

mountain! Yes, even this mountain is pregnant with so much to share with the people of this city. This mountain carries a divine message and gives the good news of the birth of the Báb in this city.' Later, when I saw the hill myself, I wondered how this girl of such tender years had perceived such things in this mount. The mount looks exactly like a pregnant woman who is lying down.

"Up until the time that she grew older and was arrested, she often went on the rooftop to look at that pregnant mountain. She said that the mountain was blessed, because the sacred eyes of the Blessed Báb had gazed upon it."

Mona was just turning seven, and she had this gift of spiritual perception. The more we look the more we might see how powerful her father's example was for her. His life was becoming the pattern she chose to follow. Yadu'lláh had his own pilgrimage coming.

The House of the Báb in Shiraz is one of the great holy sites in the Bahá'í Faith. It's where He was born in 1819 and where He lived most of his life. It is where He declared His mission to His first follower, a young religious scholar named Mulla Husayn. This was on the night of 22 May 1844. Every year, Bahá'ís celebrate that event and tell the story of that night and the wonderful conversation between the two.

Yadu'lláh had never been to the House of the Báb. He was also so humble that he didn't feel he deserved to go. He told his family, "I shall not visit the Blessed House of The Báb unless he calls me himself." Of course, that was impossible. The Báb had died more than a hundred and twenty years earlier, so He couldn't call him. Or could he?

One day the phone rang and Yadu'lláh was given an address to make a repair on a television set. This television was owned by the mother of the person who took care of the House of the Báb. She lived right there! So Yadu'lláh went and did the repair. When he was done and he was all set to go, the woman asked him, "Don't you want to visit the Blessed House? There is nobody there and I will let you in."

He said it was the happiest day of his life. One source tells the story:

> He walked around the yard several times and then up and down the stairs, kissing the edge of each step; finally, he entered the room where The Báb had first declared his mission, bowed his forehead to the ground, and immersed in spiritual ecstasy. Every time he talked about this visit with family or friends, his eyes would fill with tears. [7]

This was the man that Mona looked up to and learned from in her early life. Maybe the actions of Mona and Amu seem odd to you or like something you can never imagine yourself doing. I want to tell you that no one who met Mona or her father thought they were strange. They felt the embrace of their love and there was no awkward feeling. As one Iranian friend remembered Amu:

> "Anyone who had met him could not forget him. Just by visiting with him, you could understand the real meaning of kindness and love. His name and the word "love" would always come together."

Maybe instead of thinking of them as so different from us, we can learn from the way they behaved. We can imagine ourselves or our children in the future acting with such love for God and such spiritual awareness. Maybe that is one of the reasons we are learning about their stories, so that we can be more like them.

School

"My legs started to shake and my pulse beat faster"

The morning of the first day of school arrived. Mona and Taraneh were getting ready to meet a new set of teachers and classmates in their new city. Mona was heading into third grade.*

Across the city, I was waiting in the hallway of my house for the clock to move faster. It was my first day of first grade. I had laid my clothes out the night before, and I got up extra early. My outfit was a yellow shirt with a navy blue dress over it, with white stockings and black shoes. It was our school uniform, and I liked it. The time came, and I headed out the door on the 10- to 15-minute walk to my school. I didn't need anyone to walk with me, I knew the way.

When I got to school, a lot of the other children were crying and clinging to their mothers. I was very attached to my mother (and still am!), but I wanted to go to school. I had watched my sisters and brothers going all these years. I was curious about where they went and a little jealous about something they were able to do that I couldn't.

My school was a private school of grades 1 through 5 run by a female principal named Mrs. Sultani (*Sultání*). The schools in Iran at that time allowed boys and girls to mix. That changed during the Revolution when they separated boys and girls into different schools.

---

* Mona had only just turned 7, but in Tabriz her parents had arranged for her to start school at 5, a year earlier than other children. This is part of the reason there is confusion about Mona's age in the published accounts.

I was eager to learn all I could at school: to read and write, to add and subtract, and to meet new friends. Children are naturally happy to learn. They are good at it, until obstacles start coming in their way.

In the school yard, we learned to stand and sing our national anthem. It was full of praise for our country and our king, the Sháh. In class, they taught us reading and writing. Right away, though, I was treated differently than the other students. It was because I was a Bahá'í child, and my teacher was prejudiced against Bahá'ís. She would make bad comments about the Bahá'ís in front of the class, so everyone would learn that I was different and somehow bad. My chance to make friends was getting smaller. It turns out she was prejudiced against me for another reason too.

So my teacher started drawing letters from the alphabet on the chalkboard and we were supposed to copy her. I picked up my pencil and started to draw the letters as best I could the way she had. The teacher came over to me, took the pencil out of my one hand and put it in the other. I am left-handed, so it was only natural for me to pick up the pencil with my left hand. I tried scrawling with my right hand a bit, and she nodded her approval.

She went back to instructing the whole class, and I decided that I liked using my left hand better. When she saw me doing this, she quickly came back over, grabbed my left hand with the pencil in it and squeezed it so the pencil pressed hard against my knuckles. Tears gathered behind my eyes, but I fought the urge to cry. This woman was discriminating against me because I was left-handed. She then called me the devil in front of the other children because I was Bahá'í and left-handed!

In Iran and in other countries, there is a superstition against left-handed people. Some people believe we are somehow possessed by the devil. This is a stupid idea. Science shows that 1 in 10 people are left-handed, and it's because of the way their brain works. But some people resist reason and science when they think their religion is teaching something different. This is one reason Bahá'ís believe we need new Messengers of God from time to time. They show us the difference between truth and superstition. They clean the Faith of God like it was a mirror that had gotten dirty after so much use.

My father found out about this treatment and came to the school and complained to the principal. The principal went and scolded the teacher, but she still found a way to get what she wanted. She would place me in the middle of a row of students all sitting on a bench and using the same table. Because I was in the middle, I couldn't use my left hand to write or else I would knock against the girl to my left and disturb her writing. She thought this way I would be forced to write with my right hand. And I did, while she was watching. In class I would write the way she wanted, and at home I would do my assignments the way I wanted, with my left hand.

Just as she had found a way around the principal's order, I had found a way around hers. She would see my assignments and know I had done them left-handed, but she couldn't do anything about it. I was in first grade and I was already learning more than my school lessons. I was learning to secretly work around the authority. That's not a great lesson for a six-year-old.

But you can't unlearn abuse. Once it happens to you, it leaves its mark. You go on, but you're different. To this day, I have trouble writing. I learned to use my right hand, but I never like the way it looked, and my left hand isn't practiced and takes too long. As a result, I have trouble expressing myself through writing even though I have no trouble doing so verbally. Then again, God provides. As fortune would have it, I ended up marrying a writer.

School in Iran teaches a mixture of things: some that are useful and good and some that are harmful and prejudiced. As Bahá'í children, we learned to develop a thick skin against the prejudice of the people around us. We did not fight back, although sometimes we did stand up for ourselves when we felt like we were being treated unfairly. Still, we were encouraged by our parents and our community to do well in school. The Bahá'í teachings say we should pursue excellence in all the sciences and arts and other areas of human achievement. Therefore, many Iranian Bahá'í children and youth are at the top of their classes. This is annoying to the religious leaders because they want to prove that Islam is superior.

Mona did extremely well in school. Both her teachers and her classmates liked her a lot—those who were not infected by the disease of prejudice. As it says in *The Story of Mona*:

> When she entered the third grade in Shiraz, she was quickly recognized as an excellent student and was considered one of the most outstanding in the school. She also had a beautiful singing voice and a genuine love for those around her, especially younger children who would often surround her when she arrived at school just to be with her.[8]

She grew attached to her teachers and friends. Even in first grade, back in Tabriz, she would cry if one of her teachers left the school for another position. This was a quality that continued and even increased as she grew—this sense of care, concern and empathy for others. To be honest, it would be a source of considerable pain in her future. Mona was passionate about people, and it hurt her when people were discriminated against or when people were not treated with respect. She herself cared so much for others that she had a hard time understanding how others could be so careless.

When she was 12, she wrote the following essay about her time in grade school. It's kind of funny, but it's clear she had felt hurt by teachers' behavior. It begins with the class monitor, a fellow student, telling everyone to get ready:

" 'Children, children, the teacher's coming. Go take your seats—
now stand up!'

" 'Stand up and shut up!' some teachers say, acting like we have
offended their fathers. Some say, 'You may sit down.' Some say
nothing and take their place in front of the class. Some of them
frown and glare, and with a pen in one hand and a ruler in the
other, they begin questioning and leading the lesson, here and
there kicking students out, and so it goes on and on …

"The whole time I spent in grade school, it was the same. I always
wanted to be a teacher just to tell the students this is not how
teachers should be. The teacher is not a creature that everybody
should fear and run away from, not daring to talk to them. But
there was something about whenever I set foot in the school and
the name of the teacher was mentioned: my legs started to shake
and my pulse beat faster, and so I would forget my decision to
become a teacher. I asked myself, why are the teachers so selfish,
proud and ill-natured? We have been taught that the teacher is
like our mother, a spiritual mother to whom we are indebted.
One day when I was in third grade, I went home and asked my
mother, 'Do all spiritual mothers have rulers and hit their kids?'
My mother had no answer for me. I looked into her eyes and
waited, but heard nothing. She said nothing, but this had really
become a riddle for me. Are the teachers our spiritual mothers?"

This was obviously not an essay for school or else she might have
had to face that ruler again. Mona loved to read and write just for her
own interest and expression. She had a curiosity and a passion for
learning that was not crushed by having some bad teachers. And she
had lots of different subjects she was interested in. Like many
children, Mona was drawn to creative activities and the arts from a
young age. Her mother said:

"She loved crafts such as embroidery, carpet weaving, mesh weaving, engraving, painting, and lace weaving. Often when she was a very small child in Isfahan, she noticed the engravers from behind their shop windows as we walked through the streets, and ran to look at them. She looked with such passion that the artist usually stopped work and invited her to go in and give it a try. This always made little Mona very happy, who always accepted the artist's invitation with joy in her eyes and ran to try her hand at engraving. I always watched how her father looked at her with love and admiration and how he always thanked the artist for giving Mona a chance to try the craft."

Having supportive parents can make a world of difference. Her mother was a professional seamstress and could share with Mona skills such as sewing. And Amu always nurtured the young Mona in her unique set of interests. In addition to handicrafts, Mona loved many other arts, such as painting, poetry, music and dance. With some of these, such as painting and calligraphy, her father was able to teach her or at least participate alongside.

"Father and daughter used to sit together at times practicing their painting, and talking about it. Mona's father was a good calligrapher, and Mona used to try to practice calligraphy with him. Sometimes they talked about music for hours."

Amu didn't himself always have the skills or the knowledge she was seeking, but he could encourage her and try to facilitate her learning. This process began with simply listening, and both parents recognized the value of this. According to her mother,

"When Mona spoke in her usual way filled with passion and excitement, we listened to her with great interest and enthusiasm, even though we had gotten to know her and always knew what she was about to say as soon as she began speaking. We listened as though we had no idea of what she wanted to convey, asked her questions, and encouraged her to continue speaking, which in turn developed her thoughts and ideas. Sometimes, in the middle of her speech, a new idea would approach her mind, and she would stop to say that it would be best if she said something else or did something else. We – especially her father – always helped her in this process."

The connection between father and daughter was based on a deep respect, one that went both ways. He didn't try to make her exactly like himself, and he didn't force her to live up to some standard to please other people. Mona's father nurtured her to grow to be the person she was meant to be. His child was a seed that with the water of love and the sun of nurturing would grow and blossom into a beautiful and unique flower that God intended and that only God could foresee. Every child should be raised like this.

Mona showed a profound respect for her father, as well, not just for what he did for her, but for who he was. She used a similar image of flowers in bloom, as her mother recalls:

"She made a beautiful handicraft, which explains the story of our family. It is the image of a beautiful bird that is carrying a branch. The branch has three flowers: one of the flowers has not bloomed yet; one is fully bloomed; and the other is half bloomed … [T]he flower that is not yet bloomed is symbolic of the son we lost; the fully bloomed flower is symbolic of Mona's father; and the half-bloomed flower is symbolic of Mona herself. [The branch containing these three flowers] is [symbolic] of a gift that the bird is presenting to Bahá'u'lláh from our family."

Mona and her father would communicate just by looking into each other's eyes. This connection grew as Mona grew older, even to the point where her mother would sometimes feel left out. But as she later said, their looks "did not contain any negative attitude or complaints or sadness. They were filled with love, affection and joy." There was just something about the tie between these two souls— and it was a bond that would last through the worst possible circumstances they could imagine. On occasions when her father was away,

> "Mona busied herself by reading and doing other things. Sometimes, she went onto the rooftop, or walked to the mountains to look at the city's beautiful scenery and to pray for the safe return of her father. Whenever she was away [from her father], she was drawn to the roof in order to expand her horizons and to create a bigger life in her mind."

In the end, Mona's development, both of mind and heart, was more stimulated at home than at school. It was there she gained her thirst for understanding and her joy in discovery and in artistic creation. Her parents' loving and caring example brought out not only Mona's talents, but also her spiritual qualities. Because of the family's modest means, in some cases, she had to go without material things. Then there was such sweetness in the detachment she showed.

> "Mona was in love with [the sound of] piano, and admired Beethoven deeply. She always tried to listen to his music whenever she could. Her father had promised her to buy her a piano as soon as it was possible for him to do so; however, pianos were very expensive and impossible for us to afford. But Mona used to try and comfort her father by praising the most inexpensive musical instrument of the time, which was the flute. She used to say, 'the flute has a soul-stirring and soul-awakening effect. God willing, I will learn to play it ... ' At times like that, Mona's father looked into his daughter's beautiful eyes and smiled quietly with pride ... "

Adolescence

"While her tears came streaming quietly down"

In 1977, Iran was still acting like a western country. The Sháh was still in power. Girls wore short skirts walking in the streets of Shiraz, while the disco music of the Bee Gees and Abba was playing loudly from the shops.

In 1977, Mona's mother and father were thinking back to their days as pioneers. They were determined to try again. It's not that the family was not happy or active in the Bahá'í community. When they arrived in Shiraz, Amu had immediately set to work with service and teaching activities, and his wife and children participated, as well. It's just that they felt they could do more. As Mrs. Mahmudnizhad remembered it:

> "We yearned to be pioneers... [W]e wrote a letter addressed to the National Spiritual Assembly of Arabia.* We gave this letter to a relative and asked him to deliver it to the National Assembly. In that letter, we offered to move to any place that required pioneers, and waited in anticipation of a response ..."

To add to their dilemma, Amu was asked to take on a new responsibility in the Shiraz Bahá'í community. Mr. Vahdat asked him to be his assistant in his role as Auxiliary Board Member. Mr.

---

* A National Spiritual Assembly is an elected body that oversees the affairs of the Baha'i community in a country. There was at that time one central Assembly in the Gulf region and was titled the Spiritual Assembly of Arabia. (TN: Gloria Shahzadeh)

Vahdat was the father of Mahvash, the friend who took us out to lunch for Naw Rúz.* Mr. Vahdat and his family were dear friends of our family's, and he was an important figure in my youth. He had been a colonel in the army and was respected by all, and yet he had a gentle manner and a soft voice. As Auxiliary Board Member, he had a lot of responsibilities in seeking to protect the Bahá'í community and to encourage its growth. Of course, he needed help and was turning now to Amu to be his assistant. Still uncertain about the future, Amu accepted this new role, and they waited for word regarding pioneering.

Mona turned 11 in 1977. Age 11 is the gateway to adolescence, and the few years that follow are key in a person's development. This is when we start to change from girls and boys into young women and men. This is when we start to become individuals, distinct from our parents. We make choices—sometimes rational, sometimes emotional—that mold the attitudes, personality and character we will walk through life with. And these choices are taking place at a rapid rate. Bahá'ís often call kids this age "junior youth."

Like all junior youth, Mona loved her friends. She had lots of friends, including Muslims and Bahá'ís. She loved all alike, and treated all equally. When she opened the door to friends of whatever age, she was filled with excitement. She would exclaim, shake their hands and welcome then in. When she saw someone she loved, she'd get tears in her eyes and run and hug them. She'd shout, "O my God! I want to hug you and squeeze you in my arms!"

At the same time, she was dignified and moderate. She would show care and affection for all those she greeted, not just her good friends. She didn't discriminate or create "cliques" that make some feel special and others jealous and left out. Mona loved to talk to

---

* See pp. 9-10

people about spiritual things and about her Faith, but in positive and non-judgmental ways.

Her care for others spilled outside her home into the homes of her neighbors. One of her neighbors shared this beautiful memory with Mona's mother:

"When she came home from school, she used to come to our home and fill it with joy and happiness. We were used to having her there. She used to go straight to the stove and check on our food. She looked at the food with interest and enthusiasm, and, if it was something she liked, she exclaimed with excitement saying, 'Mrs. K-----, you are so fine!' I enjoyed hearing her make this comment, so I always tried to cook something that she liked. She then used to come to your own home, and, if you had cooked something that our children liked, she would bring some to our home and we would all eat together."

Mona loved children. She said when she was in their presence she felt like she was in the presence of God. What a remarkable thing to say! This was a key aspect of her character, and we will see later on how this love for children would become eternally connected with her name and memory.

Like many junior youth, Mona loved her room. After her sister, Taraneh, got married, Mona had decorated the room herself. Her mother recalled:

"She had spent little money, but the room was very beautiful. She made the curtains and the bedspread herself with a blue-and-white checkered cloth. [...] She prepared an album of her art works ... She made flowers with tissue paper of different colors. She died panty hose with different color dies and, using wire, made beautiful artificial flowers. She always used the least expensive things she could find around the house to create beautiful works of art. She even used elastic paper to make exquisite flowers, and it was never clear as to what was used to make them. Friends always wondered as to how these flowers were made."

Mona had made artwork for her wall that spoke of her love for people and for nature and for her faith. At the same time, the room was simple and tidy, just like Mona herself was clean and organized.

Like most junior youth, Mona was playful and generally joyful and happy. She did, however, have a lot of responsibility for such a young person. Her mother has recounted how Mona "attended to all of the housework":

"I used to work as a seamstress [at home] and had no time for the housework; therefore, Mona did everything, from housecleaning to laundry, to cooking and baking."

This was a bit shocking to me, because I was raised by a mother who would not even let me help in the kitchen. My responsibilities at that age were to my schoolwork. Still, Mona seemed to approach this responsibility with care. Her mother tells the following story about when Mona was 13 or 14:

"One day, I had gone out with one of my friends; when I returned, I found that a few of Mr. Mahmudnizhad's Muslim relatives from Tehran had come to our home in Shiraz. Mona had prepared everything for them to bathe, had prepared a lovely spread for dinner, and had set the dinner table with great taste. I was astonished, inasmuch as we did not have much at home with which she could have prepared dinner, and yet she had managed to prepare a beautiful meal. I asked her if our guests had helped her with the work, but she answered in the negative, stressing that she had done everything herself."

Mona loved puzzles. She loved dance, from ballet to Indian dances that portrayed stories. She loved traveling and visiting historical sites. In and around Shiraz, there are so many historical places. You can go visit a garden that is 500 years old or a mosque more than 1,000 years old. You can go to Persepolis—just a one-hour drive away—and see the remains of a 2,500-year-old city. And Mona had a powerful imagination and intuition that made visiting such places more intense. Her mother recalled the experience the following way:

> "[S]he could actually see the laborers of the past ages come and go while building the structure. She heard the voices of the kings as they passed by, and even heard the galloping of the horses. She also saw the buildings being ruined, which made her look at the world and regret as to why everyone came and went without leaving anything of value behind. She then used to sit and pray for them, while her tears came streaming quietly down."

Her mother goes on to say how this characteristic of Mona's was very strange for her. This degree of sensitivity seemed to be a secret that her mother could not penetrate. Her sister describes a similar feeling in the face of Mona's deep sensitivities:

> "I was her sister, but never understood how close she was to God. She is a mystery, at least for me. Mona was quiet and kept everything inside. She would never talk about her insides, her emotions … "

It seems the only one who really understood these more puzzling aspects of Mona's was her father. And the two of them just spoke of it through their eyes.

In adolescence, all young people need some way to express their thoughts and feelings, including those feelings that are difficult or painful. From what her mother and Taraneh say, it seems like Mona did not talk about such feelings openly at this age. The way she chose to express her deepest thoughts and feelings was through her writing.

One method was through letter-writing. Letters were much more common before email and social media. You basically had three ways to communicate with someone: phone them, visit them face-to-face, or write them a letter. Mona had family and a growing number of friends in different cities, and she would write them letters, post them in the mail and some days or weeks later, she would receive a reply. This was one way in which Mona could communicate her feelings.

Another method was through poems and essays that she would write for herself. These contained some of her deepest thoughts and feelings, and we are lucky to have a number of these preserved by her family.* Mona would write out her dreams and experiences. She poured out her hopes and her ideas. She also spoke of her pain and frustration in a way she couldn't yet with speech.

Like most all adolescents, Mona hated injustice. Even small examples of it. For instance, she didn't like when people were late or otherwise wasted her time. She herself was highly responsible and naturally got upset when others took advantage. There is something about this age where young people begin to see very clearly the differences between what the adults around them say and what they do. They often respond with anger.

The short essay in the previous chapter about terrifying teachers is part one of a three-part essay called "Which teacher, which method."† It seems she used this essay to track her relationship with

---

* See Appendix A for additional translated poems and essays not included in these chapters.

† See p. 48

teachers. Part two is the angriest of them. It shows Mona's displeasure with something that happened to her in eighth grade.

"Those times passed, and I went on to higher grades. Then I came to dislike teachers in other ways.

"When I was in eighth grade, we were supposed to have a grammar test on a Saturday in the month of March. I studied hard and came to school prepared. But the other students were lazy and hadn't studied. The teacher came into the class and told us to take out paper. But when the first question was given, one of the students began to cry. At the second question, she cried harder. The teacher asked, 'What is the problem?' The student said, 'Ma'am, we didn't think you were serious about the test.' The teacher then closed the book and said, 'Well then, the test will be next week.' It was that simple. 'The test will be next week,' not even thinking that the students didn't study because they didn't want to miss their weekend fun.

"From that day, I hated that grammar class and that teacher. That weekend, all my family had come to our home and in the afternoon went out to Salt Lake. I really wanted to be with them, but I only joined them for lunch and was with them only a little while. Then I went back to my room and studied. I heard their laughter, but told myself, 'It doesn't matter. Instead, I will get a good grade on my test tomorrow. It's worth it.' So when the test was canceled, I was furious. I got all choked up and right there my tears came. I didn't want to cry in the class, but the tears kept coming harder so that I wanted to scream. I asked for permission to leave but that creature didn't let me. I cried so much, so much. That day will never be erased from my memory."

You see how young Mona was unable to express herself outwardly but kept all her feelings inside. This is how many young people feel sometimes. The good news is that as we grow older, we can learn to express our feelings verbally in a way that addresses the problem or the injustice. We don't have to keep it all bottled up or blow up with rage. We can learn to speak directly, rationally and effectively. Mona would eventually learn this, and Wow! What a power she gained when she did!

One "adolescent" thing Mona never showed was disobedience to her parents. This is partly cultural. In Iran and in many non-western countries, it goes against the culture to rebel against one's parents. This doesn't mean it doesn't happen, just that it is not as common as in the West.

Now rebellion against one's king? That's a different story.

We began this chapter talking about 1977. What a difference a year can make. In 1977, disco was in the air. In 1978, it was Rebellion that was in the air. Different groups were joining together in opposition to our king, the Sháh. Mob violence was erupting here and there. Fear started to drive people's behavior. The women who had worn short skirts before now would wear long veils covering up their whole bodies.

In 1978, the Mahmudnizhad family finally got word back regarding their pioneering request. Mrs. Mahmudnizhad explains the unexpected result:

> "After one year, the person with whom we had entrusted the letter came back and returned to us our letter without having made the delivery as he was requested to do. We were very sad and even tearful because of the fact that he had not given the letter to the National Assembly; however, after a little while, Mr. Mahmudnizhad considered this as a good omen and said that this must mean that our existence in Iran is required. We will stay in Iran and will serve in this country."

It seems that the infinite math of God was here at work and His Hand was moving into place the players and setting out their parts all for some greater purpose. Perhaps in the end we will glimpse it.

Revolution

"You have to get out of your home!"

It started to get bad in the summer of 1978. The demonstrations throughout Iran were huge and violent. The people were all uniting against the government of the Sháh, and he was powerless to maintain order. Power was shifting to the leaders of the Revolution, and they were looking for targets to satisfy the people's rage. The Bahá'ís have always been an easy target. The teachings of Islam clearly protect older religious minorities such as Christians, Jews and Zoroastrians. The newer Bahá'í Faith is, however, considered by Iran's religious establishment to be a heresy—that is, a false and misleading religion.

So the clergy would curse the Bahá'ís in the mosques, calling them devil-worshipers, lovers of the Sháh, spies for Israel or America. What they accused depended on their mood that week. Then their followers would go out and attack. They would terrorize the Bahá'ís, beat them, set their houses on fire, drag them through the streets, sometimes killing them. This first happened in villages, but it would soon arrive in Shiraz too. That was in the winter of 1978/79.

One morning we noticed that our house and some of the other Bahá'í houses around ours had been marked with a red X. We didn't know what that meant. Was our family being targeted for something bad? Someone said it might just be the electric company marking where repairs were needed.

Early the next morning, we woke up and saw smoke in the air. One of our relatives, who was a Muslim, came to our home and found my Dad:

"They are burning Bahá'í houses in the Saadiyeh neighborhood!"

"What?"

"You have to get out of your home!"

My Dad immediately thought of my older sister Nahid (*Náhíd*) and her family. Their home was close to that neighborhood. We all gathered up quickly and left our house. We made it safely to the home of one of my uncles, who was Muslim.

We were worried, though. There were actually twelve of my family members living at Nahid's home. This included Nahid, her husband, and their four kids, plus my other sister, Giti (*Gítí*), her husband and THEIR four kids. Giti's family had been staying with Nahid while they waited for their own home to be finished.

Nahid was at home alone with her three-year-old son when she heard loud voices from outside. She looked out and saw people coming down the street towards her home. She grabbed her son, jumped in her car and took off without even thinking to grab her purse. All her belongings, all those of her family and all those of Giti's family were left behind.

The mob broke into the house and looted the place, and then they set it on fire. Everything of value was stolen. Everything else was burned.

Giti's husband was nearby when he heard what was happening. He rushed to the house. He saw neighbors running away with their property and the house on fire. There were soldiers standing in the street. He pleaded with them to stop this and help put out the fire. They said they had no orders to do so. The people who were there to keep order would not stop the chaos.

Hundreds of Bahá'í homes were looted and burned that day. This was not just in Shiraz, but in neighboring towns and villages. Bahá'ís there were sent running from their homes into the mountains, and many came down into the city.

I remember it was 7:30 p.m. when one of the leading mullas in Shiraz, Ayatollah Dastghayb, came on the TV and told the people to stop burning houses. As you may have guessed, those red X's had been put on all the Bahá'í houses to tell the mobs which homes to loot and burn.

One of my relatives came to my uncle's house and told us this. He was part of a political group called the Hujjatiyeh, who hated Bahá'ís. He said his group had marked all the X's.

It turned out, however, that our house was safe. When the mob came to burn it, our neighbors stopped them. There were two well-known mullas in the neighborhood. The houses were close together and they were afraid for their own property.

Still we didn't dare return home, so we stayed with my uncle a whole month. Every day we were uncertain what was coming next. Order was breaking down everywhere. There was a 6 p.m. curfew, and the army apparently had orders to shoot anyone caught outside after that.

One day I had a toothache, and my mother was able to get an appointment with a dentist. We went and he gave me penicillin, which is a common antibiotic. I took it and hoped my tooth would heal.

That night, I began to shake. A little bit at first, then more. My jaw started jumping up and down, clattering. My family didn't know what to do. There was a curfew and we couldn't go find a doctor. I was in shock, shaking violently, jumping up so much that I broke my tooth in half! My family put a cushion in my mouth to keep me from doing any more damage. They held me, tried to comfort me and prayed. Eventually, I came out of shock and the shaking got less and less.

The next day they took me to the dentist, who shared the obvious news: I was allergic to penicillin and should never take it again. I later had that tooth removed, and to this day, I have a gap on the lower right where my first molar should be. It's a physical reminder I keep of that time.

We were lucky that we had family we could stay with. All of these Bahá'ís whose homes had been burned, where would they go? Some had relatives or friends that had room, but many did not.

Everyone was doing what they could. The Mahmudnizhad family assisted some of these homeless friends. Mrs. Mahmudnizhad explains:

"Our family was witness to approximately 300 Bahá'í houses going up in flames. So many houses were looted and their furniture taken away. Bahá'ís were stranded in the mountains and deserts. Some had come from different cities like Jahrum, Burazjan, Bushihr and were staying in the homes of other Bahá'ís or in the Bahá'í Centre.

"Mr. Mahmudnizhad used to bring them to our home, and I would prepare a meal for them and encouraged them to take a bath and clean up. Mona watched them as they shed tears. We lived on the fifth floor and we could easily watch some of the houses in our neighborhood burn. Sometimes the Bahá'ís who lived in those houses, would come to our apartment and watch with us as their home went up in flames.

"However, Mr. Mahmudnizhad who had a great sense of humor did not allow anyone to stay sad and used to make everybody roar in laughter to an extent that they would forget their sorrows and become happy for giving something in the path of God."

Amu was working, on the one hand, to cheer up these unfortunate friends. On the other hand, he was working to address the problem with others on the Spiritual Assembly. They are the group of 9 people who oversee the affairs of the Bahá'ís in a city or town. Amu served on the Assembly in Shiraz as the secretary, which is one of the main officers.

The Spiritual Assembly didn't know what to do. All of these people needed places to stay. Some lucky ones had family, but many did not. Many of the Bahá'ís had opened their homes, but it was not enough. The Shiraz Bahá'í Center was large, but it had been taken over by the Revolutionary Guard. That was the armed group that supported and protected the new government. They used the Center, which was a place of peace and goodwill, to store their guns and ammunition.

That was not their only problem. Members of the Spiritual Assembly also had to worry about their safety. The Revolutionary Guard was targeting them for arrest and imprisonment. All their meetings had to be in secret therefore. A small committee of youth was assigned the task of arranging meeting places and informing the Assembly members right before the meeting. My brother, Daniel, served on that committee, as did Simin Saberi (*Símín Sábirí*), a young woman in her early 20s who would be martyred with Mona.

One day Daniel saw members of the Spiritual Assembly come out of their meeting looking very sad. He asked them if they were okay. They told him they had so many homeless Bahá'ís and not enough room for them all without the Bahá'í Center. They felt the only solution was to go and try to persuade the authorities to let them have the key to the Bahá'í Center. But this was too risky, so they didn't know what to do.

"I'll go," Daniel said. "I am young and single. You all have families."

"But you might never come back home."

"I'll take the risk."

So Daniel managed to make an appointment with Ayatollah Mahallati, who was one of the two most powerful religious leaders in the city. The Spiritual Assembly told him if he wasn't back by noon, they would assume he had been arrested.

We all prayed—my family and the Spiritual Assembly.

Daniel arrived at the Revolutionary government's office. He had no idea what was going to happen. There was a long line of others waiting as well, and the room was full of guards with guns. They asked him what he wanted.

"I need to speak with Áqá [Master]."

Now Ayatollah Mahallati was very old and deaf, so he had a secretary who wrote things down for him to read. This secretary was overrun with people with requests for the Ayatollah, and he was eager to get rid of Daniel.

"What do you need?"

Daniel tried to avoid mentioning the name "Bahá'í" at first. He kept bowing and gesturing to try to get the attention of the old man.

"There are some sick people who need help."

"So take them to a hospital."

"They went, but they sent them away."

"So tell them to go home."

"They don't have homes."

Finally, he just had to tell the truth: "I am here on behalf of the Spiritual Assembly of the Bahá'ís of Shiraz, and I would like to get the key to the Bahá'í Center. As you know, we have lots of homeless families with nowhere to go."

The secretary got very upset. He started verbally abusing Daniel and the Bahá'ís and didn't write anything for the old man. Daniel knew he was going to prison.

Ayatollah Mahallati interrupted the secretary and asked him what it was about. The secretary angrily wrote what he wanted. Mahallati gave Daniel a look and wrote out on a piece of paper, "Give them permission to use one of the buildings." He then put his stamp on it.

The secretary was shocked and handed the paper to Daniel. Daniel read it.

"Actually, I don't need this. I need the key."

Can you imagine the secretary's face? Mahallati interrupted and indicated that they should give Daniel the key to the Bahá'í Center.

Daniel walked out of there with the key, but not believing what had just happened. He arrived back at 12:30 p.m. Everyone thought he was gone, for sure, but there he was. And for several months the Bahá'ís were able to use their Center to meet the needs of all those displaced families.

Talk about Daniel in the Lion's Den!*

Once they had the key, the Assembly opened the rooms in the Bahá'í Center to families and they set up a large tent in the yard for single people and young people. My sister, Giti, and her family, all six of them, moved into the Center until they could get their house ready. Nahid and her family went to stay with relatives.

My family clustered around the Center, and my older siblings helped out however they could. They and other youth were organizing their efforts to fill all the tasks that needed to be done.

---

* This refers to a story in the Bible about a miracle involving the prophet Daniel, which took place in Ancient Persia.

Help started to arrive from other cities. They sent clothes, food and other supplies.

As an eleven-year-old, I was having fun. School had been suspended for everyone, so I would come to the Center in the morning and leave at night. My nephews were around my same age, and we were always racing around. The youth committee saw our energy and decided to give us a job. We were put in charge of managing a children's library. So we created a nice room with chairs and books on the shelves. The kids who had lost all their things could come and read or sign out books.

All in all, we had a lot of activities to make up for missing school. I have so many good memories from that time. Meanwhile, the Revolutionaries were going forward with their plans.

One day the Revolutionary Guards came with guns and demanded part of the Bahá'í Center for their own use. At the time, we were having a little children's class. We were in the middle of prayers when a guard with a gun came into the room. The sight of the gun startled us all.

I stood up and told him, "We haven't finished our prayers yet."

He stopped and hesitated. "Okay, but hurry up!" And he went back outside the room.

I don't know where I got the courage to say that.

Eventually, the Revolutionary Guard took back the whole Bahá'í Center, and we never had access to it again.

What happened to the Bahá'í Center, however, was nowhere near as important as what happened to the House of the Báb. The first belonged to the Bahá'ís of Shiraz. The second belonged to the whole Bahá'í world, and everyone awaited word of its fate.

I remember visiting the House even as a small child, and I consider myself one of the luckiest people in the world to have had this opportunity.

Mobs had vandalized this Holy Spot from early on, one time after another. They saw it as an important symbol to knock down in their effort to destroy the Bahá'í community. But it remained the property of the Bahá'ís until government officials took it over in summer 1979. Ayatollah Mahallati himself determined to oversee the destruction of what he called "The House of Heresy."

Several times they tried to demolish it, and several times they had to stop. There were freak accidents where people were hurt or killed in trying to knock it down. We Bahá'ís naturally took this as a sign. They kept trying and the sacred House was completely demolished during the night in December 1979.

News of this event quickly spread through the Bahá'í world, shattering hopes and breaking hearts. My brother was part of a crew who took a video of the destruction. That night we and several other Bahá'í families were able to watch the video. Everyone was crying. That video was then sent to our World Center in Haifa, Israel. It was evidence of a terrible act that will be remembered for centuries.

A few days later, the Bahá'ís began to pick through all the rubble. They took out any artifacts or anything that might someday help rebuild the House. A Bahá'í friend had a storage area in a town called Akbarabad, about forty-five minutes away. All these items were taken there.

There were lots of children and youth who were eager to help. I remember our friend Hedayat Siyavushi (*Hidáyat Síyávushí*) picked up me and some other friends in his little "Folex" car. This is what Iranians called the Volkswagen Beetle. Hedayat had a great sense of humor, and he was a lot of fun to be around. Today was a serious day, though. He took us to the storage area and gave us the task of picking up and separating all the little pieces of glass from the broken stained glass windows. We were told that in the future the House of the Báb would be built again, and they would use these original materials. We were so careful not to miss a single piece. I considered it a great bounty to be part of this recovery effort.

In 1982, Hedayat was arrested, and he was executed in January 1983.

The site of the House of the Báb would eventually be bulldozed and turned into a parking lot. They also dedicated the neighboring mosque to the 12th Imám[9], a mysterious Shí'ih leader who disappeared when just a child. There is a bitter irony here because Bahá'ís believe the Báb to be the Return of the 12th Imam.

Amu and Mona visited the holy spot one last time on 19 November 1981. It was only an empty area of rubble at that point, but Mona was very moved by the visit. Remember that Mona had a gift for recalling the history and spirit of a place she was visiting, even places far less important than this one.

When she came home, she asked her mother if she could come inside with her shoes on. Usually Persians take their shoes off before entering a house. Mona felt she had holy dust on her shoes and she didn't want to take them off yet. She walked inside as if she were still walking on holy ground. She needed to express her feelings so she went into her room and poured her heart onto paper.

In January 1979, the Sháh and his family got on a plane and left Iran for good. He had been king for four decades, and he was now being forced out by the uprising of millions of Iranians. A couple weeks later, a religious leader named Ayatollah Khomeini got off a plane in Iran after 14 years in exile. He was the new leader of Iran and oversaw the making of a new government called the "Islamic Republic of Iran." This new government eventually took control of the Revolution, which had been supported by people with all sorts of political views, including communists and atheists.

The Islamic Republic wanted to destroy all those it considered its enemies. This included political groups that were willing to kill to get what they wanted, and it also included ethnic minorities such as the Kurds. It also included religious groups who were peaceful but just believed differently. The most hard-hit group in this last category was the Bahá'ís.

In her book, Olya Roohizadegan[*] (*Ulyá Rúhízádigán*) describes how the Revolution shifted from the Bahá'ís' perspective. There was chaos and destruction at first, and then it turned to an oppression that was focused and used violence for a purpose. Olya wrote:

> By the end of 1979, fourteen Bahá'ís ... had been killed by individuals or mobs, or have been executed by the authorities, often after prolonged torture. Hundreds more were homeless, jobless and penniless, their houses looted and vandalized, their shops, offices and farms seized and their valuables stolen. All over Iran, Bahá'í Centres, cemeteries and holy places had been confiscated by the authorities, and the House of the Báb, the most cherished Bahá'í property in the country, had been leveled to the ground.

> At the beginning of 1980, a new stage in the repression of the Bahá'í community was initiated by the government. A proclamation was made banning Bahá'ís from government and teaching jobs, and Bahá'í children were suspended first from universities, then from schools. Of course, the order was not immediately enforced on everyone, but it gave the Bahá'ís of Iran advance warning of what lay ahead.

---

[*] Olya Roohizadegan was a Baha'i who lived in Jahrum, just outside Shiraz. She would eventually be imprisoned along with Mona and would later write a book called **Olya's Story** about her experiences.

It was not long before news began to reach us in Shiraz of raids on the homes of several prominent Bahá'ís in Tehran, including members of the National Spiritual Assembly. Arrests soon followed.[10]

The new authorities had a plan to uproot the Bahá'í religion by targeting its leaders and by denying its people their basic rights.

Mona's Response to Revolution

"It was then that I decided to do my best
to help these children."

As Bahá'í children growing up in Iran, we had all read stories about the early believers and martyrs. They had suffered so much, and yet they had shown such amazing courage and faith in their difficulties. We read their stories and were inspired by them. They just seemed, however, like stories from a time long gone. We never realized those kinds of times might come back. Now news was coming to us about the arrests of Bahá'ís around the country and then the terrible news of executions. The time of heroes and martyrs had returned.

Mona was 12 when this change came. When she heard the news of arrests, violence, discrimination, and deaths, she was very sad. But when she saw the courage the Bahá'ís showed, her faith grew stronger. She started spending more time in prayer, especially at midnight. The persecution started hitting close to home, as friends of the family were arrested in Shiraz and other places in the country. Mona showed her feelings in her drawings. Taraneh remembered,

> "[Mona] drew a picture with someone crying, and his or her head is bowed down beneath his feet and is full of tears like a sea, but so shameful that he cannot be in the Presence of God. Like in the long obligatory prayer, it says, 'Thou dost perceive my tears ...' "

The long obligatory prayer was written by Bahá'u'lláh and is something that many Bahá'ís say every day. In the section mentioned above, the person prays to God basically saying, "You see my tears and my sighs. You hear my groaning and crying." It ends not by asking God to take away the pain, but by asking Him to help her focus on His beauty and follow whatever He decides. God is not just a Father who gives rules; He is a Friend or a Lover that we turn to with affection. When we are in love, we do what our beloved wants just out of a desire to please them. This is how Mona was seeing her relationship with God and His Messengers. The Bahá'í writings spoke of Bahá'u'lláh as "The Blessed Beauty." They are full of beautiful ideas like this.

Mona was turning for guidance and comfort to the Bahá'í writings, which are like an ocean for the soul to swim in. Her mother recalls,

"Sometimes, father and daughter used to sit up all night studying Bahá'í books and psychology texts. They soared the infinite worlds together and entered the realm of discoveries. They discovered realities, heard the unheard and saw the unseen; at which point I was left behind, because I could not even imagine [the things they experienced.]"

Mona was trying to understand why the world is the way it is and how we should respond. She was searching for ideas that she could then turn into action. She was gaining a vision of the way the world could be and should be. Then she was going to act in a way to bring that about. Her mother spoke of Mona's ideal vision of the world:

"She imagined a world in which ... people have rid themselves of prejudices, bitterness and enmity and are standing united hand in hand ... She has written an essay based on the fact that the world would be such a beautiful place if there were no wars, if arms and weapons would not be sold, and if the world would follow the Bahá'í Teachings and become united. She explains how the world could progress if all the resources that are exhausted for making weapons could be used for provision, health, sciences, industry, agriculture, and trade. She argues that such a world would become another world in which there would be no tyranny or injustice, where everyone progresses, and where all the people will live a good life in peace, harmony and affection together."

Mona was courageous in sharing her vision. She was eager to talk to her friends and classmates who were not Bahá'ís about this beautiful vision. Because of her joy and enthusiasm, many of them were eager to listen and ask questions. In her school, she would make wall magazines where she'd write articles with illustrations on enlightening subjects. In school essays, she would often end the essay with a Bahá'í quotation. There were, of course, limits to how outspoken she could be. The authorities were creating rules that severely limited free speech. And so a healthy and harmless exchange of viewpoints could now be considered a crime.

In one school essay, she shared what she did over the summer as well as some of her goals and values.* She talks about spending time with her friends and swimming, doing housework, and showing hospitality to visitors. Then she says,

"Also, I read a series of books that had been suggested to me. Mostly these were history books—the history of the lives of the early martyrs, and for each book I would write out questions and answers or copy out some beautiful sentences in a separate notebook. Those were the things I did each week, plus, well, a bunch of other things, and in this fashion the day would become night."

---

* See Appendix A for the complete essay on the writing prompt "What was your main responsibility for the summer?"

Mona mentions reading mostly "history books … about the lives of the early martyrs." She was not reading about the martyrs of early Islam, but those of the Bahá'í Faith. You can see, however, how that lack of detail makes it possible for her to tell the truth but not get in trouble. This is what we call "hikmat" in Persian and Arabic. It means using wisdom when you speak.

Mona was reading books such as *The Dawn-Breakers*, which is a famous history of the early years of the Bahá'í Faith. Her mother comments that when she read this book "she was so immersed … that she felt and witnessed every event that was described" in it. Taraneh talks about Mona reading a book about Anís, a youth who clung to the Báb's side as they were shot by a firing squad. The young man could not shield his beloved Master from the violence of 750 bullets. Taraneh says that after reading the book, Mona drew a picture of a girl being hanged—not alone, but with other women. Mona was clearly imagining herself in situations like the heroic ones she was reading about. This picture would be particularly prophetic.

Mona speaks of copying out "some beautiful sentences." This likely refers to the Bahá'í writings, which she loved to turn into one art or another. And then she says, "plus, well, a bunch of other things." Mona of course could not at this point speak openly in a school essay about her Bahá'í activities.

Those activities included basic community gatherings that she had participated in since she was a small child. There were children's classes, and the classes for junior youth that she attended. There were devotional gatherings, where she would often chant in her lovely, soft voice. There was the 19-Day Feast, where Bahá'ís gather in homes or centers to pray and consult on community affairs. She often recited poems and sang songs at Feast. She would sacrifice and give money she had saved to the Bahá'í Fund, which supported all the community's activities. Her family had always found something to give, even in the poverty of their pioneering. These were all regular parts of being a Bahá'í. Such activities were now considered illegal by the government.

Mona wanted to do more. She was always precocious. This means that she was always a little ahead of her age. For example, she was a year ahead in school, and she was very sensitive and spiritual for such a young person. Now she wanted to join in with the older youth in their classes. In the essay about what she did over her summer, she wrote about going to an Arabic class on Wednesday evenings. She says she didn't get out of that class what she was hoping. What she was hoping was to take the Arabic class that her father was teaching the youth. He had to be fair, though. Fifteen was the age of maturity for Bahá'ís, and she was only 13. That was frustrating for Mona.

She also wanted to teach her own Bahá'í class for small children. Remember how much she loved children. She applied to a committee that oversaw all the classes in Shiraz. She got back a rejection saying that she wasn't yet old enough. Hearing this news, she burst into tears. Her parents tried to comfort her and tell her the time would come soon enough. And as a junior youth, she knew just how wrong they were.

Mona knew she was ready to work with children. She was already doing it. It actually started in secret: One morning before school, Mona's mother saw her daughter putting some disinfectant, a towel, and some clean clothes in her bag. Mona didn't say anything about it, but she said she would be a few hours late after school. The same thing happened two more times that week. When it happened a fourth time and there was still no explanation, Mrs. Mahmudnizhad got angry.

Mona had just come home and jumped into the shower before her mother could say anything. Her mother opened the bathroom door halfway and shouted, "Why don't you go back where you came from?" And she walked away, upset that her daughter was keeping secrets from her.

Mona came out of the shower, and she was crying. "Mother, if I tell you the truth, will you allow me to go back there and continue my service?"

Service? Mrs. Mahmudnizhad wasn't sure what kind of service this was. She told her, "If what you are doing is right, I will even help you in your work, otherwise I will punish you. Now tell me!"

Mona wiped some of her tears and began to speak. Last week, her teacher had taken her class to an orphanage. The children there had melted Mona's heart. She was so moved that she volunteered to help out there. She told her mother about the first time she went:

"One of the kids came forward and asked me if I would like to be her mother. Without thinking, I sat and took her little hand in mine, kissed her beautiful face and told her that I would love to have a lovely daughter like her. A few days later, I felt that the little girl was expecting me, so I went to see her at the orphanage, but I found her sick in bed. Her beautiful eyes were swollen and red. As soon as she saw me, she said, 'Mom, you came!' Then the other children came round me and asked for my name. I told them that I was their mother.

"Their clothes were filthy. Their hair was a mess and they had not even washed their faces. The little ones who were barely a year or two had to share their bed with two others. They were all sick and had diarrhea. They were not wearing any diapers and their beds were full of filth; consequently, their hair and faces were infected with germs. Nothing was sanitary, and the children cried together in such a way that even a [heart of] stone could be moved to tears. It was then that I decided to do my best to help these children, so I asked the person in charge to allow me to go there a couple of times a week to bathe the children … [N]ow when I go there, as soon as the children see me they call out and say, 'Mommy Mona is here.' "

Mona would bring them biscuits, cheese puffs, storybooks and crayons. She continued,

"I sit down in the middle, while they hover over me by caressing my hair or sitting on my lap, and they show me the sort of affection that every child would like to show his mother. In this way, I can somewhat provide for them something which would in some way make up for not having a mother.

"Mother, there is no pleasure greater than this! I clean the smaller children; I bathe them; I put them in diapers; and if there is any time left, I take them in my arm and give them milk from a bottle. They then put their arms around me and touch my eyes and ears with their little fingers and go to sleep with a smile on their lips. In this way, I do what I can for them and consider myself the most fortunate mother in the world."

For three years, Mona visited the children in the orphanage. It was only when she was arrested and imprisoned that she stopped going. When her mother was sharing this story many years later, it was clear how deeply moved she still was by her daughter:

"How old do you think Mona was [when she started visiting the orphanage]? As God is my witness, she was only 13 years old. How do you think she purchased the biscuits, cheese balls, crayons and books? Her father used to give her a monthly allowance of 50 Tumans. He had also put some coins in a tin can and told her to take money from there for her taxi and transportation costs. However, since Mona didn't want to burden her father financially, she got up very early in the morning and, after saying her prayers, walked to school—which was quite a distance away—instead of taking a taxi. She also walked back from school. She did this regardless of the season or how hot or cold the weather was. In the summers, she worked in a supermarket and used her wages to buy gifts for the children and her friends ... Yes, dear Mona served Bahá'í and non-Bahá'í alike, and her goal was service to humankind."

It was with deeds such as this that Mona started to become known as "The Angel of Shiraz." All the while, she was living openly and speaking freely as a Bahá'í in a country that was increasingly hostile to her faith.

Other Bahá'ís had different opinions about how Bahá'ís should behave. It is important to know that Bahá'ís work for unity, but they don't always agree on everything. Some Bahá'ís wanted to be very careful and not call attention to themselves or let anyone know they were Bahá'ís. Given how difficult things were getting in Iran, this could be a very hot topic.

One incident shows how this clash of ideas could be painful, and particularly for Mona who was so sensitive. It involved the part-time job she had making a little money to spend on her children and other things. Mrs. Mahmudnizhad tells the story:

"Mona worked in a supermarket which was owned by two Bahá'ís. She would go there very early in the morning, and would weigh things like beans, lentils, peas, etc., and would package them in a bag ready to be sold. Of course, this wasn't one of her duties, as she was a salesperson, but she liked to help the owner of the store who was the father of one of her friends, and she would do any extra work that she could.

"One day, when one of the owners walked into the store, Mona approached him with joy to welcome him and said, 'Alláh-u-abhá.' He was upset that Mona had said 'Alláh-u-abhá' to him in the supermarket. He complained to the other owner that Mona could ruin their business in this manner and should not have said 'Alláh-u-abhá' in the store. Mona had apologized and said that she would say 'Salaam'* from thereafter, but he had not yielded in his anger.

"Dear Mona came home very upset, to an extent that she contracted a fever and became sick. She said, 'We have to sacrifice whatever we have for the Faith, our belongings are not worth anything. It is not important to me that he treated me this way, but if it were someone else working for them, she would have been deeply hurt.' She left her job at the store with a broken heart. She stayed awake all night communing with God, and prayed for the storeowner.

"It was from then forward that she entered a world of visions and witnessed everything in the realm of dreams."

---

* *Salaam* literally means "Peace," but it is used like "hello" in English.

Dreams and Visions

"I realized that I had not been asleep"

Dreams are a natural part of our lives, and we don't always take much notice of them. Sometimes they frighten us or leave us confused. Sometimes, they are so beautiful we have to share them with others. Sometimes they go further than that, and it seems like we have entered not just the dream world but the world of the spirit. We meet people who have passed on to that world and they share some wisdom or offer some sign that connects us and awakens us.

The most meaningful dreams of my life happened during the time of the Revolution and the several years that followed. This was not just true for me. I believe this is because we were always praying. Our lives were so full of urgency. The threat of injury, prison or death was always there, but we were also concerned with our spiritual lives. Were we overcoming fear and anger and blame through our prayers? Were we still united as families and as a community? If we were not united, what was the point of being a Bahá'í? Unity was the lesson and the gift we had to offer the world. Unity and a renewed faith. And for that, we turned to prayer, lots of prayer.

Mona's dreams during this period were very meaningful, too. She would share them with her family and would often draw or paint the images from the dreams. They showed how her spirit was closely connected to the next world. For example: Mona started to set her mind on the question of justice for the leaders who were terrorizing her community and the rest of Iran. She wondered, What kind of punishment would these men face for their crimes against humanity? They were responsible for so much violence and death.

One day her mother noticed Mona had been sad for some days. She asked her to share what was bothering her. Mona hesitated until her mother gave her her full attention, and then she opened up:

"For months, I have been thinking about the end of those who take captive innocent people, torture them, and finally execute them; those who are truly at fault and brainwash a number of naïve people to go astray … I have been asking Bahá'u'lláh repeatedly to show me the sort of punishment that these people receive.

"A few days ago, when I was deep in thoughts, I had a vision of a big and beautiful amphitheatre, in front of which was located three circles. The middle circle was a pool of blue, beautiful, water. Immediately after that was roundabout of grass and beautiful flowers. The third circle was a roundabout full of shiny, colorful, stones, which had nine gateways, one of which led to the amphitheatre. The stones were beautiful, and when the sun shone upon them, it gave them even more dazzle and beauty. I had lost myself in their beauty and started to throw the stones up in the air to enjoy their sparkle and dazzle.

"Suddenly, I saw Bahá'u'lláh before me and became ashamed of my childish behavior. Bahá'u'lláh noticed that I had felt ashamed, so He came forward and began to do what I had been doing. He, too, threw the stones up in the air to watch them. He then smiled at me and told me to follow Him inside the amphitheatre so that He could grant my desire.

"I walked into the theatre and saw a movie screen before me. Bahá'u'lláh started the projector and told me to watch."

Mona continues the story saying she recognized two prominent men on the movie screen. The picture was quite vivid and clear. She saw one of them lying on a bed with the fingers of one hand stuffed in his mouth and the other stuffed, as she describes, "under his body." No matter how hard he tried, he was not able to release his hands. She then saw the other man sitting with the fingers of both hands in his mouth. This man, too, was unable to free himself from his predicament. She continues:

"At first, I thought that their punishment was very mild, and suddenly desired to feel what they were feeling. As the thought passed through my mind, I began to feel their pain and realized how utterly painful and frightening was their condition. Suddenly, I lost my composure and began to scream saying that I did not wish to see any more. Suddenly, the light of the projector was turned off and I got back to my earlier condition. Bahá'u'lláh reminded me that I, myself, had begged Him to show me how they were being punished."

This had a big effect on Mona. She started praying that God would forgive these men. This is a sign of a strong soul—when you can pray for your enemies, those who are doing you harm, and mean it.

There are many interesting aspects to this dream. One is that Mona showed the same persistence—you could call it stubbornness—to God or to Bahá'u'lláh when she wanted an answer as she would sometimes show to her mother. Another is that this single-mindedness is not criticized by Bahá'u'lláh. His love covers over any criticism, and He simply answers her request. As it says in the Bible: "Knock, and the door will be opened to you." He also does not criticize her for playing with the stones, which she feels embarrassed about. He joins her in tossing the stones up in the air. This is very much like the way Bahá'u'lláh acted in His earthly life.

There is a story of a boy of four or five years old who, while the grown-ups were resting, found a bag of sugar. He put a handful in his mouth and filled both his fists, and when he walked out of the storeroom he ran into Bahá'u'lláh pacing in the hallway. Bahá'u'lláh did not shame the boy or even give him a critical or sad look. He looked at him with love and understanding and said, "It seems you like sweets." He then picked up a plate of candies and offered the boy one.[11]

The way of love is so often about understanding and allowing people their freedom. God allows all of us freedom. He knows the best way to reward goodness and to punish evil. Our job as individuals is to learn the way of love and forgiveness and to allow Him to take care of justice.

A key element of learning love and forgiveness is empathy. This means extending your feelings beyond yourself to include the feelings of others. You don't think of another as separate from you, but as united with you. For example, Mona had a friend who lost both of her parents in a few months' time, and Mona longed to comprehend her friend's feelings. She wrote about this and asked God, "Now that You have given me the bounty of having my parents, at least allow me to understand the loss which my friends feel by being deprived of theirs." In her dream, Mona reached out with empathy even to those who persecuted her community.

Her capacity for empathy could even be disabling to her. Her mother recalled one such time:

"One day in her biology class, her teacher was speaking about children's paralysis and was explaining the disease. When the teacher looked at Mona, she noticed that Mona's tears were streaming down and that her body [seemed] to be paralyzed. Bewildered, the teacher asked Mona if there was anything she could do, but Mona only smiled back at her. Yes, she had begged

God and prayed to feel everything and see everything as it was, even pain. When her teacher discussed this issue with us, her father and I tried to convince her to change her biology course to sociology. Although she did not quite agree with our decision, she obeyed and began her studies in social sciences."

While our main focus should be to learn love, forgiveness and empathy, we must also learn to stand up for what is right and to speak the truth. As a young Bahá'í female in Iran, Mona was pushed by her society to be silent and to blindly obey an unjust system. We see how, in her dreams, Mona was practicing speaking out in powerful ways. She was also telling the future. When she was only 12 or 13, Mona dreamed about her father and his coming death or martyrdom. She wrote the following about this dream:

"Last night, I dreamt that my father was martyred. My desire, his desire, had been fulfilled in the realm of dreams. My father was martyred in the path of truth; in the path of Bahá'u'lláh. In my dream, I realized that it is no longer my imagination or a story, but rather it is the absolute truth ...

"In the state of devotion, while still asleep, I told my father, 'Blessed are you, blessed are you for having attained the presence of the Manifestation of God, Bahá'u'lláh ... In my dream, I found myself consumed with pride. I was so overwhelmed with joy that my soul did not seem able to be contained in my body ... I saw myself addressing a number of non-believers, telling them how proud I was of my father, who, being a Muslim and a follower of the Shi'ite sect, had searched for the light of truth and found Bahá'u'lláh. I told them that my father had persevered in the face of hardship and given his life because of his faith in Bahá'u'lláh.

"I told them that my father had passed through the seven valleys and that he had recognized each valley before stepping into the next. I then explained to them the seven valleys, and recalled my father as I went through each valley.

"I then became aware of my surroundings and saw myself drenched in my tears. I realized that I had not been asleep, rather I had stepped into the world of visions. I will always be proud of such a father. I love him and appreciate him, and, and … "

Mona speaks of her father crossing "seven valleys." This is a reference to a book by Bahá'u'lláh called *The Seven Valleys*. That book describes the soul's journey from selfishness to selfless devotion to God, and it breaks down that journey into seven steps. These steps are symbolized by valleys, the low areas between hills or mountains. The early stages include the Valley of Search, the Valley of Love, the Valley of Knowledge, and the Valley of Unity. In her speaking out, Mona was showing both her understanding of the book and her father's spirituality.

Mona says she had stepped into the world of visions. It is easier for us to understand dreams than visions. Is a vision a dream we have when we are awake? Is it a momentary awakening of our souls into the world of spirit?

I had a glimpse of this kind of experience myself one time when I was deep in prayer. It scared me, actually. Some people, however, are able to stay in that experience longer. Mona was one. This was not something she talked about with me. She was not a show-off. Her mother has shared these stories with us. These experiences were an important part of her daughter's life.

She had at least one such experience as a child. Do you remember the story of Mr. Samandari? He was the old man who had a vision that baby Mona would one day make "the world to cry out." That same trip when he was visiting the family in Yemen, he had a photograph taken with Yadu'lláh and young Taraneh. In the picture, Mr. Samandari's hand is over Taraneh's head. Now, as a child, Mona would always gaze enviously at the photograph wishing that she could have met Mr. Samandari. Her mother picks up the story:

> "She immersed her thoughts so deeply in this until she experienced what she had desired. One day, when she was about 8 or 9, she ran towards me with tears rolling down her cheeks and said, 'Mother, I saw Mr. Samandari put his hand over my head.' I asked how this could have happened since Mr. Samandari wasn't there, but she said that she had met him in her room that day in a vision."

What a persistent will Mona had! What perseverance at that young age, and as she grew. And what perseverance she would be called on to show. As Jesus said,

> Ask, and it will be given to you; seek, and you will find; knock, and it will be opened to you.[12]

Mona's room

Maturity

"The soul of every Prophet of God, of every Divine
Messenger, hath thirsted for this wondrous Day"

"That day also passed and now I'm in high school. Here I've seen good teachers, very good teachers, some of them much better than what I imagined a teacher could be back then. Now, to make a long story short, there were certainly some teachers that from way back I got to know outside of school. Those teachers didn't use force or imposition. I spent at least two hours each Friday morning* with one, and those teachers were books—books that were especially for me, books that told me, 'Just give me two hours of your time per week. Only two hours.' I loved that teacher because whatever I wanted to learn, it would teach. Those two hour sessions came and went, and I gathered them up. I learned wonderful things far beyond what the school books taught and I drew out their usefulness. In my heart's core I was instructed by them, and put them into action and I was successful. My teacher taught me how to pass from the dark and narrow pathways where it is hard to see. It taught me how to persevere. It taught me the way to prosper is perseverance. It taught me how to persevere during spiritual tests.

"My teachers said to me, 'The life that you have in this transient world you see about you, this is not life,' and it said, 'The real life is in the other world, where you will realize all your lofty dreams

---

* Friday is the holy day of the week in Islam, and it is the one day of the week that students don't go to school.

of this world,' and it said, 'Therefore, my daughter, strive to find the Truth in this world, that in the other world, you may be united with it.' My teacher said to me, 'Don't just think that me and my words are enough.' It told me, 'Humanity needs to DO many things that they aren't doing, many things that pen and tongue cannot say.' My teacher told me many things and taught me many things, many things."

This lovely piece is the third and final part of Mona's essay "Which teacher, which method." This is the same essay that had described the "creature" teachers in the earlier sections. This portion was written later, as she says, when she was in high school. There is a clear difference in the maturity level. Mona was finding an education beyond what school could offer.

Mona saw her 15th birthday as an important milestone in her life. Remember that 15 is the age of maturity in the Bahá'í Faith. This doesn't mean you leave school, get married, get a job and buy a house at 15. It means, at that age, we become responsible for our own spiritual choices and development. We can no longer just say "I belong to this religion because my parents raised me that way." Just like there's a time when the mama and papa bird nudge their young to use their wings, the age of maturity is the time for the fledgling soul to fly.

Many young Bahá'ís around the world celebrate this day with a little ceremony of signing a registration card. This is a way of officially "declaring" as a member of the Bahá'í community. Mrs. Mahmudnizhad recalled her daughter's "declaration party":

"She was extremely excited on the day that she was registered as a Bahá'í. On the next day, she invited her non-Bahá'í friends and told them that it was her birthday. Her friends were amazed and reminded her that she had just celebrated her birthday a few days earlier; but she told them that it was now her spiritual birthday. She told them that this was her real birthday.

"On that day, with great excitement, she prepared a macaroni-dinner by herself and made a cake. When her friends arrived, she played some music and they danced and then they had lunch. Once she was certain that they had enjoyed themselves, she invited them to sit and listen to her. She then addressed them saying, 'I was, until today, considered someone who was born into a Bahá'í family; but, from today forward, I AM a Bahá'í and fully responsible for my behavior and my actions.' She then shared with them some of the Bahá'í Teachings.

"Her friends listened to her intently and congratulated her on her second, or rather spiritual birthday, wishing her ever-increasing success."

Now that she was 15, Mona could apply again to teach a Bahá'í children's class. Sure enough, she was assigned to the Children's Education Committee and she was able to begin teaching a weekly class with young children. According to *The Story of Mona*, the topics of the classes included:

the study of the great religions, developing spiritual qualities, encouraging the children to put their talents and education to the service of their fellow man and especially learning to appreciate the oneness and diversity of the human family.[13]

As with the orphans, Mona made sure to provide materials for the children, such as pencils, crayons and booklets. In the booklets, she would write prayers for the children to memorize. She herself had been memorizing more Bahá'í prayers and writings. This was at the suggestion of the National Spiritual Assembly of Iran in case one day the friends* lost access to Bahá'í books. The nine members of that National Spiritual Assembly were captured on August 21, 1980. They were never heard from again.

On 1 May 1981, we were devastated to hear news that the previous night the authorities had executed three of our dear family friends: Mr. Yadu'llah Vahdat, Mr. Sattar Khushkhu, and Mr. Ehsan Mehdizadeh.† Our family immediately went to the Bahá'í cemetery, where we were met by pretty much the rest of the Bahá'ís of Shiraz, including the Mahmudnizhad family. This was the spot my mother visited every Friday to pray and grieve for my oldest brother, Dariush (*Dáríúsh*), who passed away when he was 21. Cars kept arriving, with more and more people pouring in—hundreds, if not thousands, including Muslim mourners as well.

There were guards with guns inside and outside the cemetery. Inside, the bodies were being prepared for burial, and the guards would only let in immediate family. Of course, Mr. Vahdat's wife and daughter were absent because they were both in prison. Mahvash would only be held for a couple weeks total, but Mrs. Vahdat was arrested with her husband the previous June, was brutally tortured, and was imprisoned for several years.

The guards kept telling the Bahá'ís to leave. No one paid any attention. They were chanting prayers and weeping. Some mourners wailed and hit themselves on the head and chest with grief. At one point, we all began to sing the prayer "Is there any Remover of Difficulties save God?" We sang it 19 times. Can you imagine the hundreds of voices of young and old, men and women singing together? We posed no threat to the guards, but they were frightened

---

* "Friends" is a term Baha'is often use to refer to one another.

† These names transliterated are Yadu'lláh Vahdat, Sattár <u>Kh</u>u<u>shkh</u>ú, and Ihsán Mihdí-Zádih.

by the size of the crowd and by our solidarity. They insisted we leave, but still no one moved.

Then, a gentleman came and told the crowd that the Spiritual Assembly had met and asked that all the Bahá'ís leave immediately. And just like that, the crowd of Bahá'ís turned and—to the guards' great surprise—got in their cars and went home with no questions. A few days later, we all attended a huge memorial gathering at the cemetery to honor those dear souls. From that time onward, the government outlawed Bahá'ís gathering in large groups and the bodies of our martyrs would be dumped without notice in unmarked graves and without Bahá'í burial.

Soon after, Amu was offered a new position. He was already serving as Secretary of the Spiritual Assembly and teaching classes for youth and adults. Now he was appointed to be an Auxiliary Board Member, replacing Mr. Vahdat. This new role came with new duties. These duties extended over the whole Fars province, so he started to travel and spend even more time away from home.

This began to affect Mona. He included her in his activities as he was able. For example, he allowed her to attend the adult classes he was leading about the Bahá'í Writings, and she worked hard to memorize right away the prayers and writings they covered. Sometimes, however, he would be gone overnight or for several days. Sometimes her mother would go with him as well. Mona, of course, needed to stay home and go to school. My sister, Monir, often went and stayed with Mona overnight when her parents were gone. Mona shared her feelings:

Why did he have to be away so much? The youth and other people got to see him more than she did. She missed him. He was the one who understood her more than anyone in the world.

Monir was a safe person to talk to. She knew the situation but was not directly involved. They discussed the extraordinary times they lived in: Her father was sacrificing and helping to hold the Bahá'í community together. There was no one else who could give this service. Mona knew how deeply he loved her. She felt better after talking it out, and she was more determined to serve and to sacrifice.

Perhaps she remembered in those moments that she herself had asked God to show her what it felt like to be deprived of her parents.

One of Amu's duties was to visit with young people whose parents were Bahá'ís but not active in the community. You can imagine these young people were being discriminated against because they were Bahá'ís, and yet their families did not always practice the Bahá'í teachings or participate in Bahá'í community. These young people didn't necessarily know much about "their faith" except that they were being punished for it. Mrs. Mahmudnizhad explains:

"His aim was to talk to them and give them moral support. It was at times like this that Mona used to go with her father with a determined spirit to help the pre-youth and the youth of those families. She used to try to associate with them and to arrange deepening classes for them.

"Yadu'lláh had great handwriting and used to reward the friends for their services by a gift of a calligraphic piece. One of Mona's duties was to find the appropriate quotation for that specific individual. Mona also used to help with the illumination and beautification of the calligraphic pieces."

Several years ago, my sister gave me two of these calligraphic pieces that Amu had given her. They are quotes from Bahá'í writings written in Amu's beautiful handwriting and decorated with pictures cut out and added by Mona. These two pieces are a bit faded now, but still precious to us. We have them framed and hanging on our wall. What's so meaningful about the pieces is that they have some of Amu and some of Mona in them.

They would visit those unfortunate friends who had loved ones in prison, and would meet with them after the prison visits. They would listen to the news and to their grief. They would offer comfort and boost their courage. Before they left, Mona would leave behind coupons for gasoline (petrol) without letting them know she had done so. The war with Iraq was now on, and gasoline was being rationed. According to her mother, Mona would do everything she could to get these coupons.

As things got worse and worse, the household worked together as a team. Amu would go house to house visiting the Bahá'ís with both his wife and daughter. The family moving together drew less suspicion than if Amu went alone. Amu was not only engaging in his service, he was trying to model Bahá'í behavior for his daughter. According to Mrs. Mahmudnizhad, there was never any conflict between her husband and herself about Mona's involvement in Bahá'í activities.

At this point in Shiraz, the whole Bahá'í community from top to bottom was under threat. *The Story of Mona* offers this description:

> The persecution of the Bahá'ís extended to every level of society. While the Islamic authorities tended at first to single out only the more prominent members of the Faith for arrest and execution, cancellation of pensions, freezing of bank accounts and dismissal from employment, they extended their repressions even to the school level by expelling numerous Bahá'í children, especially those attending high school and university. They were only to be allowed to continue their studies if they denied being Bahá'ís.

Bahá'í children, even when they were still allowed to stay in school, were forced to sit apart at the back of their classrooms, as "unclean infidels" and were not allowed to touch the other children. In one instance a Bahá'í child was forced to wash the brick floor of his classroom and sent home with bleeding hands, because he had refused to recant his Faith. [14]

The need was overwhelming. Mona tried to arise for the sake of these children, as well. After school, she would change out of her school uniform, put on a chador and walk to the homes of children who were not getting their proper schooling, no matter what their religion. She'd work with them on basics like reading and writing. She would write down the birthdays of poor children in her notebook, her mother remembered, "and visit them on those days with flowers, candy and fruit" even when "they lived on the small streets of the remote areas of the city." She would visit a home for disabled children and help them to walk and exercise. As her mother recalled, "the children would fight and cry over her to give them exercises; however, she always tried to be fair and used to give exercises to three different kids each time she went there."

Her mother also said,

"She spoke to Bahá'í parents whose children were no longer allowed to receive an education, consoled them and gave them courage to endure. If there was any news from the Universal House of Justice*, she … communicated the message bringing joy to their hearts."

So many Bahá'í children were being kicked out of school, but Mona herself was still attending. That meant that while there were more people to visit, there wasn't any more time. When she learned a friend of hers was expelled, she said, "Good for you. Now you can

---

* The elected body that oversees the world Baha'i community.

study the Bahá'í books one year longer. Pray that I will also be expelled."

Mona's service to the Faith had grown so rapidly she found she barely had time to complete her schoolwork. This was the same girl who, not long before, used to study so much that her parents went to the principal, who told her, "We need professors, but not crazy professors." The stress on Mona was so overwhelming she thought of giving up her Bahá'í activities.

What do you do when you're overwhelmed like that? Do you make an abrupt change and drop your responsibilities? If not, how do you keep from burning out? How do you adjust and keep your important commitments but let go of some of the smaller priorities? What if all your commitments seem important? Everyone needs to eat and sleep, right? These are the questions that mature individuals face all the time.

Mona didn't know what to do. One day she was so tired and felt like she was at the end of her rope, so she went to her father for guidance. Other parents might say, "Hey, focus on your school." Or "You're just a kid, now is when you need to be having fun!" What did Amu say? Amu went to the bookshelf, took down a book and read the words of Bahá'u'lláh:

> Great indeed is this Day! ... The soul of every Prophet of God, of every Divine Messenger, hath thirsted for this wondrous Day ... An act, however infinitesimal, is, when viewed in the mirror of the knowledge of God, mightier than a mountain ... This is a Revelation, under which, if a man shed for its sake one drop of blood, myriads of oceans will be his recompense.[15]

He didn't answer her question directly. He didn't tell her what to do. He simply provided the larger vision, which can be found in the Bahá'í writings. Mona herself decided what to do. She resolved to put her anxiety behind her. Part of the problem was allowing her mind to focus on stress and on the negative aspects of life. She could instead concentrate on the good and the opportunities of life. She would do her best to serve humanity day by day, as God's Providence allowed.

In the passage from Mona's essay that opened this chapter, she discusses her two-hour study sessions on Friday and their power for her. Now Mona was no longer satisfied with just two hours a week of extra reading. A hunger was pushing her to want more from the day than what God had provided.

If you peeked in Mona's room in the middle of the night, you would probably find her awake. She scheduled out her time in the early morning from 1 to 6 a.m., planning for each hour a particular subject to study, a book to read or a time for prayers. She might be studying a Bahá'í book or Arabic grammar or a book on psychology or self-improvement. She was trying to cram in as much understanding, as much awareness into her day as possible. Her mother claimed she was only sleeping two or three hours a night.

The household chores, schoolwork and service activities of the day didn't allow her enough time to satisfy her intellectual and spiritual hunger. Maybe the quiet of night inspired her. Alone with her window open and the midnight breeze, Mona would chant and her voice would mingle with the sounds of the street at night and greet and wake the birds of the morning.

When she got tired, she would pace the room. During a break, she would sometimes gaze down at the street five levels below and at the gentleman at the corner shop. It was before dawn, and he was already at work preparing his soup (*ásh*) for his morning customers. Mona would call out to him in her mind:

"It's just you and me, Mr. Ásh-maker. We're the only ones awake. You are getting ready to feed the stomachs of the people, I pray for them to feed their souls. How can they sleep? Don't they know what Day this is?"

Steps of Courage

*"Without a word of hesitation, He placed
the cape around her shoulders"*

Mona was in Grade 11 in the fall of 1981. One of her classes was a Religious Literature course. Of course, the school's idea of "religious literature" was only texts that were acceptable to the narrow-minded Shí'ih clergy that now ran the government. One day her teacher assigned the students to respond to the following prompt: "The fruit of Islam is liberty and freedom of conscience, but you must taste it to understand." The students were to read their papers out loud in front of the class. This assignment clearly showed the teacher wanted to divide the Muslim students from all others.

Mona was not happy about this. This teacher was so *porrú*! There's no really good word for that in English. It's like saying someone is full of gall. Gall is bold, shameless behavior, but it literally means bile—the bitter fluid produced by the gall bladder. When someone is *porrú*, it can leave that taste of bitterness in your mouth. And for this teacher to call what this new government represented "liberty" and "freedom of conscience," it just put that taste in her mouth.

Of course, Mona had no problem with Islam. Bahá'ís fully accept Islam and the divine station of its Prophet Muhammad and all of the other Prophets spoken of in the Islamic holy book, the Qur'án. Bahá'ís believe the Qur'án is the Word of God. But the difference between the Bahá'í interpretation of the Qur'án and that of this government was like the difference between sweet and bitter.

Now Mona could not just use *hikmat*, "wisdom", to write her way
around this. Whatever she wrote, she would need to read out loud in
front of everyone. She had to write something she believed. The final
essay she wrote is lost, but a draft of it was found. It begins as a call
for free speech, but then goes as far as openly proclaiming
Bahá'u'lláh as the Promised One.

'Freedom' is the most brilliant word among the radiant words
existing in the world. Man has always been and will ever be
asking for liberty. Why, then, has he been deprived of liberty?
Why from the beginning of man's life has there been no freedom?
Always, there have been powerful and unjust individuals who
for the sake of their own interests have resorted to all kinds of
oppression and tyranny ...

Why don't you let me be free to express our goals in this
community; to say who I am and what I want, and to reveal my
religion to others? Why don't you give me freedom of speech so
that I may write for publication or talk on radio and television
about my ideas? Yes, liberty is a Divine gift, and this gift is for us
also, but you don't let us have it. Why don't you let me speak
freely as a Bahá'í individual? Why don't you want to know that a
new religion has been revealed; that a new radiant star has risen?
Why don't you push aside that thick veil from your eyes?

Perhaps you don't really think that I should have freedom. God
has granted this freedom to man. You, his servant, cannot take it
from me. God has given me freedom of speech. Therefore, I cry
out and say, "His Holiness Bahá'u'lláh is the Truth!" God has
given me freedom of speech. Therefore, in clear words, I write,
"Bahá'u'lláh is the One whom God has made manifest! He is the
founder of the Bahá'í religion and His Book is the Mother of
Books ... [16]

Now I doubt she actually was able to read the whole essay aloud. Her teacher insisted that she stop and sent her to the principal. The principal called in Mona's parents: This behavior was unacceptable! The parents begged him not to expel her. This man was not friendly to Bahá'ís, but he hesitated to kick her out. Maybe he realized how popular she was with teachers and students and how it might create more trouble if he did. He agreed that Mona could stay, but she could never discuss the Bahá'í Faith again at school. They all agreed, and she obeyed the agreement from then on.

Let's remember: this is the same girl who in eighth grade sat in her chair unable to say something to a teacher who unfairly canceled a test. Now she was trumpeting aloud her religion that was illegal in the eyes of her country.*

Mona had found a new courage. Some called her fearless. But does that mean that she had no fear when she did this? Don't you imagine when she said this that her hands might have been shaking a little bit? That her palms might have been sweaty and her heart racing? That her voice was trembling? At least at first. Courage is not a lack of fear. Courage is moving through the fear because you believe that what you are doing is right. And each step of courage you take, your fear has less control over you. Is courage even possible without fear? Courage is like a muscle that must be exercised, and fear is simply the weakness we build up from. And even the strongest can never escape weakness completely.

The group that inspired the most fear in Iran was the Revolutionary Guard. This was a special military group created by Ayatollah Khomeini early in the Revolution. It was like an army that

---

* After Mona was arrested, the school delivered a report of this behavior to the prosecution. One source mentions that the Hujjatiyeh group now controlled the school's administration and they were eager to help the authorities against the Baha'is.

swore allegiance not to the country itself but to the leaders of the
Islamic Revolution. So there was the regular army that my father and
Mr. Vahdat had belonged to, along with my nephew and countless
other Iranian youth. By 1981 that army was engaged in a
heartbreaking, bloody war against Iraq. The Revolutionary Guard,
on the other hand, was made up largely of uneducated and fanatical
young men from villages around Iran. They were not there to fight
foreigners. They were there to force the Iranian people to submit to
the will of the Islamic Republic.

In short, the Revolutionary Guard was the ruthless instrument by
which the clergy maintained their grip on power. For Mona to speak
up in class to a teacher, who had no connection to the authorities,
required one level of courage; for her to speak up to a member of the
Revolutionary Guard required another. One day Mona was visiting
her neighbors who were Muslim. A cousin of her friend was visiting
the family, as well. He was a member of the Revolutionary Guard.
Mrs. Mahmudnizhad picks up the story:

> "As soon as he saw Mona, he said to her, 'You are a Bahá'í, aren't
> you?' When Mona responded in the affirmative, he continued
> saying, 'We have decided to destroy you all. First we will arrest
> all your leaders and execute them, and then you will all convert
> to Islam and follow the Shi'ite religion.'
>
> "Mona then told him: 'You are getting ahead of yourself, slow
> down and listen to me. Yes, you come with your weapons, take
> us in by force, put us behind bars and even execute us, but your
> success will end there! Each and every one us believes in the
> Bahá'í Faith, and [you will not succeed in destroying our Faith]
> even if you cut our bodies in small pieces, for every part will
> separately cry out saying, "I am a Bahá'í!" In fact, just now,
> because of what you said I reached a certitude that the Bahá'í
> Faith is the absolute truth. So you see the harsher your behavior,

and the harder the adversity, the stronger will our faith and certitude become. So here is your chance, do endeavor to attain your goal!' "

Evidently, the encounter did not go any further than that. How could someone respond to Mona's bold statement except by either backing down or spiraling into violence? Mona was now speaking her truth to someone who saw her as the enemy. The great test of courage and integrity is if you can stand up for what is right, no matter what the outcome. But to do that you have to KNOW what you're standing up for is right. You cannot just have some faith. You have to be absolutely certain. You have to have certitude. Mrs. Mahmudnizhad said:

> "One of Mona's paintings is reflective of the certitude she had reached. The painting is in three phases. The first phase shows a house of a Bahá'í family which is set on fire by the enemies of the Faith, while she is praising God and raising the call of 'Yá Bahá'u'l-Abhá!'* The second phase shows her being tortured in prison, while again she is raising the call of 'Yá Bahá'u'l-Abhá!' The third phase shows that a bullet is shot through her throat. The bullet comes out of her throat from the other side shouting 'Yá Bahá'u'l-Abhá!' "

This idea of experiencing suffering in three stages is surprisingly consistent in Mona's paintings and dreams. These phases also seem to represent stages of spiritual strength and courage. In the spring of 1982, Mona took a trip to Isfahan, a city about 6 or 7 hours north of Shiraz by car. She was visiting some of her friends when a similar vision struck her. Her mother said,

---

* Yá Bahá'u'l-Abhá means "O Thou the Glory of the Most Glorious" in Arabic. It is an expression used by Bahá'ís in times of emergency, difficulty, or excitement. (Pronounced: YA-ba-HA-ol-AB-ha)

"One day, when she was sitting in a taxi going to the home of her friend, she was carried away in her thoughts and had a vision, which she then put on paper. She drew three steps.

"On the first step, you see the picture of her father being hanged, underneath which is written, 'The first stages of love are to lose one's head, to lose one's life, to persevere in the path of calamity; they are the first and last.'

"The second step signifies the home and belongings of her [parents], which were confiscated after [her father's] martyrdom. She has also drawn a cross over it, and next to it has drawn the picture of a woman who is watching the scene in wonderment. The woman is me, whose husband was martyred and who lost her home and belongings and was left without a refuge.

"On the third step, she has drawn a picture of herself being hanged, underneath which is written, 'Our aim is to give our lives, to sit with the lovers of God, to be enthralled with the love of friend and stranger alike, and to adore the one true God.' "

Mona gave this drawing to her friend as a gift in an envelope on which she wrote, "Accept this from the bottom of my heart, because all the love you've stirred in me is in the ink and the contents of the envelope."

The most well-known of Mona's dreams also takes place in three stages. This is the dream of the three colored capes. She had this dream in the summer of 1982, just a couple months before she was arrested. It is a complex dream and, in its way, beautifully encapsulates her life. She wrote about this dream in her diary, and the story was included in *The Story of Mona*:

She had been saying prayers with a small group of friends for several hours. After they left her home, she was so moved by the prayers that she went into the living room and sat down in front of a photograph of 'Abdu'l-Bahá, meditated quietly and then fell asleep.

In her dream, she saw 'Abdu'l-Bahá chair and desk, with a vase on it, as in the picture before her. She was very happy and said: "How happy I am to see your desk and chair." At the same moment she saw Bahá'u'lláh entering the room. The Blessed Beauty [Bahá'u'lláh] went out into an adjoining chamber and brought out a box containing a beautiful red cape. He unwrapped it in front of her, saying, "This is the cape of martyrdom in my path. Do you accept it?"

Mona was speechless … Finally, she said, "Whatever pleases you … "

Bahá'u'lláh put the cape back in the box and returned to the adjoining room bringing back with him a second box, containing a black cape which he unwrapped and said:

"This black cape symbolizes sorrow in my path. Do you accept it?" Mona replied, "How beautiful are the tears shed in Thy path."

He put the cape back in the box and again returned to the other room, emerging with yet a third box containing an elaborately beaded blue cape of the same design as the others.

Without a word of hesitation, he placed the cape around her shoulders, and said: "This is the cape of service." Then he seated himself in the chair and said to Mona: "Come and take a picture with me!"

Mona was breathless with astonishment at the bounties being showered on her and could hardly walk. She looked up and saw a man sitting behind an old-fashioned camera covered by a cloth. Bahá'u'lláh repeated his instruction but Mona could not move.

Then Bahá'u'lláh took her arm, saying, "Mehdi, take our picture." And he took a picture of them together. The flash of the camera wakened her abruptly and she pleaded tearfully to be able to finish her dream and then fell asleep again. Bahá'u'lláh had left the room. Only the photographer remained, carrying the tripod and camera on his shoulder as if to leave. He turned around and asked Mona to convey his love to his children. But Mona could not tell which "Mehdi" he was since there were many people by that name in the long history of the Faith and in her own community. But still he looked familiar to her. "Mehdi" was busily tying his shoes and noticed that Mona did not recognize him. As he was leaving the room he turned and said, "I am Mehdi Anvari." Mona instantly recognized him as one of the Bahá'ís of Shiraz who had previously been killed.[17]

How well Bahá'u'lláh knew Mona's heart. First, blue was her favorite color. Second, the stages of Mona's spiritual evolution were laid before her, but in reverse order. It was the summer of 1982, and she was not even fully 16. Service was the garment she wore, and beautifully so. The other garments would wait, for the moment.

The dream also shows how real and close the world of spirit is when we live in a state of prayer. Dr. Mehdi Anvari (*Mihdí Anvarí*) had been executed on 17 March 1981, a little over a year before Mona had this dream. She didn't know him well, because his family had pioneered to a town a few hours away called Abadeh. He was part of a large well-known family in the area. His son, Nayer (*Náyir*), was my teacher in Bahá'í classes when I was a junior youth.

This dream had a profound impact on Mona. Her mother has shared her memory of Mona at the time of the dream:

"One day, very early in the morning, we awoke from the sound of Mona's cries. We got up and ran to her room. She was standing in the middle of the room, with tears streaming down her cheeks and her hand placed on her chest, saying, 'I feel Bahá'u'lláh's hand here!' [...] Mona always felt Bahá'u'lláh's fingers on her chest [as He closed the button on the cape], and even reminisced about it several times in the prison."

Waiting

"I am a soldier of the Blessed Beauty,
and I will not leave my post."

Everyone knew Amu would be arrested. By summer and fall of 1982, Bahá'í leaders around the country were being arrested everywhere. The government was now fully organized behind its goals. They planned to wipe out our Faith by imprisoning and killing our leaders. Nine Auxiliary Board Members—including Mr. Vahdat—plus a Continental Counselor* had already been killed or disappeared without a trace. In the past year, the members of a new National Spiritual Assembly (formed since the disappearance of the previous one in 1980) had been arrested and executed, as were members of Local Spiritual Assemblies in cities such as Hamadan, Tabriz and Tehran.

The fact that Amu avoided arrest so long surprised everyone. The fear and the waiting for his arrest were not easy for his family. Knowing that your loved one could be taken away and executed at any time is very difficult to live with. The tense wait even inspired some strange rivalries: Apparently, Mona and Taraneh argued about who would get their father's books when he was executed. Their deeper concern for his safety was no doubt behind such a quarrel.

---

* A Continental Counselor is a position that supports Bahá'í community on a a national or continental scale, compared with the Auxiliary Board Member's regional focus.

His wife was the one most concerned. When he was appointed Auxiliary Board Member, she became especially anxious. Mrs. Mahmudnizhad said:

"I knew that this would guarantee his arrest, because he was also the secretary of the LSA of Shiraz. I was worried that his workload would increase and that he would have to work night and day, which would endanger his health. Of course his appointment ... put his life more at risk as well."

Some Bahá'ís were escaping to Turkey or Pakistan and then settling in countries that would offer asylum. Amu, however, would not talk about escaping or moving to another city or village.

Our family was in a different situation. And, just a few months before arrests in Shiraz would sweep up so many of our dear friends, we moved.

My sister, Shahin, had married a wonderful young man named Saeid Rezaie (Sa'íd Riḍáí). Saeid had attended Pahlavi University in Shiraz and earned a degree in agricultural engineering just before all Bahá'ís were expelled. After graduating, he moved to the northern part of Iran, to a province called Mazindaran. He and a friend planned to start an agricultural endeavor and to serve the Bahá'í community there. He would come back to Shiraz to visit family as much as he could, and we would see him and hear of all his activities. One of these times when he came to visit, he showed his interest in my sister and asked her out. His trips back to Shiraz increased. It was a 13-hour drive, but he would travel all the way just to see Shahin for a short time, and then he would get back on the bus and return home.

When my sister and he got married in 1981, she moved to the north with him. It was so hard for us to say goodbye, even though we knew she would be happy with Saeid. My parents started talking about moving there to be close to her. We heard there was a house available, and the owner wanted to find a Bahá'í family to rent to. This was in the middle of nowhere, on a highway between the cities of Sari and Qa'em Shahr. The community there was in need of support from a pioneering family.

My family consulted with Mr. Mahmudnizhad, and he encouraged us to go. So in August 1982, we packed up and got ready to move. I remember when Mona and her family came to say goodbye at a gathering we had at my brother's house. That was the last time we saw each other.

When we got to Mazindaran, we had a hard time finding a high school that would enroll a Bahá'í. All of them rejected me, except one school called Vali 'Asr in Sari. That didn't mean it would be easy. This was still Iran after the Revolution. On my first day of high school, the students were gathered together to demonstrate against the "enemies" of Iran: America, England and Israel. I refused to take part, because this goes against the Bahá'í principle that the world is one country. As a result, the principal said she would not allow me into the class. For several weeks, I went to school and sat in the schoolyard every day with nothing to do, waiting for them to change their minds, while they waited for me to change mine.

The school was quite far from our house, which was right next to the highway. The local people knew it as a Bahá'í home. People used to come and throw stones at our house and break windows. One time they shouted they would attack the house and rape the girls, so we had to go and stay at a friend's house for a week or so, until that group got tired and gave up. These are just some examples of the difficulties we faced there. Still, they were nothing compared to what was about to hit our beloved city of Shiraz.

No one expected Mona to be arrested. Yes, Mona had her dreams and visions about imprisonment and martyrdom. Still, the government's pattern was clear: they arrested mainly men, sometimes women, but never girls or children. Now with hindsight, we see how that pattern was changing. Mona's mother explained:

"One day she came home and said 'Mom, there is a man who is always following me wherever I go. At first I thought that his destination is in the same direction as mine, but when I noticed that he is always behind me, I realized that I am being observed.'

"I told her, 'Be more careful.'

"She responded: 'Then I won't be able to continue my services. I think that he is appointed by Baha'u'llah to follow me, because, when he is walking behind me, I don't have to deal with the boys harassing me on the streets. * He is like a brother who is protecting me, but I feel bad that he has to wait on the street for hours for me to finish my business in a home and return. Sometimes, I even let him know from afar before I go in that I may take a couple of hours or more. I am used to it, and am in no way scared or worried about it.'

"Afterwards, we realized that he was a Revolutionary Guard who had followed Mona everywhere making a list of all that she had done and all the places she had visited."

Of course, Mona's father had been followed and harassed by such spying guards. The family's phone line was tapped. Their mail was being opened and read. These were regular aspects of the police

---

* Boys on the street often follow the girls as they are walking. They try to engage them and ask for their phone numbers. Girls usually ignore them even though they are very persistent. This is an annoyance but is not considered to be threatening or "stalking" as it would be in other parts of the world.

state that Iran had become. It is a sign of Mona's growing spiritual vision that she could call this guard a brother. It may also be that she was trying to assure her mother, who no doubt would be more nervous about this news than Mona.

In October, rumors were flying around that the Revolutionary court in Shiraz was making its list of arrest warrants. In mid-October, Mr. and Mrs. Mahmudnizhad went to a meeting at the home of Olya Roohizadegan, who was one of his assistants. Olya tells the story:

> A minute after he and his wife had arrived, the doorbell rang. I looked out of the window and saw three bearded men, obviously representatives of one of the Islamic groups. Before I opened the door, I asked the Mahmudnizhads to go out through the back door and wait. The men were from the local mosque, and said that they had come to find out how many people were living in our house so that they could give us the proper number of food coupons.

> The next day Mr. Mahmudnizhad came to our house again. He told me, "After we left your house yesterday and got out of earshot, my wife and I could not stop laughing at the thought of Bahá'í houses being surrounded by armed guards before they dare ring the doorbell!" [18]

Amu again was using laughter to break the tension. A few days after the incident at Olya's home, a group of youth came to visit Amu and to reason with him. Mrs. Mahmudnizhad explained:

> "The [Bahá'í] youth ... begged him to leave Shiraz, inasmuch as they feared that his arrest was inevitable. However, Mr. Mahmudnizhad told them that he was a soldier of the Blessed Beauty and that he would not leave his post.

> "They offered to come and place a peephole on our door, so that whenever the revolutionary guards came to take him, we would

know by looking through it and would not open the door. In order not to hurt the youth, Mr. Mahmudnizhad agreed to their suggestion, so they came and installed the peephole and went."

Even their Muslim neighbors down the hall tried to help out. The husband came one day to speak to Mrs. Mahmudnizhad, and said, "Let us keep your furniture in our home, so that if they come to loot your apartment, you will have something to live with later. We will keep them safe for you."

"When I saw that they meant well, I accepted their offer. They came -- the parents and the girls --and moved some of our furniture and clothing to their apartment. They also placed our books under the bed. When Mr. Mahmudnizhad came home and noticed some things were missing, he said, 'How come one of the carpets is missing?' "

Amu asked that everything be brought back. He said to his wife, "Do you want me to be ashamed for not having anything to give in the path of the Blessed Beauty? Do you want me to sacrifice my home empty of its carpets?"

Isn't it interesting that he would allow his friends to install a peephole but not to hide his belongings? To his wife, these situations seemed very similar, but Amu saw an important difference. The second example showed attachment to worldly objects. He was willing to sacrifice so much more than his belongings for his faith.

So it seemed that the arrests would come any day, but Amu and Mona were still going around visiting Bahá'í friends. They were not hiding inside. They went again to Olya's home. She asked Amu a question that was on the hearts of all the Bahá'ís:

"How long do you think this will go on? How long will the Bahá'ís have to suffer such prejudice and oppression under Khomeini's regime?"

Amu was tired. He was not sleeping enough. His ulcer had been bothering him. Everybody around him was anxious. He knew that at any moment the sword was going to fall, he was going to be arrested and what they would do to him was anyone's guess. Mona probably had her own thoughts about this, but she waited for her father to speak. He looked at Olya lovingly and spoke.

"My dear, study the Bahá'í writings. They have already described the calamities in Iran and in the world at large. We Bahá'ís have a difficult test before us, but we have to recognize it and remain firm. Khomeini has come to assist the progress of the Faith."

He said this with a smile of hope. Mona understood what her father was saying, but it was really hard to accept sometimes. How do we see someone who seems to be so evil and cruel as a friend? There were moments when she could glimpse this, but others when anger got the better of her.

He continued, "This is only the beginning of the revolution on this planet. Calamities [Great difficulties] will continue to occur until humanity has reached a higher consciousness, and until we all practice the unity of mankind and live together in peace and harmony."[19]

The Arrest

"Not a leaf falls off the tree unless by the Will of God"

Two days later they came. It was 23 October 1982. It was evening, almost 9 p.m. on a school night, and Mona was studying. Mrs. Mahmudnizhad explains:

"[W]e hosted a gathering for Mr. Mahmudnizhad's assistants who had come from in and around Shiraz to consult with him ... Mona was wearing a green blouse and a green and cream checkered skirt, and looked particularly handsome with her green eyes and straight long hair. She spent all day serving the guests, and, once they had left, she started to study for her English exam, which was scheduled for the next day. Mr. Mahmudnizhad said that he would help himself to some dinner, and I went to take a bath because I was exhausted. I had just come out of the bathroom and was still wearing a towel on my head when I heard a violent knock on the door.

"By force of habit, I automatically asked who it was without looking through the peephole, and reached the door in no time. In the meanwhile, I could hear our Muslim neighbor telling whoever was behind the door that we were not in. I looked through the peephole and saw five revolutionary guards standing outside with their weapons. They were forcing their weight against the door and were trying to break it and enter our home. I told Mr. Mahmudnizhad, who was sitting behind his desk writing, that there were revolutionary guards behind the door."

According to Olya's account, Mona shared the following:

Four armed guards pushed their way into the house. My father asked them to identify themselves. They said, "We are the guards of the Revolutionary Court of Shiraz. We have a warrant to enter your house from the Public Prosecutor of Shiraz." My father calmly asked to see the warrant, and one of the guards handed him a piece of paper. My father looked at it and said, "Please come in, the house is yours to search." [20]

The four rushed in and began to search the apartment, while the fifth stayed in the hall by the stairs to keep out any curious neighbors. Remember, the apartment was not very large, only two bedrooms, a living room, dining room and kitchen. The guards told Mona and her parents to sit on the couch and not to move, but Mona pushed back. Mrs. Mahmudnizhad explains:

"Usually, as soon as they entered a home, they asked the women of the household to put on their Islamic attire; but they didn't tell us anything to that effect on that day. Mona stood up and said that she wished to cover her hair, but they told her that it was not necessary and ordered her to sit down again. She said, 'I have to obey the rules of the country and cover my hair!' But again they said, 'No.' Finally Mona stood up and said, 'You are neither my father nor my brother, and I must, in accordance to the laws of Islam, cover my hair when in your presence.' She went to her room and put a shawl around her hair.

"One of them remained to watch us, and the others went to Mona's room and looked through everything. They even took out the sheets that were kept over the mattress and the blanket by safety pins. They did not bother to open the safety pins; they just ripped the sheets apart to look under them. Believe me, it was like we were attacked by the Mongols; everything was a mess.

One of the guards was standing guard by the stairs and had warned all the neighbors not to come out of their apartments before midnight.

"I was very worried about my husband and told him that I thought they were going to take him. I was also shivering; however, he told me to look at 'Abdu'l-Bahá's photograph and recite the 'Remover of Difficulties.' He started reciting the prayer himself, and Mona and I joined him. The guard who was standing in front of us ordered us to be quiet, but we paid no attention and finished reciting it -- but of course only one round of it!"

The guards found a family photo album with pictures of Bahá'ís in it. Some of these individuals were dear friends of the family, and some of them had been executed. The guards considered this evidence of some crime.

"Do you know who this is?" one guard said.

Amu looked and said, "This is a picture of Mr. Bakhtavar."

Mr. Bakhtávar was a well-known Bahá'í scholar who was executed in July 1981 in the city of Mashhad. The guard sneered and felt this was proof that they were spies or enemies of Iran or Islam. He didn't understand that this family was proud of their friend, not just for his intelligence or scholarship, but because of his faith, his sacrifice and his dedication to all humanity.

This nonviolent family sat with a guard pointing a gun at them. Three others were turning Mona's room upside down looking for things. Mona still believed it was just her father they were going to take. He was sitting between her and her mother on the couch. Every once in a while, they would each trade looks and the feelings would start to bubble up to the surface, and they would try to push them back down.

Mona put her focus on studying her English. She would occasionally ask her father for help, but each time she had a question she would ask permission to speak from the guard pointing a gun at them. The guard soon got tired of this. He told her to be quiet and stop asking questions.

"I have a test tomorrow. You guys leave, and I am the one that has the test."

But the guard insisted. "No. No more questions."

It was getting close to midnight when news came that no one was expecting. Mrs. Mahmudnizhad explains:

"The three guards who were searching Mona's room came back after three hours with a plastic bag full of Mona's writings. They then turned to Mona and Mr. Mahmudnizhad and told them that they were taking them to the station.

"I immediately rose to my feet and shouted, 'She is only a child, where do you think you want to take her? Take me instead.' "

The head guard said, "You should call her the little Bahá'í teacher. Look at this poem. It is not the work of a child. It could set the world on fire. Someday she will be a great Bahá'í teacher."

Mona's mother began to beg them not to take her: "If you want to take my husband, OK, but where are you taking this sixteen-year-old girl at this hour of the night?!"

The guards were getting angry at the delay. They expected everyone to fear them and obey them without thinking. "Don't say, 'This little sixteen-year-old girl! You should say, 'the little Bahá'í teacher!' "

Mona stood up suddenly to calm her mother down. "Mother, why are you begging them? Why do you think they are taking me? I haven't bombed a bridge or set a bus on fire. They haven't found drugs or guns in our home, and I haven't committed any crime!

Mother, don't you know why they are taking me? Because I am a
lover of the Blessed Beauty …"

"I suddenly shivered in my skin and sunk into the couch. Her
father was looking at his daughter with tremendous joy and
pride. He was enjoying his daughter's extraordinary courage,
and his bluish green eyes were sparkling with joy."

As Mona told the story to Olya, her father tried to calm her
mother:

"Farkhundih, don't worry. I love these brothers like my own sons
and I am sure it is the will of God for them to be here now and to
take Mona and myself away with them. Just leave everything in
God's hands and don't worry about Mona. These brothers look
upon Mona as their own sister." [21]

Isn't this an astonishing thing for someone to say? Time and
again, Amu strove to see with the eyes of the spirit to the oneness of
the human family, even when people were hurting him. We also can
see how he was calling on these men's higher selves to treat Mona
with care and respect.

"Mona went to her room to put on her coat, and one of the
guards followed her there; but she told him to wait outside, as
she had to get dressed.

"They had filled a few bags full of books and photo albums to
take with them. [While inside her room] Mona looked through
the bags in order to try to get a clue on what they wished to
interrogate her about; and, in doing so, she found a few letters of
repentance* which she hid under the bed and other safe places …

---

* When Baha'is were attacked by fanatical mobs, they would be threatened
with death if they didn't recant their faith. In the chaos and confusion, many
would say whatever the mob wanted to hear. They later realized what they
had done and regretted it. The Spiritual Assemblies would accept letters of

Therefore, [by hiding these letters] Mona was able to save those friends from yet another severe test.

"In any case, Mona put on her coat, opened the door and passed through the guards looking like royalty. She stood before me in great beauty, grace and courage, and said, 'Mother, this is not a prison, it is a courtyard. It is not a dry well, it is the exalted moon! Do not worry; I hope to see you soon!' She said this and walked outside of the door.

"Mona's father had also changed and was ready to go. He … turned to one of the guards and said, 'My friend, will you let me speak a few words to my wife?' He was granted permission to speak and turned to me saying, 'Not a leaf falls off the tree unless by the Will of God. And now, if the entire world arises to stop us from exiting this door, we will still leave on this day, at this hour, at this minute and this second; because this has been ordained for us by the Will of God.' He then said, 'See you later' and stepped outside of the house."

"repentance" from such individuals, and they could be welcomed back. As secretary of the Assembly, Mr. Mahmudnizhad had such letters in his possession. If these were found by the authorities, those Baha'is could easily be targeted again.

Mona and her Father

PART TWO

Arrival at Prison

"I felt as if I was standing on a balcony
and getting closer to the moon"

I said goodbye to my mother and left with my father and the guards for Sepah. ... They took us in a yellow Renault, they blindfolded us and had us bend down with our faces against our knees so we don't see outside. They took us into Sepah's prison ... I was taken to a room where they insulted and belittled my beliefs and yelled at me. They separated me from my father and I was body searched by a female guard in another room. Then they blindfolded me again ... [22]

These are Mona's own words about that night. Thirty-eight Bahá'ís, both men and women, were arrested that night in Shiraz. They were taken to Sepah jail, which is still in the city limits. These were individuals who were active in Bahá'í service. Mona was the first Bahá'í female to arrive. Blindfolded, she was given one end of a rolled-up newspaper to hold while a guard held the other end and led her down a long corridor. These ignorant people believed that Mona, who was the essence of purity inside and out, was "unclean" and would somehow infect them! She was brought to a large, dark room that already held more than 40 women. Most of them were sleeping or trying to sleep. The air in the room was damp and stuffy. The room had glass windows with metal bars. It was already crowded and women had to lie on their sides to sleep.

I was standing in a large, dark room and for a while I couldn't see anything. My eyes had not yet adjusted to the darkness of the cell. A prisoner came up to me and directed me to a space on the floor in the corner where I was obviously supposed to sleep ... I guessed the time to be just before midnight.* She gave me two thin, dirty blankets.

It took a while, but eventually I got used to the darkness and could see. The cell was like a hall, and many young girls and women were sleeping on the floor. I didn't know anyone, as I was the first Bahá'í in that cell. I had no idea where my father was. I lay down in the corner and silently said prayers ... [23]

So was Mona afraid? Was she angry at the injustice of her arrest? Was she worried about her father and her mother? Anxious about what was to come next? Mona was human, after all, so she may have felt all of these things. But her dominant emotion was something else: gratitude.

"When I first arrived in prison, I prostrated and kissed the ground in praise of the Blessed Beauty. The people in the prison gathered around me and asked about my crime. I told them that I had committed no crime and that I was merely a Bahá'í. They looked at me with great pity and said, 'You are considered more of a criminal than us; we feel sorry for what is to befall you.' I felt like laughing, but I controlled myself! You see, I was proud of myself. I was there for the sake of the Cause of Bahá'u'lláh, in the sort of place the Desired One Himself and His family and children had spent time for a long while. But I knew that my prison was far different from His prison. How can one compare the [fine] weather of Shiraz with the [foul] weather of Akka? But yet the bounty of God was bestowed upon me, and I was in great joy. I brought to memory the prison of Siyah Chal*, and was

---

* The Síyáh-Chál, or "the Black Pit," was the Sháh's terrible underground dungeon where Baha'u'llah was imprisoned for four months.

immersed in happiness for having been counted as one of His chosen ones and for having been given a tiny portion of what had befallen my Beloved. I gave praise to Bahá'u'lláh and prayed and meditated."

And then:

I felt as if I was standing on a balcony and getting closer to the moon. But the worried look on my mother's face was still before my eyes. I prayed for her perseverance and for my father's too. I decided to go to sleep like the others and wait until tomorrow to see what destiny had in store for me.[24]

Mona tried to settle down to sleep, just as the Bahá'í women began to arrive. The first one who came was someone she didn't recognize:

I was lying there, deep in thought, when the cell door opened and a woman came in. I didn't recognize her. I found later that she was Mrs. Iran Avaregan [Írán Ávárigán], but I didn't know she was a Bahá'í at the time. I got up and went to the washroom, then I returned and went to sleep.[25]

Mrs. Avaregan was upset and worried when she arrived. She had been arrested with other Bahá'ís and was not sure where they had been taken. She herself recalled seeing Mona when she arrived:

"I tried to go to sleep, but I was very worried … Suddenly, I noticed that a beautiful girl was sleeping next to me. When she got up to go to the bathroom, I noticed her fine figure and her silken, long hair. I instinctively found a fond feeling in my heart for that girl. I also felt a special calm by seeing her; it was incredible."

The next to arrive was Mrs. Tuba Za'irpur (*Túbá Zá'irpúr*). Mona said:

Later the cell door opened again and another woman entered. This woman kept repeating, "You must give me my pills, I suffer from very bad migraines." But no one paid any attention to her. It was Mrs. Za'irpur. I couldn't see her face properly in the dark, but her voice sounded very familiar. They brought her to our corner. As soon as she looked at Mrs. Avaregan, she exclaimed, "Iran, is that you?" [26]

Hearing her voice, Mona recognized the sound of her beloved teacher. She ran towards her and took her in her arms and kissed her.

"Mona, is that you? What are you doing here? They've even arrested you? Oh my God!"

To this Mona could only smile. Soon others began to arrive, six in total. Their joyful reunions woke up some of the sleeping prisoners. Why such joy at such a bad situation? they wondered. They would soon get to know the Bahá'ís better over the coming days and weeks and see how their love transformed the prison.

I felt a warm glow in my heart when I recognized Mrs. Za'irpur. Even though they had taken me away from my home and my loving family, I was brought to a new family in prison where all the women were like a mother to me and all the young girls were like my sisters.[27]

Life in Sepah Jail

"Blessed are those who are persecuted for righteousness' sake"

At 4 a.m., the lights went on. The Muslim call to prayer blasted from the jail cell loudspeaker. "Allah-u-akbar, Allah-u-akbar ... " The jailers had forgotten that the call to prayer was meant to be a beautiful way to awaken, to greet the day and to rekindle the flame of love for God in the hearts. Blasting it like this seemed more like a punishment.

Mona rose up and rubbed her eyes. She had only slept briefly, and now it was disorienting to be awakened in this abrupt way. The blankets she had were not much use in cushioning the hard floor or keeping out the cold, damp air. She didn't want to think about their smell or what kind of germs were on them. She reminded herself of why she was here and whispered a prayer of gratitude and another for steadfastness.

The other Bahá'í women were all beside her and were rising, as well. Some of them were middle-aged: Mrs. Za'irpur, Mrs. Avaregan, and Mrs. Nusrat Yalda'i. The others were only in their 20s: Zarrin Muqimi, Simin Saberi and Akhtar Sabet.* Each of these young women had been very active in Bahá'í community life, and all three had served as assistants to the Auxiliary Board. They were all unmarried as well, and this fact was one of the accusations used against them!

---

* Transliterations: Nuṣrat Yaldá'í, Zarrín Muqímí, Símín Sábirí, Akhtar Thábit.

Mona looked around and was now able to see the conditions of the place. There was no way it was meant to hold this many people. There weren't enough toilets, sinks or showers to meet the needs of the 80 to 90 women being held here. There was barely enough floor space for them all.

Olya gives a detailed description of the poor conditions there:

Our accommodation in Sepah consisted of two adjacent cells, each about four by six metres. There were as many as forty to fifty people in each. All crammed together there were political prisoners, murderers, prostitutes, drug addicts and women who were mentally or physically ill. They included people who were sentenced to death, pregnant women and even nursing mothers with babies.

There were hallways on each side of the cells, two of them very narrow and the other two about 1.5 metres wide. There were two toilets and two showers in the wider hallways — completely inadequate for so many people.

Each cell had two windows secured by iron bars. The air inside the cell was stifling since we could not open the windows and so many people were all packed together. It smelt of vomit. I soon discovered why. The general lack of hygiene and poor food in the prison regularly led to sickness and diarrhea. We all suffered from it, but the drug addicts suffered more than most. They seem to be sick all the time. In one corner of the hallway there was a television which was controlled by the guards. All they showed were scenes of the war against Iraq, official demonstrations, or religious programs directed by the mullahs.

The floor was covered by an old dirty carpet, and our sleeping facilities were limited to two very thin, dirty army blankets each, one to sleep on and one to cover ourselves with. When additional prisoners arrived, we had to share our blankets with the newcomers. The Bahá'í prisoners were supposed to keep to one side of the cell so that they wouldn't "contaminate" the rest, so we were allowed to sleep on only one side in a row. This left us so little space that we had to sleep curled sideways because there wasn't enough room to turn onto our backs. There was a heater in the hallway which was turned off at night and sometimes even during the day, which meant that the prison was so cold at night it was hard to sleep.[28]

Despite the bad conditions, the first couple of days were like a joyful reunion for the Bahá'í women. The interrogations had not started and the food wasn't yet so bad. Mona and the other women were still riding the high of the spiritual feelings of gratitude and purpose. Just as Jesus said, "Blessed are those who are persecuted for righteousness' sake, for theirs is the kingdom of Heaven,"[29] these friends had found a heaven in this awful place.

They chanted Bahá'í prayers with voices full of feeling and devotion. Mona joined her lovely voice with the others, and they sang beautiful Bahá'í songs. The other prisoners and even the guards were moved by this. They were attracted, drawn to this group of people who obviously had committed no crime. It seemed the Bahá'ís would break the walls of the prison with their spiritual power.

It was harder for the families on the outside than the prisoners those first few days. Mona's mother and Taraneh were filled with worry about what might be happening to Amu and Mona. They didn't even know if they were still alive. They went to the prison day after day, but none of the officials would tell them anything. When they asked for permission to see them even for a few minutes, they would be insulted and mocked. Still they kept coming back to Sepah for any word on the condition or whereabouts of their loved ones.

News of the Bahá'ís' songs and prayers reached the Religious Magistrate, Ayatollah Qazá'í. He was a corrupt, fanatical man who, like too many others, used religion to gain power and forgot that its purpose was to promote love and unity among people. The Magistrate gave an order forbidding not just the chanting and singing of the Bahá'ís, but also their prayer. They were not even supposed to say prayers silently to themselves, and they would be punished if they were caught by the guards doing so. The Muslim prisoners were warned to stay away from the "unclean" Bahá'ís, and they would be punished if they disobeyed. So murderers, prostitutes and drug addicts were told to stay away from the innocent Bahá'ís.

Mona was still Mona, though, and she didn't see the world in black and white with Bahá'ís on one side and Muslims on the other. She had spent her life, guided by her father's example, showing love and friendship to all. For their part, the Muslim prisoners—including the murderers and drug addicts—were all drawn to Mona for her sweet and loving nature. Olya said they called her *zendání kúchúlú*, or "the little prisoner."

After the first few days of their imprisonment, things changed for Mona and the others. The Bahá'í women were separated from each other and sent, blindfolded, to various rooms where interrogations and tortures had begun. The same thing was happening with the Bahá'í men. Of course, there were many more of them who had been arrested.

Before the women were separated, they decided as a group that they would not say anything about their Bahá'í activities. They had broken no laws. Since severe restrictions on Bahá'í meetings in Iran had begun, the Bahá'ís had only met in small, informal settings. They

were very worried that if they did talk, they might give up
information about Bahá'í friends. This could possibly be used as
evidence against the friends. They would respond to their
interrogators with silence no matter what.

They did not realize how much information the Revolutionary
Court had already collected on Bahá'í activities. The interrogators
were full of misunderstandings, but they knew a lot about who was
who in the community. And generally speaking, the harshest
treatment was given to the most prominent Bahá'ís. Mrs.
Mahmudnizhad shared the following account:

> "The members of the Local Assembly received, without
> exception, 74 lashes each, and were sent to solitary cells. The way
> that the lashes were administered was that the prisoner was
> made to lie down on his stomach and his hands and feet were
> tied to the bed. Then using a three-layered cable, or a gas hose, or
> a whip, the prisoner was lashed.
>
> "There was a man by the name of Abdu'llah who was called to
> do the whipping. He was supposed to put the Qur'án under his
> arm and whip the prisoner with the sort of force that would still
> enable him to keep the Qur'án under his arm; however, he was
> cruel and never used the book. He raised the whip as far as he
> could, and lashed the prisoner with all his might.
>
> "The men were whipped on their naked bodies and were left on
> the bed with blood streaming down their flesh, so that they
> would be whipped again on the next day on their injured bodies.
> This was done to pain the prisoners to a state that would move
> them to recant their faith."

Four of the Bahá'í women were whipped in this way. They
included Mrs. Za'irpur, Mrs. Yalda'i, Mrs. Mihrí Vahdat-Haqq, and

Mrs. Mahbúbih Mumtází. Mrs. Za'irpur shared her terrible experience with Mrs. Mahmudnizhad as follows:

"I was whipped because they claimed that I was lying about my name. My name is Tuba, but they insisted that it was Qudsíyyih and that I was lying. I kept swearing to God that I was telling the truth, but they would not hear of it. They made me lie on the bed and gave me a whipping. I was in a bad state and contracted a fever. I was also suffering from a migraine headache, but I endure it all.

"An hour later, they summoned me again for interrogations. This time, they accused me of being a member of the Spiritual Assembly and whipped me again. No matter how I tried to tell them that they were mistaken and I was not a member of the Assembly, they did not believe me. They laid me down again on the whipping bed and tied my both hands to the bed. They then tied the big toes of my feet together, fastened my ankles to the bed, and whipped me. Suddenly I felt as if my big toes were broken and separated from my body. They gave me 40 lashes and I was screaming of pain when they stopped the lashes.

"They then took me to a cell, which was supposed to be for solitary occupancy, but was housing 5 prisoners because of lack of space in the prison. The other four people in that cell were political prisoners. My body was swollen and I was in severe pain; thus I needed extra space. Therefore, the other four prisoners sacrificed their space and sleep and took turns standing up for 2 hours at a time to allow me more space to sleep.

"I spent the night in severe pain and was running a high fever. My feet were swollen beyond measure; so one of the prisoners suggested that I should cut the soles of my feet to allow the dead blood to leave my body. One of them had taken a piece of dried cement from the prison yard and had rubbed it against the floor to create a sharp edge. They used the dry cement to scratch the soles of my feet, and some blackened blood left my feet until red blood started running out. The pain was unbearable, but the guards came in again and took me in that condition for further interrogations. I was threatened to be whipped again, if I did not admit to the 'truth'!"

The Revolutionary Court had created a four-stage system of interrogations and trials. The first stage it seems was in some ways the harshest. It included day after day of verbal abuse, unending questioning, and often torture. The goal was to get the Bahá'ís to provide "evidence" against themselves and others, to break their spirit and, ultimately, to recant their faith.

Near the end of her first week in prison, Mona was blindfolded and led to what she thought would be the first stage of her interrogation. Instead she was led to the basement where they tortured prisoners. The officials knew she wasn't planning to talk.

She was led to a room where she heard a familiar voice. "Mona, tell them whatever you know."

It was her father's voice, but like she had never heard it before. It was quiet and filled with pain. This gentle, loving man had been tortured so severely, beginning with the 74 lashes described above. Mona was still blindfolded and wasn't sure though if it was really him there. She had heard that the prison officials would tape the voices of their torture victims and then play them back for relatives. She didn't say anything.

The prison official threatened her father that if she didn't start to talk, she would be tortured just as he had been.

Mona blurted out, "I am ready."

Amu spoke again, "Please convey the truth as you know it. We have no underground secrets or anything of that sort. If we have rendered any service to the community, we have only fulfilled our religious duty. Therefore you should clearly state what position you hold."

"In what capacity are you asking this of me?" Mona asked.

The interrogator answered: "In his capacity as the Secretary of the Spiritual Assembly and as a member of the Auxiliary Board!"

Mona recoiled at this. "The Auxiliary Board Member and the Secretary of the Spiritual Assembly are both outside prison right now. If they were to give me such instructions, I would obey them; however, my father is a prisoner like myself and has no authority."

Her refusal to talk upset the mulla in charge, and he sent Mona away from her father. It is unclear whether Mona herself was tortured.[30] Many of the women received the bastinado, where the soles of their feet were mercilessly whipped. They were then forced to walk on bleeding feet while they were taunted by the guards. Mona did not like to talk about her interrogations in Sepah. She said it would bring her "down to the world of accusations, ugly words and improper questions."

Whether she was tortured physically is not so important. What happened TO Mona is not nearly as important as how Mona RESPONDED. The actions of cruel and power-hungry people should not be our focus. Our focus should be on the heroic deeds and words of those souls we wish to emulate.

So Mona was brought back to her cell with her mind thrown into confusion. She and the Bahá'í friends had sworn not to answer questions during interrogation, but now her dear father and role-model was telling her to talk. Had her father somehow been broken by the interrogators? Had he been so badly tortured that he had given up or lost his judgment and was now helping the prison officials to get information? She just couldn't believe this about her father. Then again, maybe he was afraid of what might happen to her, his beloved daughter, if she didn't talk. If she could only see his eyes—those eyes she knew so well -- she might then understand.

Mona barely had time to sort through these questions before she was taken away again. She was brought back into the presence of her father. The interrogators had been pushing him with threats to Mona if he didn't persuade her to talk.

He begged her: "Dear Mona, my daughter, whatever you know, tell them."

"The eyes are the windows to the heart," Mona said. "Perhaps if you would remove our blindfolds and I could see my father's eyes, I might be moved to accept his request."

Her father made the same request.

The interrogators felt they were close to winning. They went along with the idea and took off the blindfolds. Father and daughter saw each other. She ran into his arms. What had happened to him? She saw how badly his body had been battered, but no, there wasn't time – she looked in his eyes. She looked for that light inside that she knew so well. Had it been dimmed or put out by these difficulties?

He looked back at her. Both hearts swelled. She saw that same light in his eyes, a light that was undimmed by shame. She hugged him and kissed him with tears falling all around. They were prodded to hurry by the interrogator.

Father looked at daughter, uncertain if he'd ever see her again. "Answer them bravely and honestly. We have nothing to hide."

The First Stage of Interrogation

"If you only say you are not a Bahá'í ..."

Mona returned to the prison cell and shared with the other women that her father had told her to talk. The women consulted together. All of them respected her father, but now they were confused. Some thought they should keep on with their silence. Others felt that he was right and it was best to tell the truth. Tortures had already begun. They didn't want pain or fear or anger at injustice to cloud their decisions. They needed to pray and meditate on it. Mona told them she had made her decision.

The next day, her interrogation sessions started. Prisoners would be brought into a room, sometimes alone, sometimes with others, but there was no interaction allowed. There would be a mulla there, an Islamic judge overseeing the interrogations of several prisoners, along with other officials and guards. The scene is further described in *The Story of Mona*:

> The revolutionary guards are usually masked and the prisoners blind-folded, and made to sit facing a wall. At each stage the victim is verbally abused, asked the same questions over and over again, and often asked to write down the answers since the majority of the revolutionary guards and many of the interrogating judges are illiterate, while their Bahá'í victims are often well-educated. The interrogators demand to know the names, addresses and telephone numbers of all the Bahá'ís in a given city, then in all of Iran, then around the world. At each

stage the prisoner is asked to deny their Bahá'í beliefs and become a Muslim ...

At various times, prisoners were interrogated verbally and required to stand blindfolded for hours on end while they answered. At others, the prisoners were seated facing a wall and handed a set of written questions.[31]

Speaking of her first day of interrogation, Mona recalled the following to a fellow prisoner:

The questions they asked were as follows:

What is your religion? What do you believe in?

Were you born in a Bahá'í family? Date and place of birth.

Name of the school you are studying at. Which grade?

Have you ever taught in a Bahá'í class?

When did you declare and who was present at that session?

Names of the members of the Local Spiritual Assembly of Shiraz and the members of the Bahá'í National Spiritual Assembly.

What activities do you do as a Bahá'í?

Names of the members of the Bahá'í committees in Shiraz.

Write about the Bahá'í administration. How many members of the Universal House of Justice are Persian and how many are not? What nationalities are they?

Names of all the prominent international Bahá'í administrators in the world.

Have you ever been on pilgrimage?

How much have you donated to the Fund?

Who was the chairperson of the feast and where was it held?

Who did you vote for this year?

Have your parents been members of the Local Spiritual Assembly?

The names of the Bahá'ís you know.

Are you willing to recant?

I answered all the questions very frankly and my answer to the last question was, "I am a Bahá'í and I will never recant." The interrogator said, "If you refuse to recant your Faith, we will execute you." And I told him that I would rather be killed than recant the Faith I believe in."[32]

That was day one. These sessions would go on for long hours, day after day for a week or so. They would last from 10 a.m. to 4 a.m.—that is, the next morning, only to start up again a few hours later. The prison officials used this kind of schedule to throw the prisoners off balance, trying to get them to renounce their religion.

During all the endless hours, I was praying and begging Bahá'u'lláh to give me the strength to remain steadfast all during this nightmare … One day, the Mulla told me to write all the details of my life …, as well as my activities as a Bahá'í, all of which I again described very frankly. [33]

At one point during her interrogations, the Mulla told her: "If you only say you are not a Bahá'í, you and your father will be freed in no time. But if you continue being so stubborn, I will see to your being executed myself."

You might wonder what you yourself would do in that situation. Would you doubt your faith? Would you just say you denied it to be let free? You also might wonder whether Mona had doubts about her faith.

The first thing to know is the Bahá'í teachings say we should act with wisdom but we should not dissemble, or pretend not to be Bahá'ís to avoid persecution. The other thing is Mona's faith was not based simply on imitating her parents or others. She had worked to understand it herself, so her faith was not "blind" but was a conscious knowledge. The foundation of her belief was strengthened further by her pattern of service and by her constant prayers. Her faith had become the lamp that lit up her world; how could she turn to the darkness?

She replied to the Mulla: "I am a Bahá'í and I will never deny this fact."

At another point, the Mulla asked Mona about the very same book she had proclaimed aloud years earlier in a dream. *The Story of Mona* recounts:

> [T]he Mulla asked her about Bahá'u'lláh's writings on *The Seven Valleys*, to which she gave a detailed reply, but was ignored. The Mulla then asked her to say a prayer. She asked him if he really wanted her to do so and he replied sarcastically, "Yes." Mona then folded her arms, closed her eyes and started the prayer, but was cut off by snide laughter from the Mulla.[34]

Mona was asked about why she visited the homes of those Bahá'í children who had been expelled from schools. She responded by asking them a question of her own: "When you deprived our children of an education, did we not have a right to give them lessons in love and affection as well as in the sciences? Yes, I visited those homes and consoled those families."

All the while, the prison officials were doing all they could to confuse, disorient and terrify the Bahá'ís. The guards would lead a group of prisoners blindfolded into a courtyard, line them up and tell them they were about to be shot to death. The prisoners then heard the terrible sound of gunfire and waited for the bullets and the release of death, but nothing came. Only mocking laughter. The guards had aimed their guns in the air. This was just one example of how Iran's regime tried to convert souls to the "Straight Path" of Islam.

One day around 7 p.m., Mona was spending another exhausting day in interrogation when she was told to put on her blindfold. This was weeks after her arrest, though who could be sure, since one day blended into another in this terrible cycle of interrogation? She was taken with five other Bahá'í prisoners down a hallway in a direction she didn't recognize. Where they were headed, she didn't know.

All this time, Mona's mother and sister had no idea what was going on with their loved ones. It was the same for all the Bahá'í families. Then there were the families of other souls unjustly imprisoned—political prisoners, for example. The new regime hated Bahá'ís, but they also hated members of political groups different than their own and they suppressed them with extreme violence. Mrs. Mahmudnizhad described the experience of families waiting for news of their loved ones' fate.

> "I used to go to the Sepah [prison] two times a week; once for Mr. Mahmudnizhad and once for Mona. It was a commotion outside of the prison. The families of the political prisoners were mingled with the Bahá'í families, creating a huge crowd outside of the prison.
>
> "Once the crowd had gathered, the families of the political prisoners were called and the names of their dear ones who had been executed were announced. At such moments, the families would throw down on the floor the fruit, which they had brought for their dear ones, and would start to cry and moan."

After the executions were announced, the prison would give the names first of those who had been transferred to the larger, main prison at Adelabad and then those who were allowed visitors that day.

"We had to wait until the very end in the hopes of getting a visit with our dear ones. We used to go there at 1:00 p.m. and stay until it was dark and cold, only to be told that we were not allowed a visit that day. We did this for four weeks, and were fed up with the situation, but did not know what to do."

It was Friday, 19 November 1982 and as I sat by the window looking out at the people moving around on the streets below, going about their normal lives, oblivious to what was going on around them, I lost control. I couldn't stop crying. It was as if a dam, at last, had burst. I was calling to God out loud, "Oh God, I want my child; I want Mona from you. I haven't even heard from her; I want my baby." I looked up at the sky and cried, "The little birds are free but my little bird is trapped in a cage." [35]

The following day she got up, determined to try again. She bought some oranges, apples and sweet lemons, washed them, put them in a bag and headed off to pick up Taraneh to head to the prison.

"As usual, we were kept waiting until it was dark, but the Bahá'í women could not stand it any longer and started to plead their case. They shouted saying that it was not fair that they were coming so often to the prison without being permitted to get any news of their children. They demanded to receive permission for a visit that day.

"One of the authorities there by the name of Ja'fari, who was the head of the police station, stood facing the [revolutionary] guards with his back to us and shouted, 'Why do you bother us so much, go about your business.' He pretended that he was addressing this to us, but by using his left hand—which the guards could not see—he signaled us to go in. He then stood against the bars himself to allow the Bahá'ís to go by him. He also managed to distract the guards and the other visitors by picking an argument with a couple of the Bahá'ís.

"When the revolutionary guards outside of the prison noticed that some of the Bahá'ís were about to go inside, they tried to go after them on motorcycles, but it was too late and the Bahá'ís had entered the building."

So Mr. Ja'fari, who was part of the civilian police, showed compassion toward some of the Bahá'í families by allowing them in. Mona and five other Bahá'í women had been called from their interrogation rooms for this hastily-arranged visit. Now there were at this point three other Bahá'í women in prison, but they were being held in solitary confinement and were not allowed visitors. Frequently, when a prisoner was badly abused, they would not be allowed visitors.

This visit would be brief, only a few minutes. It would be silent. They would not be able to talk to the prisoners, nor should they talk to each other. When they were asked to leave, they should leave. Mrs. Mahmudnizhad picks up the story:

"They brought our dear ones and made them stand against the wall. They were veiled and we could only see their beautiful faces. The area on which they were standing was no more than 2.5 meters in length. A thick glass wall separated us from the prisoners. They had each lost a few kilos. When my daughter Taraneh saw her sister in such a state, she began to shed tears uncontrollably; but Mona signaled to her with her hands to wipe away her tears."

I was looking at them [the prisoners] and crying. Mona indicated in motions that I shouldn't cry. Quickly, I wiped my tears away. I couldn't tell her, my beautiful bird, that my tears were from the joy of seeing her.[36]

The Black Cape

"Even as a slave, sitting under a sword hanging on a thread"

In prison, there were moments of joy and bittersweet moments of tenderness and care, such as that silent visit among family members. There were moments of selflessness and small acts of service and love. Many of these would never be written down. Those that were recorded are told and retold as precious memories—the glimmering actions of souls so purified by difficulty that they became spiritual gold, worth so much more than any piece of metal. These souls were so transformed that no amount of evil treatment could lead them to respond with evil. This is the victory. This is their eternal glory. This is why songs, poems, stories, plays and books sing their praises and will continue to do so for centuries to come.

These were not happy, carefree times. Heroes do not emerge in days of plenty and freedom. These were days of violence, of cruel insistence, of the deep, dark shadows of hatred and prejudice. This was when the ignorance of the many was manipulated by the ambitious few. In such times, the innocent are often crushed. Innocent victims often instinctively respond with fear and even anger. These heroes and heroines even overcame that limitation when they learned to see their ill-treatment as a divine blessing. The black cape of suffering is a beautiful garment when seen through spiritual eyes.

The new Faith of God is like a tree. The prayers and good deeds of its followers are like drops of water to help it grow. Sometimes, envious people will try to cut down the tree and destroy the new

Faith of God. Those who suffer persecution are like guards who stand to protect the tree no matter what violence the envious people use. They may bleed and they may fall, but their pure blood is a magical ingredient that makes the tree stretch out its limbs and leaves and grow more beautiful than ever. As it says in a prayer by the Báb:

> Great is the blessedness of those whose blood Thou hast chosen to water the Tree of Thine affirmation, and thus to exalt Thy holy and immutable Word.

The Báb had experienced great suffering—years of it, at the hands of the government until His final martyrdom, when His precious blood was spilled out onto the earth. Bahá'u'lláh faced 40 years filled with pain and suffering. He experienced a living martyrdom, afflicted by anxiety and trouble and sorrow that bled His life away drop by painful drop. As He said:

> I have been, most of the days of My life, even as a slave, sitting under a sword hanging on a thread, knowing not whether it would fall soon or late upon him. And yet, notwithstanding all this We render thanks unto God.[37]

The government of Iran was growing ever more violent. Did it think that if it destroyed all those elements of society that went against its ideas, Iran would be purified? How wrong the persecutors were to believe that violence against the innocent could ever bring a purification.

On the 29th of November, 41 more Bahá'ís were arrested. This included 11 women. That same day, Mona and her group of prisoners should have been sent home and returned to school and work and other socially beneficial activity. Instead, they were sent to the main prison, Adelabad—meaning "the abode of justice."

The authorities did not tell any of the families about the move. The following Saturday, Mrs. Mahmudnizhad went to Sepah prison hoping to see Mona again. The guard at the gate told her about the transfer. The visiting time would be the same, but Adelabad was almost an hour's drive. She told the story:

> Anxiously, we rushed to Adelabad. As soon as I saw Mona in the visiting room I snatched up the receiver and asked her how she was. She had caught a cold, and had piled on all the clothes she had, one on top of the other, to keep warm … [S]he had caught a chill because of the cold, wintry weather and having only one blanket to sleep on.
>
> I looked at her slight figure muffled up against the cold and lost my self-control. "Please forgive me for crying," I apologized, "but I can't help it. I miss you so much, my darling."
>
> Strong as a rock, Mona held back her tears; I could see them welling up in her eyes but she managed to control herself. She tried to cheer me up: "Mama, we are very comfortable here. Compared to the last prison, this is like a mansion. They give us breakfast, lunch and dinner! It's almost luxury!"[38]

Mona was being truthful. In some ways, Adelabad was better than Sepah. It was larger, more relaxed. Visits were allowed on a regular basis. The severe interrogations she faced in Sepah were over. Prisoners were able to interact more, and the relations between the Bahá'ís and the other prisoners were going well.

It was still very difficult. The prison was cold, damp, overcrowded and very dirty. Adelabad was built to hold a large prison population, and the women's section had three floors of small individual cells all connected with balconies and stairways. It was overflowing now, and the Bahá'ís were put on the third floor. Each cell had one or, at most, two beds, but now with three women assigned to it. Mona was among the many women sleeping on a cold, concrete floor, still with only two thin blankets. The prisoners would pile on all the clothes they had and yet never feel warm. It was now December and only the beginning of a cold winter for Shiraz. But Mona did not dwell on these things. Referring to that same visit, Mrs. Mahmudnizhad said:

> Mona always tried to comfort us. She was always concerned about others, showering us all with her love and happiness. Before the visit was over she told me, 'The minute you find out they have brought Father here, bring him extra blankets so he won't catch cold.' When the time came for me to leave, Mona kissed her fingertips and put them up against the glass partition. I did the same, and after that whenever we said goodbye we did the same thing. [39]

Mona told her mother that she had written and mailed them a letter. This was surprising, since prisoners weren't even supposed to have paper. The letter did arrive in a few days. In it, she addressed her family, including "my mother who is dearer to me than my life and my kind sister." She wrote about God's great bounty to her even though she felt unworthy to serve Him. "Dearly beloved of my heart and soul, pray for us so in all conditions we will be content." She asked them "not to be overtaken with sorrow" and again asked them to pray, "because we are in need of your prayers."[40]

The possibility of release probably seemed further away now they had been transferred to the main prison. They were soon to enter the second and third steps of their criminal processing. All the interrogations at Sepah had yielded files of thick stacks of paper that the government considered "evidence" against them.

The 41 new prisoners were put through the same kind of interrogations at Sepah and then sent to Adelabad. Olya Roohizadegan was in the group arrested on 29 November. She was imprisoned for a time in Adelabad before being released in mid-January. She wrote out some details of the conditions there:

> Prison food consisted of a tiny piece of bread and cheese for breakfast; cooked white beans for lunch; and bread, yoghurt and dates in the evening. All the fruit we received from our families had to be handed over and then shared between all the prisoners. Of course, Bahá'ís were left till last, so naturally the best fruit had already been taken by the time our turn came.
>
> A more annoying problem was how to wash our clothes. The prison authorities considered our garments to be contaminated and so we had to manage our washing the best we could, using soap and a small bucket in our cells, with water splashing all over our feet. We didn't have anywhere to hang the clothes, so we draped them over the cell bars with the bucket strategically placed to catch the drips. Because of the cold and damp, it used to take four or five days for clothes to dry.[41]

She goes on to comment that given the cold and the need to wear all their clothing, "the decision to wash an item was not taken lightly." She says one of the worst aspects were the toilets and showers.

> There were only three of each for the whole of the third floor, and they were always dirty. They had no doors – whether for security reasons or from neglect it was hard to say – so someone had to stand guard whenever we used them. This was a daily indignity we women all felt keenly. Moreover, with 150 prisoners on our floor, we had to take it in turns to use the showers, which often meant going for days without being able to wash at all.[42]

Those who were addicted to drugs seemed to suffer the most. These women were going through severe withdrawal, their bodies shaking with craving for their particular poison. They were given no medical treatment as they might receive in a civilized facility. They would scream and writhe, get sick and be unable to clean themselves.

With these conditions plus the physical and psychological wounds of torture, sickness and disease were inevitable. Now, if you don't know already, one fairly universal characteristic of Iranian Bahá'ís is an intense concern with hygiene. One of the early Bahá'í quotes we memorize as children is "*Nezáfate záhere har chand amrí-ast jesmáni, valí ta'sír shadíd dar roháníyat dárad.*" This is a quote by 'Abdu'l-Bahá that is translated, "*And although bodily cleanliness is a physical thing, it hath, nevertheless, a powerful influence on the life of the spirit.*"[43] One can see how these prisoners would be tested not just with their steadfastness in faith, but also with their steadfastness in filth. Could they remain patient and tolerant in handling this dirty, foul-smelling, repulsive environment and the people in it?

Mona was naturally inclined to cleanliness. Remember, this is the girl who at 3 tried sweeping up the patio right after a bomb hit it. Perhaps she had already absorbed the quote mentioned above. But Mona had also been trained to handle filth. Think about all those years she spent volunteering in the orphanage caring for children living in squalor. She had done all the housework at home, according to her own mother. Then there are all those years of following her father in visiting and paying attention to the needs of people who often were worse off than herself.

Because of this, Mona was better prepared for prison life than many. She had developed critical spiritual qualities: She was accustomed to difficulty and hardship. She had learned to be content with little. She could put other people's needs before her own. She had so much practical experience in serving others that cleaning up and nursing a drug addict back to health might seem little different than attending to an orphan child left neglected in her crib.

This is one of the great lessons we can take from Mona's story. Yes, she did great, heroic things in prison—the most amazing of which we haven't even gotten to yet. But Mona did not become a spiritual hero overnight. She had trained for this spiritual marathon all her life with her father as her coach and her own faith and will-power as her trainer.

Her Trial

"Young girl, what do you know about religion?"

In January, Mona was wakened one morning at 4 a.m. and told that today would be the second stage of her interrogation. An hour later, she was put in a car headed to the office of the Assistant to the Public Prosecutor. After more than a month of waiting, this was a sign that things were moving. The women were starting to get called to trial, some even getting offers of release.

The official looked through the stack of papers that Mona had filled out in those long, difficult interrogations. They had all been stuffed into a file with her name on it, along with other forms and reports, including details on her life and family, her daily activities and movements. The file could hardly contain all the pages. It had been passed around callously and was covered with the finger prints of unholy men. Many of these men had been placed in positions above their ability and could not even read or understand what she had painstakingly written. She had wrestled with herself about what exactly to include. She tried to answer the questions while protecting the names of individuals who were still free. She also had tried to be as truthful as possible to show anyone who would read the obvious innocence and benevolence of the Bahá'ís. She had hurt her hand from writing so much. But the eyes that looked at these pages, whether literate or illiterate, all saw just one thing: guilt. It was as if they were looking in a mirror.

The official began to ask Mona questions. They were the same old questions she had been asked more than 2 months ago here in Sepah prison. Mona tried to answer sincerely. She tried to see the good in the man in front of her. Perhaps he would listen with a sense of justice. She was asked about her beliefs.

"I believe in God and all His Messengers who have revealed a Holy Book. We consider them all to be Messengers of God."

The official replied: "You are accused of being a member of the Zionist movement, who are spies."

"Bahá'ís have nothing to do with politics." She tried to explain the history again, "The state of Israel was founded only 35 years ago, while the Bahá'í Faith was founded 139 years ago. We only have spiritual organizations."

The prosecutor wasn't listening. "There remains only one way for you, you should either recant the Faith or you will be executed.'

Mona said she would rather be executed.

Now here we glimpse one of the motivations behind these interrogations. From one point of view, these officials at every step in this process seem to be aiming at one thing. It's not necessarily killing or even causing pain to the Baha'is. Do they really want to execute a beautiful 16-year-old girl? Do they actually believe she's a spy? It's possible. But isn't it also possible that they just want her to deny her belief, give up and change sides? It's clear they don't want to actually engage in a rational discussion or consider her explanations. Everything they say and do is trying to persuade or bully or torment her into saying one thing. Is it "I give up!"? Or maybe "You win!"? Have you ever played a game and found yourself so completely absorbed in that game that all you could think about was winning? Did you ever find yourself doing things you would not normally do in order to win? Sometimes, people fall into this state of mind in real life, and the results can be very damaging.

After almost a full day of this back and forth, the Assistant Prosecutor had a change of heart. Or maybe it was just a change of approach. He offered to release Mona if she could raise 200,000 Tuman in bond. That was about $35,000 US at the time.

Mona felt a little surge of hope inside. She had prayed so much, and worked so hard to keep her mind focused on God's will, even if that meant prison, even if that meant execution. However, what if God's will was that she should be free?

That surge of hope was soon checked by realistic thoughts. How could her family possibly afford that? Even in better times, they couldn't afford a second-hand piano for her. Would the Bahá'í community be able to raise that kind of money? There were now a number of prisoners being offered release on similar terms. Would some be freed and not others? All these thoughts began to crowd in, so Mona breathed and felt herself reaching out for help with detachment. There was no way she could know the answer. She would just need to pray and wait and see.

Mona's mother got a phone call that day telling her Mona was being interrogated at Sepah. She said:

"I rushed to the Sepah Prison as fast as possible and was able, with great difficulty, to obtain permission to visit with Mona. I was shaking with joy when I saw her. I took her delicate body into my arms and kissed her beautiful face.

"Tears of joy filled her beautiful green eyes, too, and she said to me, 'Mother, the prosecutor has told me that I would be freed if we pay them two hundred thousand Tumans, but I beg you not to do anything rash, because I am quite happy here. Please, mother, be sure to consult about this with the others.' "

Mrs. Mahmudnizhad was then in such a hurry to find a way to arrange Mona's release, she didn't even stay the full 20 minutes of their visit. She left after 10 minutes, and Mona watched as her mother rushed out with the high fever of hope in her head.

Mrs. Mahmudnizhad's thought was to put up their apartment for a bond. This would mean instead of giving the court cash for bail, they could hand over the title to their property. The problem was the family still had a mortgage on their apartment, and the authorities would not accept property that was not fully paid for. *

Mrs. Mahmudnizhad realized she would have to consult with the Spiritual Assembly about what to do. This is what Mona meant when she said, "be sure to consult with the others." Remember that the Spiritual Assembly was operating in secret because of the danger. It had new members since the arrest of Amu and the others, but its authority as an administrative body was still the same. Mrs. Mahmudnizhad said:

> "So I went home and contacted one of the friends and conveyed the details. He told me that 'they' would consult about it and contact me the next day. On the following day, he called and said that we should not give in to the request of the authorities in Mona's case, because it would set a precedent and they would start arresting our youth in order to extort money from us. He also said that today they are asking for 200,000 Tumans, but it will be 400,000 tomorrow and 600,000 the next day, until they will start asking for a million and maybe more."

Now we see another possible reason the Iranian authorities were arresting and holding Bahá'ís: money. There are numerous cases where the officials would say to the Bahá'í prisoners things like, "We

---

* In Iran as in other countries, it is common for people to own apartments and not just to rent them.

see you're innocent, so we'll release you as long as you pay this large amount of money in bail." Of course, bail is not meant to be paid by people known to be innocent. They should simply be freed and not charged. These officials were trying to imprison Bahá'ís and push their families to hand over large sums of money and property. It was very unlikely they would get this money and property back.

This decision of the Assembly was difficult for a mother to hear. She knew it was correct, but it meant her lovely young daughter would not be freed. She also had to wait almost a full week before their next visit when she could break this discouraging news to Mona. In the meantime, Mona would have to walk that tightrope suspended between hope and not knowing, known as detachment.

Then Mona was called to the third stage of her processing, only a few days after her meeting with the Assistant Prosecutor. This would be her trial before the judge who oversaw the sentencing of all the Bahá'í cases in Shiraz, the Religious Magistrate Ayatollah Qaza'i. If there was a Grim Reaper in Shiraz, he was it.

This third stage was short but intense for all the Bahá'í prisoners. It might last 15 minutes, certainly no longer than an hour. But the threat of death hung in the air. It was perhaps in this arena that the Bahá'ís best showed themselves to be spiritual champions. Their heroic courage, their inspired words, and their crystal pure statements of truth are awe-inspiring. Mona's performance there was no exception.

The Religious Magistrate began by insulting Mona and trying to humiliate her. He told her, "Your parents have deceived and misled you. They have forced you to imitate them in following the Bahá'í Faith."

"Your honor," Mona replied, "it is true that I was born into a Bahá'í family and initially learned the Faith from them, but I want to assure you that I've exercised my own reason and accepted the Faith after my own investigation. One doesn't become a Bahá'í by imitation, only by individual investigation of the truth. You have access to several of our books, you can read them for yourself to confirm this. My parents never insisted on my becoming a Bahá'í."

This Magistrate looked at her astounded and said, "Young girl, what do you know about religion?" You see he was an Ayatollah, the highest ranking religious title in Shí'ih Islam. He believed that he was the expert on religion and that Mona was just an ignorant schoolgirl.

"Is there a better proof of my faith than the fact that I was dragged out of school to be brought here and undergo long hours of trials? Can't you see that it is my belief that has given me the confidence to stand in your presence and answer your questions?"

This was an impressive answer. The Ayatollah asked Mona to say a prayer.

She said no, she couldn't do that.

"What do you mean?"

"You would have to sit respectfully with your hands folded before I would do that."

The Magistrate was not used to taking orders from prisoners, and he refused at first. But after a moment, he went along with it. Mona put aside the "evidence" file the Prosecutor had put in front of her. She breathed in and began to quietly recite a prayer by 'Abdu'l-Bahá:

O God! Refresh and gladden my spirit. Purify my heart. Illumine my powers. I lay all my affairs in Thy hand. Thou art My Guide and My Refuge. I will no longer be sorrowful and grieved. I will be a happy and joyful being. O God, I will no longer be full of anxiety, nor will I let trouble harass me ...

In the middle of the prayer, the Ayatollah started waving his hand, interrupting Mona. She stopped and waited, but he remained silent. Mona wondered: Had he been moved by her prayer?

After a moment, he regained his former attitude: "Why didn't you chant the prayer? On the night you were arrested, the guards found many tapes of your chanting. Your crime is quite obvious: you were misleading young people by making recordings of prayers and your beautiful voice."

"Your honor, in your opinion is the chanting of prayers a crime?"

"Yes. What harm did you find in Islam that made you turn to the Bahá'í Faith?

"But I do believe in Islam, your honor — because the basis of all religion is the same. However, I also believe that, according to the needs of human beings in different ages, God sends us different messengers and laws to guide us. But if by Islam you mean the hatred, murder and bloodshed in this country, a sample of which I have witnessed in prison, that is why I've chosen to be a Bahá'í."

Now you know that this certainly affected the courtroom. Did it get so quiet you could hear a pin drop? Did people stir in their seats or speak out in anger? Who was this young girl to say this to the man who decided whether she lived or died? There were no friendly faces in that room for Mona. She was on her own without even a feeble-willed, court-appointed lawyer. But she had the Concourse on High behind her, filling her with the strength to speak and a shining sword of truth to slice through the dark veils of superstition.

The Magistrate could have said and done a number of things. He chose to shut the matter down: "We must obey the Qur'án. You must either accept Islam or face execution."

"I kiss the order of execution," Mona answered without hesitating.

She was taken back to Adelabad, still not knowing what her fate would be. That rested with Ayatollah Qaza'i. Despite her penetrating testimony, or perhaps because of it, he re-authorized her release. This time he set the bond at 500,000 Tuman—two and a half times what it had been only days before.

The following Saturday was January 15th. Mrs. Mahmudnizhad walked into the visitation with a heavy heart and a disappointing message to share.

> "I tried to convey this to her in a roundabout way. Oh, how beautiful was her response to it. She put down the phone and kissed both of her hands and blew the kiss in the air for the members of the Spiritual Assembly who had blessed her with that decision. She did this three times. God only knows just how submissive she was to the Will of God."

Mona with her Father and Mother by the sea, in Bushihr

The Mother's Arrest

"I wish to go home."

Six of the Bahá'í women were released, including Olya. About fifteen remained in Adelabad, including their youngest prisoner. The ones who gained release were sent off with love by their fellow prisoners. They were given lists of people to visit and to hug and kiss. They gave back assurances of prayers, of support from the outside, and that they would tell the stories of what the prisoners had experienced. They walked out the door with mixed feelings of happiness and relief in reuniting with their loved ones and regret and a sense of survivor's guilt in leaving their comrades.

The full emotion of those moments is hard to comprehend. As Olya was leaving, Nusrat Yalda'i had tears falling down her face and said, "If only I could sneak into your pocket and come with you." [44]

Inside, the women struggled to keep up their strength and their hopes. They supported and encouraged one another. The women all marveled at the story of Mona's trial and comforted her for the lost opportunity of her release. They knew how difficult this must be for her mother, as well, to be separated from Mona. The young women all tried to hold back tears for their mothers that were on the outside. Zarrin had just watched her mother walk out the doors into a free life, but without her daughter. Roya, who was closest to Mona in age at 22, reached out and held her mother, Izzat, who shared a cell with her. Roya, brave and detached, was so full of life, while her selfless mother centered her thoughts on the safety of her daughter and the other young women.[*] Mona watched them, lost in thought.

Like many of the family members on the outside, Mona's mother tried to keep occupied. Many of them would just go and hang around outside Sepah in case any information was available. This was something that the Spiritual Assembly had encouraged them to do. Mrs. Mahmudnizhad would go a few times a week. Thursday, January 20th was one such day she decided to visit.

Taraneh had driven her over, bringing her baby girl, Nura (*Núrá*), in the backseat of the car. It was late morning on a winter day. Little Nura was sick with pneumonia. While Taraneh tended to her, Mrs. Mahmudnizhad walked over towards the entrance where the family members would congregate. Not long after, Taraneh saw an official talking with her mother and then watched her mother signal to her and then follow the official inside. Mrs. Mahmudnizhad's odyssey was about to begin.

She followed the official into a large hall, which led to a series of interrogation rooms and also to the Prosecutor's Office and the Executive Office. This official—known as Interrogator #5—had been interrogating Mona, and he remembered seeing Mrs. Mahmudnizhad around in recent weeks and months.

"Are you the mother of Mona Mahmudnizhad?"

"Yes."

"I have a few questions to ask you in relation to Mona."

Her heart sank in her chest. She was afraid that she would have to answer his questions exactly as Mona had, or else he would accuse Mona of making false statements. She might then be given the 74 lashes.

"No I'm not here to answer your questions."

---

[*] Ru'yá Ishráqí and 'Izzat Ishráqí

"Excuse me, and why not?"

"I am not your prisoner."

"You are not my prisoner?"

"No."

Mrs. Mahmudnizhad then realized she had just walked herself into a trap. The Interrogator told her to sit and called a guard to watch her. He walked into the Prosecutor's office and came back out soon afterwards waving a paper in front of her eyes. It had the signature and seal of the Public Prosecutor.

"Now you are my prisoner."

The Interrogator took her to room number 5. The first thing he did was to roll up a piece of paper and throw it at her. She tried to catch it, and her chador was moved back. She still had a headscarf underneath that, but he started chastising her about her veil moving back and how he had seen her neck. The first stage of her interrogation had begun.

Mrs. Mahmudnizhad stayed calm.

"Do you know what I just threw at you?"

She bent over and picked up the paper, opened it to see that it was a map of the world drawn by the Guardian, Shoghi Effendi, illustrating the Ten Year Crusade. You remember that was the call the Guardian made for Bahá'í pioneers back in 1953 to spread the Bahá'í Faith to virtually all the countries in the world. That was the call that Amu had responded to with all his being when he left for the Arabian peninsula.

Mrs. Mahmudnizhad answered, "It is what it says here on the paper, "The Ten Year Crusade."

He repeated his question. She repeated her answer. His question. Her answer. His question, her answer.

"I cannot continue this line of questioning with you," he said. He picked up two files with thick stacks of paper in them, one considerably thicker than the other. She would soon learn these were her husband's and daughter's files, which had been assembled during their first stages of interrogation.

"Where was your daughter, Taraneh, born?

"Qatar."

"And where was Mona born?"

"Aden."

"Obviously you are an international spy and yet you claim that you don't know what that paper is! It is that same plan in which you participated."

The interrogator seemed to know quite a bit about Bahá'í history. The externals of it, anyway; the core of it he completely missed. He continued on with similar questions for seven or eight hours. Mrs. Mahmudnizhad was getting extremely tired. She wasn't allowed to use the bathroom or drink a glass of water. If you remember, she had trouble with her kidneys, and she was in dire need of both.

The last two hours he spent hovering around one basic topic that seemed to fascinate him: "We put you people in prison, we torture you, we whip you, we are unjust to you, we insult you, and finally we kill you; will you not arise to take revenge on us?"

"No."

"No? Why not?!"

When you think about it, this was actually a very rational concern. From his point of view, he had seen people fighting most of his life for power, one group on the bottom planning its vengeance against the group on the top and just waiting for a moment of weakness. Again, the prisoners were becoming mirrors of the suspicions and inner character of the authorities.

Despite her fatigue and mounting discomfort, Mrs Mahmudnizhad tried to reach him. "Our aim is to achieve peace and the unity of mankind. If we return the same to you as we've received, we would be exactly as you are, and the revenge will continue to the end of time. In the end, no one will win as a result."

This went on for hours, with Mrs. Mahmudnizhad answering in different ways trying to get through to him. Was he really listening? It's possible. But in a way though, the one who was changing was she. She had never had to be the authority in Bahá'í discussions. She had her opinions, which she shared freely, but always her husband had been the one to whom people looked for answers. Now the interrogator was only looking at her.

She gave answers that were grounded in Bahá'í principles and writings: "Enmity and violence are the characteristics of the beasts of the wild, and seemly deeds are befitting of the station of mankind." "When we are able to give the gift of love and affection to humankind, why should we try to take revenge and torture them?" "We are following the path that the divine Teachings have made clear to us; teachings such as, 'Ye are the leaves of one tree and flowers of one garden … ' "

Eventually, however, she was overwhelmed with fatigue, nauseated, and about to pass out. She was no longer able to write any answers to his questions. He could see her color was sallow. He didn't stop, though. He said he'd continue his questions, but that he would do the writing himself. So it went on like that for another couple of hours. Later on, Mrs. Mahmudnizhad recalled:

"When he was finished, he gave me the papers and asked me to sign the bottom. It was difficult for me to read his handwriting, but I knew that I had no choice but to sign. It was a difficult task, inasmuch as he had written whatever he had wanted to write. It was as if I was struck on my head by a heavy stick. I was at a loss as to what to do!

"I read it carefully; crossed out the parts that he had added on his own; and signed it. When I gave it back to him, he noticed that I had crossed off some of the things he had written. He became very angry and shouted at me saying, 'Why did you do this?'

"I told him that I had to do it, because he had written things that were contrary to what I had said. He told me that I should not have crossed out anything and that I would be whipped because of it. He then said that he would obtain my whipping decree the next day from the Office of the Prosecutor, but he immediately regretted his own words and said, 'Actually, I myself, am authorized to issue a decree for you to be whipped; however, the person who administers the lashes is busy whipping the likes of you, but we will get to it another day. I will then ask him to whip you with such force that you would never again dare to cross out what I write.' "

This is almost comical, if it were not, at base, so violent. They spent a few moments in silence. She was barely able to stay conscious; he was tired, flustered and unsure exactly what to do. So he turned the decision over to her.

"You now have two options: you can go to Sepah jail or Adelabad prison. It is your choice."

"I wish to go home," she said, as surprised to hear the words come out of her mouth as the interrogator ways.

And yet, it was a Thursday night, and it turned out there was no one left behind who could drive her to the prison. Nor would there be anyone to do so the following day, which was a day off. So the interrogator accepted her suggestion! But she would have to present herself on Saturday morning or else pay 500,000 Tuman. She accepted, signed an agreement and walked off toward the exit.

There was no one in the office as she made her way out. The lights were off. It was getting close to midnight. She didn't even have money for a taxi, because they had confiscated all her belongings earlier. She hesitated. It may be better to stay in prison than be stranded on the street late at night.

She turned around and headed for interrogation room 5. The interrogation officer was getting ready to close up himself. He looked up to see her.

"Can you lend me 5 Tuman? I need money for a taxi."

He reached in his pocket, pulled out a bill and extended it to her. She took the money and started making her way out. The doors were all closed with a guard sitting behind each one. As she approached, each door was opened before her, until she reached the last one. The last door also opened, and she stepped onto the street.

The Mother's Trial

"We said 'Death' and burst out laughing"

She stepped onto the street, and unbelievably, still parked outside the prison was Taraneh! She was sitting in the car with her head resting on the steering wheel. Baby Nura was still sick and barely able to breathe, but she had fallen asleep on the backseat. Taraneh was overjoyed to see her mother.

"Mum, you came!" she cried out.

"But what are you doing here? Why did you wait so long?"

"I knew in my heart you would come back."

Taraneh began to drive as soon as her mother got in the car. They talked about what happened and laughed and cried together on the way home.

The next morning, Mrs. Mahmudnizhad communicated with a member of the Spiritual Assembly. She told him what had happened and asked what she should do. He suggested she meet with Olya, who had just been released, for some guidance. So she went to Olya's home. Olya had just returned from trying and failing to get back her belongings that had been taken when she was arrested. She spoke about Mona, how well she was coping with prison and how when Olya had been sad, Mona had recited from a beautiful tablet of Bahá'u'lláh called "The Tablet of Maryam." This is a tablet I have always loved because it reflects such kindness and love from the Blessed Beauty.

Olya told her that when she reported to Sepah, they would blindfold her and take her through long and winding hallways and up and down stairs, but that she should remain assured that she is still in the same prison. She said they would take her into different rooms, some very hot and some very cold, but not to get worried. Olya even suggested that during her hearing, she could pretend to be illiterate or deaf, so they might give her a lesser sentence. Mrs. Mahmudnizhad didn't much like this comment and left not much calmer than she had come.

That same day they had a little party for Nura's first birthday. It was just Nura, her parents and her grandmother. They put a candle in a cupcake to celebrate. It doesn't make much difference to a one-year-old. They took a photograph, which Taraneh later gave to her father. He kept it in his cell, and he told his friends whenever he looked at it he felt close to God because it reflected such innocence.

The minutes and hours slipped away until Saturday morning arrived. Mrs. Mahmudnizhad went to Sepah prison. She had one more task before turning herself in, returning the 5 Tuman she had borrowed from Interrogator 5. She tried to get in the door. Of course the guard there was used to her and the other Bahá'í family members trying to get in, so he wouldn't let her in. She insisted, but he still refused.

"I brought back the money I owe," she said.

So he must have thought she had a big bag of money, perhaps bail for her daughter's release and he flung the door open. When she looked inside room 5, she saw her husband sitting directly across from her. He was being interrogated and was writing down his answers to the interrogator's questions. There were four other Bahá'í friends sitting right next to him: Dr. Bahrám Afnán, Suhayl Húshmand, Jamshíd Síyávushí, and Farhád Bihmardí.*

---

* Dr. Afnan was our family doctor, and his practice was a few minutes away from our home. He was a loving and kind and beautiful soul, who helped me with a number of ailments. A well-respected cardiologist he suffered

"Alláh-u-abhá!" She cried out, so happy to see them.

Interrogator 5 turned red in the face. But you have to hear her tell the story:

"Once I was completely inside and saw the anger in the face of the interrogator, I regretted my action and felt that I may have done something very wrong. In situations of this sort, I usually looked at Mr. Mahmudnizhad in order to comprehend from his expression whether or not my action was wrong or right. In this instance, too, I knew that I had to seek his opinion from the expression in his eyes. When I reached him, he lifted his head softly and smiled, and I knew that what I had done was not wrong and that I should not be upset by it. Therefore, I regained my confidence, approached the interrogator, gave back his money and quietly left the room."

She was then taken to a room where other women were waiting for their hearings. When the door opened, she was knocked back by a terrible smell and didn't want to go in. Somebody grabbed her arm, however, and pulled her inside. It was Shirin Dalvand (*Shírín Dálvand*), a beautiful young Bahá'í woman she knew. There were several Bahá'í women there, and they were happy to see her, but sad at the same time because she had been arrested. They embraced her lovingly, kissed and welcomed her. The group included Mrs. Tuba Za'irpur, who was the first to greet Mona in prison, as well. The other women there—political prisoners from the Mujahidin and communist groups—watched this strange display of affection in this

---

two heart attacks from the terrible torture in prison. Suhayl Hushmand was a wonderful young man in his 20s and a mentor to us. He led a junior youth group my brother David (Dávoud) was part of and he often spent time at our home. Suhayl suffered greatly as well and was executed alone on 28 June 1983—twelve days after his prison mates. He said this was because "God has ordained that I go to His threshold with a perfectly clean soul" and he wasn't ready before. (Bahá'í World 178, 188)

fearful place. Seeing them, Mrs. Mahmudnizhad lowered her voice when she spoke.

The space was very tight. People shifted around so Mrs. Mahmudnizhad could sit on the floor.

> "As I sat down I was thinking that if this was prison, I could not bear to be in it. I wondered how the rest endured it! I had asthma and could hardly breathe there. I looked around and realized that the room in which we were sitting was the waiting area for the toilets."

She saw two stalls there, and on the doors hung belts and ropes, which were used to beat the prisoners into making confessions. Mrs. Mahmudnizhad could not stand the smell. Shirin noticed her distress.

"This is not prison, Mrs. Mahmudnizhad," she said. "They will take us to Adelabad. It is like a hotel in there. You can sleep comfortably and take showers. You will be comfortable there. Don't worry."

Shirin pointed to a pile of blankets in the corner. "When we arrived this morning, those blankets were filthy and all over the floor. The prisoners who were here before we came were drug addicts and heavy smokers, and, because they were going through withdrawal, they could not control their bladders. We folded the blankets and put them aside."

Shirin was 25 years old and had been arrested with the group of forty-one brought in on 29 November. Shirin attended University before and during the Revolution, majoring in sociology. She had written a thesis paper that was so well-researched and so thorough that her professors used it in their classes after that. The topic, coincidentally, was drug addiction and what factors made people susceptible to it.

The hearings didn't begin until 2 p.m. when the Prosecutor arrived. This would be their third stage of interrogation before the Islamic judge, the Religious Magistrate Ayatollah Qaza'i. It seemed Mrs. Mahmudnizhad had jumped way ahead in line!

The first Bahá'í to be called in was Mrs. Za'irpur. Within a few minutes, she was back and sat down again with the rest. She said she had been sentenced to death. The other Bahá'í women who went ahead of Mrs. Mahmudnizhad each went in and came out with the same sentence: Death.

This was moving all too quickly. Mrs. Mahmudnizhad tried to prepare herself. She whispered, asking them what happens inside? They said that once they were inside, the judge asked their name, looked at their file, asked whether they would convert to Islam, and when they said no, he gave them the death sentence. Mrs. Mahmudnizhad wondered at this, at what they called Islamic justice:

> "I had seen courtrooms and hearings at the movies. There was always a defense attorney. Plus, the accused always had the right to speak for himself. And of course, witnesses were always required. I also thought that hearings usually lasted at least a few days."

As she was immersed in such thoughts, her name was announced. She got up and followed the guard in. The room was rectangular, with an "L" shaped desk in it. Behind the desk was a typist.

> "He was tall and heavy with a bushy beard. He was so overpowering that even while seated, he seemed to be towering over you. The religious judge was a small, angry man, and it seemed as if he had not bathed in months."

Here was the Religious Magistrate, Ayatollah Qaza'i. He didn't care about who this was or what she thought about him, if he was small or angry or dirty. He was in charge here, and she was at his disposal. He didn't think maybe this woman in front of him now might have the last word on him for posterity.

The typist was at one end of the desk and the judge was at the other end. There was a chair in front of the judge, which was clearly meant for her.

When she had first entered the room, she had said "Salaam," or "Hello." She noticed that the typist typed out the word, and she realized whatever she said was going to be recorded and put in her file. It was clear she should sit on the chair that was placed before the judge. She remembered, however, Olya's suggestion about pretending to be deaf. She didn't sit, but placed her hand on the chair and stood before the Magistrate.

"Sit down," he told her.

She put her hand to her ear and said "Huh?" pretending not to hear him.

The angry face turned very happy, but in a twisted sort of way. He turned to the typist and said, "Do you know who this is? This is the wife of the man who spoke so eloquently and wanted to teach us the Bahá'í Faith." He of course was referring to Amu. He laughed sarcastically and then barked, "Sit down!"

She sat down. She decided to drop the deaf act. Funny, she found she was not afraid of this man. She felt a certain power or boldness, as if she were the judge and not him.

He scanned through her file and asked, "You are from a Zoroastrian background, right?"

"Yes." Before her family had become Bahá'ís, they were Zoroastrian, an old religion native to Iran. The best known Zoroastrians in the west are the Three Kings or Three Wise Men who came to worship the Baby Jesus.

"Why did you leave such a good religion as the Faith of Zoroaster and convert to Bahá'ísm?"

"Because it was my heart's desire to do that."

"This is not a matter of the heart! If, right now, you declare that you are a Zoroastrian, I will free you."

She told him she would not do that.

"Look, we respect the Zoroastrians. They participate in our demonstrations, and if you were to claim to be a Zoroastrian right now, I would immediately issue your release papers."

She responded, "Yes, you are right. As you said, they pretend to be on your side, but in their hearts it is not the same. You are also not being honest, because you Muslims have never been and will never be good to them. I remember when I was only a child how the likes of you bothered and cursed my mother on the streets because she was dressed in Zoroastrian attire."

He replied that it was that way during the reign of the Sháh, but the present regime was good to the Zoroastrians. She realized the discussion was going nowhere.

"Sir, I will not convert to the Zoroastrian religion."

"Why not?"

"Because you want to take me back to two thousand and five hundred years back. I wish you had asked me to convert to Islam. I would have liked it better."

This is exactly what he wanted. "So convert to Islam!"

She responded, "Now you want to take me back to fourteen hundred years ago. No sir, I will neither become a Zoroastrian nor a Muslim, so what is my sentence?"

"Death!" He said with anger

Mrs Mahmudnizhad became indescribably happy and said in a loud voice, "I am not worthy of martyrdom, but it would make me very happy if you were to execute me. As God is my witness, it will make me immeasurably happy, immeasurably happy!"

"You will be happy?"

"Yes"

This was not the response he wanted. He wanted fear, he wanted to prove his strength. "We are not here to make you happy. Do you know what your sentence is? We will kill your husband, Yadu'llah Mahmudnizhad. We will kill your daughter, Mona Mahmudnizhad, and you can go home and mourn their loss."

The prospect of this shot through her like a lightning bolt. She immediately rose from her seat, "Can I go then?"

"Sit down!" He shouted. He went through her file, wrote something in it, and then asked a guard to take her away. The guard started to lead her out, but she realized she didn't know what to say to the others when they asked her about her sentence. When she reached the door, she turned right around and headed back for the judge.

The guard panicked and lunged to grab her, worried that she might harm the judge. This was just the kind of disorder in which an assassination might occur. Another Ayatollah in Shiraz, more famous and better-protected than Qaza'i, was blown to pieces by a woman who hid a bomb beneath her chador.

She turned, surprised at the guard's overreaction. "I'm just asking him about my sentence."

The guard relaxed. The judge eyed her, angrily. "Death. Now get out of here!"

Her trial finished about 3:30 or 4, and the Bahá'í prisoners remained there at Sepah until nightfall. They then were loaded into a mini-bus headed for Adelabad: the men in the back, the women in the front, separated by a piece of wood and a chain mesh. For the ride, at least, they were able to see each other and to talk. Mrs. Mahmudnizhad said:

"The men asked us about our sentence, and we said 'Death' and burst out laughing. In the same manner, we asked the men about their sentences and they too said, 'Death' with roars of laughter. It was a joyous feast: one that can hardly be explained with words, one that had to be seen to be believed. We were all happy. It was as if we were all going to a wedding or a glorious party."

"Loosen your head-scarf, Mrs. Mahmudnizhad," joked Shirin, "so your husband can see you a little better."

Everyone laughed again.

Shirin looked outside the bus at the lights going by and remarked: "Enjoy the lights, take a good look. We will never see this city again."

The Mother's Arrival

"Maman joon, I have three requests of you"

Earlier that day, Taraneh waited at the Adelabad gate to be let in. Today was visiting day with Mona. Taraneh wasn't sure what she should do. Part of her couldn't believe that they would arrest her mother, too. She hoped they would ask her a few questions and let her go. And she knew Mona would get suspicious if her mother wasn't there, and Taraneh did not want to say anything to worry Mona. Maybe she should go back to Sepah and make sure her mother hadn't been released? The guards came and opened the gate for the visiting families.

Inside, Mona walked through the halls with the other women receiving visitors, stopping for doors to be opened. She needed to make sure her mother wasn't still upset about her release not happening. It had been a tough week saying goodbye to their dear friends now released and absorbing the sense that freedom was now further away than ever.

She arrived at the visitation room. She saw her sister sitting there on the other side of the glass, but not her mother. That was certainly odd. Taraneh looked very unsettled. Something was wrong.

Mona picked up the phone: "Hi Taraneh. Where is Mother? Is she all right?"

Taraneh didn't know what to say. At this point, she didn't technically know where their mother was. She didn't know whether she was okay or not. Her mouth opened and she tried not to lie: "She is in Sepah. She had to take care of some things for Father."

Her sister knew when she wasn't telling the full truth, but she also knew there must be a reason. Things could not be discussed openly here as the guards monitored the conversations. So she didn't push. Mona breathed in a prayer. Her time in prison had deepened her ability to let go of worry and fear.

They talked about other things, about Nura's birthday, about Taraneh's visit with father the previous Wednesday. Deeper than the words were the looks they exchanged. Taraneh would just watch her sister, who was gradually, week-by-week, becoming a different being. She saw such detachment, and a deep, indescribable happiness in Mona's eyes. When the visiting period was over and the phones were shut off, they touched fingertips to the glass and waved goodbye. One went back to her cell, one back to her freedom, but which was miserable and which was happy?

Sometime later, Taraneh recalled that night: "The night Mother was arrested was horrible. I couldn't believe how suddenly everyone around me was gone, and that night I cried my heart out."

When the bus arrived at Adelabad, the men were led out the back and the women out the front. Amu asked one of the guards if he might speak with his wife a moment. He had made an impression on many of the guards, even as he had made an impression on Ayatollah Qaza'i. The guards were simple men, largely uneducated and violent by training, but many of them still had seeds of decency in them. The guard agreed.

Amu caught up to his wife. He had been unable to speak with her privately on the bus ride. He was obviously concerned about her: "Please try to be comfortable. Imagine that you are staying in a hotel. Be sure to instill this in your thoughts, and try to find peace of mind. We will be together again one day, either in this world or in the realm on High."

Mrs. Mahmudnizhad didn't know what this might mean. She had been able at least to see him more or less regularly on Wednesdays for the past month or two. Would she ever see her beloved husband again?

He said goodbye and left for ward 4 of the prison. She was taken to ward 1, where the Bahá'í women were housed on the third floor. The women there had got news that the bus had arrived. Mrs. Mahmudnizhad said:

> "I saw all our dear ones from down below. They were hanging on the prison bars and looking down to see us. As I was going up the iron stairs to the third-floor, some prisoners who were with me ran ahead quickly and told Mona that I was coming."

When Mona saw the group coming, her mother among them, she gave up a little sigh, involuntary and bittersweet. She felt the tears press the back of her eyes. Mrs. Mahmudnizhad continued:

> "When we reached the ward, they all hugged me, kissed me, and welcomed me. I wish you could all have been there! The last one to greet me was Mona. When she hugged and kissed me we made no attempt to control our emotions—we both started to cry. She held me tight."

Mona put her arm around her mother and said, "Welcome, Mother. Come, I want to show you your new home." Mona led her to cell number 11. It was about 3 meters by 2 or 2.5 meters. It had only one bed and was assigned 3 people: Tahirih Siyavushi (*Táhirih Síyávushí*), Mona, and now her mother. One would sleep on the bed, one beside it on the floor, and one on the floor by the door. Their few belongings were kept under the bed.

"Have you had dinner?" Mona asked.

Of course she hadn't. Mona brought out some food she had saved from that day's breakfast, lunch and dinner. That morning, she had no idea her mother would be coming, but she knew the other women would be hungry when they got back from their trials.

As Mrs. Mahmudnizhad was fresh from the outside, the women were eager to hear news, especially about their families. As she tried to eat, she shared recent news and the stories of what the families had been doing on their behalf. They came in three at a time, in shifts, until the time for lights-out approached and everyone had to return to their cells. The women went to bed that night a little happier, feeling more connected to their loved ones.

Mrs. Mahmudnizhad was exhausted, but her mind was also reeling from the day's events. Make that the past few days. Or was it the past few weeks, months, or years? Mona walked her through their procedure for preparing for bed, brushing teeth and such. She and Tahirih volunteered to sleep on the floor so her mother could have the bed. Tahirih was 30 years old and had a loving, sacrificial nature. She was actually related to Mona and her mother (being Mona's second cousin).

At 11 p.m., the lights went out and all prisoners were supposed to sleep. The guards patrolled the area and punished anyone who was even talking.

Mona was lying on the floor next to bed. She looked up at her mother and in the dim light could see her shivering. It was cold and they had no heater in their cell, and everyone had just the two military blankets. Mona and the others had largely learned to cope, but her mother was unprepared for this, and for so many aspects of prison life.

Mona gave her one of her own blankets. Mrs. Mahmudnizhad was still shivering, but at the same time she felt bad because she had three, and Mona had one. She begged Mona to take it back, but Mona refused. She showed how she had wrapped herself in just the one.

Mona's mind was occupied elsewhere and not focused on the cold. After a little bit, she reached up and touched her mother's arm, "Mother, please wait a little while. Don't sleep yet, I need to talk to you."

Although her mother was extremely tired, the cold and her reeling brain helped keep her awake. She wondered what Mona might have to say.

The guards patrolled until midnight. After that, most prisoners were asleep, although they were able to go out to use the bathroom if need be.

Mona sat up to talk to her mother. She had been weighing in her mind what advice to emphasize. She had also had been weighing her own needs, especially her spiritual needs. Mona had found a new independence since coming to prison. Her freedom to pray, meditate and serve as she determined was extremely important to her. It was her lifeline and the key to her steadfastness. At the same time, she realized she was obligated to show her mother care, respect and even obedience. She wasn't sure she had the right balance of all these as she got ready to speak, but she trusted God would guide and assist.

Mona started by talking about how different prison life was from life outside. She told her mother she should try to take advantage of the freedoms that prison did allow and try to be comfortable. She should find time to pray alone. She should suffer within herself and not cry. "When you are among others, you must laugh and give them positive energy ... Mother, be yourself here. At decision-making times don't copy anyone. Follow your own heart. The only thing that hasn't been taken away from us is our individuality."

"Maman joon, I have three requests of you. It is possible that they may martyr father while we are in prison; they may even do it tomorrow. If such a thing occurs, you must not cry or be grieved.

You must be a source of courage to the others. At times like this, you must comfort the others.

"There is something else I want to ask of you and that is not to kiss me or show more love to me than you do to the other prisoners."

"But why not?" her mother asked. "I am happy that I am here with you. It's only natural for me to want to spend more time with you."

"Because it will make the other mothers and daughters hurt with envy, and we must not cause hurt feelings for anyone. The Blessed Beauty does not like that. If your sense of motherhood overcomes you, please take Akhtar Sabet in your arms, or Zarrin Muqimi, or Shirin Dalvand, or Mahshid Nirumand [*Mahshíd Nírúmand*] and kiss them. Show them affection and love." These were the young women there without their mothers.

Mrs. Mahmudnizhad didn't quite know how to take this guidance.

She would eventually get to know these young women better: Akhtar was 24 and a model of humility and peacefulness with an attitude of service. She was a very capable pediatric nurse in a Shiraz hospital and her manager begged the authorities to release her because she was so needed. Instead she used her capacities serving others in prison. Mahshid was thoughtful and dignified and had graduated from the University of Shiraz with a degree in Physics just before the Bahá'ís were kicked out in 1979. During her interrogation, the official made fun of her for all her education when it was he, a high school dropout, who was now clearly in power.

Mona continued: "As for my third request: it is possible that I, too, may be martyred. If this happens, I don't want you to feel sorry for yourself that your husband and daughter have been martyred. The Blessed Beauty does not like for anyone to feel sorry for himself. If you feel like shedding tears, shed your tears in the middle of the night when everyone is asleep. And when you do shed tears, don't do it for yourself, but do it for your love for Bahá'u'lláh and for the hardship that He endured during His earthly life; for those tears will be beautiful and for those tears have the sun shining behind them."

Her mother couldn't even consider this possibility at the moment. Tired and overwhelmed, she didn't argue. She felt a deep love coming from her daughter with all of these words. She would later remember how wonderful Mona was that first night, how she truly comforted her and gave her confidence.

Time in Adelabad

"How can I not help these people?"

Opium comes from large fields of beautiful flowers. It has been used in medicine for thousands of years. It has also been a terrible poison to the human mind, body and soul. Opium is a sticky paste that comes from poppy plants. It and the drugs made from it, such as morphine and heroin, are highly addictive. They don't just make the person want them psychologically. The body starts to depend on the drug. When the drug is taken away, the body goes into "withdrawal" and it is torture to the mind and body. A person addicted to opium or heroin can lose much of what makes them human, such as their reason and self-control. Their behavior becomes focused simply on getting the drug no matter what—lying, cheating, stealing, prostitution. Still, however much humanity is lost from drug addiction, the greater sin is to withhold treatment from drug addicts and make them face withdrawal alone. That sin belonged to the prison authorities.

Mona and the others watched helplessly as these women were shaking and thrashing, crying and screaming. The first few days after their arrival, they were extremely sick. They couldn't control their bladders or bowels or anything else, so their bedding was terribly filthy. These addicts and prostitutes were put in the same area as the Bahá'ís, apparently on purpose. This proved to be a test for the Bahá'í women in Adelabad.

If it were up to Mona, the Bahá'ís would simply help them, serve them and teach them. Since late December, however, the group of

Bahá'í women in Adelabad had grown considerably. All of them were dear, dedicated souls, but several of them were older and more conservative in attitude. They looked at the drug addicts and the prostitutes and they saw what many people see: They were loud and ill-mannered. They had no sense of personal hygiene, and they were infected with communicable diseases. The elder Bahá'ís worried about them all contracting disease. So they asked the younger ones not to associate with these prison mates.

There were 32 cells on their floor. There were now seventeen Bahá'ís who shared six of the cells, but right next door were these souls in torment. Mona couldn't stand having her hands tied when others needed help. One day, she came to her mother, tears welling up in her eyes, and said, "Mother, how can I not help these people? Why do you think we are in the prison? By God, we are here to help the needy. How could we ever come across people like this outside of the prison? God has planted us here so that we may help them and then guide them." She spoke of Mary Magdalene, one of Christ's greatest disciples and who is thought to have been a prostitute before her conversion. "Please let me go to their aid. Out of respect for the elders, I will go when the Bahá'ís are asleep or engaged in conversation, but I need you to help me."

Her mother accepted her wishes, and Mona got to work. Mrs. Mahmudnizhad later recalled the situation and her daughter's saintly actions:

"There was no change of bedding, so when their sheets became dirty, Mona would fold them or turn their bedding. She combed their hair and washed their faces. Every day, each prisoner was entitled to one orange, sweet lemon or apple. Mona used to collect her own fruit, extract their juice and spoon-feed those prisoners with the juice so that they might recover sooner. She used to collect tea and dates from her friends and, adding her own share, she would take them to the addicts. When the withdrawal symptoms subsided, their appetites increased, so Mona tried to keep some of her own food and gather as much as possible from everybody else and take it to them."

When their withdrawal symptoms got better and their bodies gained strength, Mona would talk with them about spiritual things. She also drew pictures for them. They particularly liked the word "Allah"—the Arabic word for God. She painted the word and they all kept a copy in their cell. It was something to focus on, to give them hope. They couldn't tell the guards it was Mona's art work, because the guards had warned them not to associate or talk to the Bahá'ís. These individuals had been so misused and misguided by Iranian society, yet ironically, the guards were worried the Bahá'ís might lead them astray.

Mona also would befriend the different political prisoners. She would talk with them, sing songs to them, and share with them the beautiful spiritual ideas of her Faith. Mrs. Mahmudnizhad remembered:

"There were three prisoners who were sentenced to death. Mona used to visit them quietly when the guards were not paying attention. They were very happy when Mona visited them, and after hearing about the Faith, they used to often tell her how blessed she was for being sentenced to death because of her faith and not because of politics or criminal offences as were the reasons for their death sentences."

They asked Mona to pray for them. These women started to wake up about 3 a.m. every day to pray for forgiveness and to fast. Before they began, they would come get Mona and she would join them.

Amu was having a similar effect over in the men's ward. For example, there was a young man from the Mujahedin* who had been sentenced to death. He said he had always been searching for the truth and now found it in the Cause of Bahá'u'lláh. It was difficult for him to accept that now he would be executed for a political movement. He had on a blue shirt, and he tore the shirt on his back into two pieces and gave one half to Mona's father.

He told him, "Tie this around your neck as a sign of our bond, and whichever one of us stays alive can wear this around his neck in the memory of the other, and in the memory of our love for Bahá'u'lláh."

For Mona's mother, prison was a hard adjustment—the harsh cold, the poor food, the foul smells, the jarring sounds, the complete lack of hygiene, the rude treatment from the authorities. Luckily, she had a community of dear friends who had arrived there ahead of her, and she didn't have to face the harsh interrogations and torture the others had. It was hard not to hover around Mona, but that can be the case for any parent of a teen. She did respect Mona's wish and tried to spend time with the other young Bahá'ís. Mona was so independent, she would spend her time praying and meditating alone, then visiting and serving all alike.

Sometimes her mother would look at Mona, so strong and mature, and it felt like the roles were reversed and Mona was the parent and she the child. Sometimes Mona would come and confide in her, and they felt like peers. Occasionally, Mona would do something sweet and girlish or she would sit and stare off, deep in thought, and it felt like the way things used to be.

---

* The Mujahedin (Mujáhidín) is a political and religious movement that advocated for the overthrow first of the Shah and later of the Islamic Republic.

The Saturday following her arrest, Mrs. Mahmudnizhad walked side-by-side with Mona down the halls to the visitation area. It had been such a long, difficult week, but she was starting to adjust. They walked into the room and saw Taraneh there on the other side. Taraneh made a big gesture of surprise and relief accompanied by a sound they could not hear. All week until that very moment, Taraneh had not known where her mother was. It was such a relief for her to see the two of them together standing side by side. The beauty of that moment would remain with Taraneh. They sat and began to talk as they had two weeks before, just with one of their seats shifted.

Spending weeks and months doing nothing in prison can really hurt one's spirits. The prison authorities made this worse by purposefully creating anxiety for the Bahá'ís. In the middle of the night, they would call one of the women's names over the P.A. system and take her away so the others thought she was going to be executed. They did this, for example, with Zarrin Muqimi, Tahirih Siyavushi and Simin Saberi. They would then send them back after an hour or two with some random excuse for keeping them so long.

Simin was brave and dedicated but also fun-loving and youthful. "When they execute us and we go to heaven," she would say, "I'm going to turn everything upside down up there to make things more difficult for the angels. That way they'll know what we've gone through down here!" [45] She was always bringing cheer to others with her active imagination.

 Mona also helped to lift the spirits of the women. Her creative mind and her positive attitude kept working despite all the restrictions. One day her mother and Nusrat Yalda'i were sitting together in one of the cells. If anyone deserved kindness and cheer it was Nusrat. She was so gentle, yet so knowledgeable, and she had been extremely active as a Bahá'í. Well before her arrest, her deep understanding of the Qur'án was admired by both Baha'is and Muslims. As a reward, the authorities made her suffer terribly with torture and solitary confinement. So this day, one of the Muslim prisoners offered her a kindness. Passing by the cell, she handed Nusrat a sour plum. This is a small green fruit that Persians love.

"I know you like these. I'm sorry I don't have enough for everyone, but I have one left for you." She had been to Sepah and was able to find some of these for her friends. "Eat it and don't tell anyone else."

Nusrat was gracious. She took the plum and thanked the woman warmly. When the woman left, Nusrat turned to Mrs. Mahmudnizhad: "I can't bring myself to eat this. Why don't you have it?"

Mrs. Mahmudnizhad said she couldn't take it.

Mona was walking past the cell right then, so Nusrat asked her to come in and she offered her the plum. "My dearest Mona, this is the only one. Please go and eat it.'

Mona didn't taarof. She took the plum and left. Everyone figured that was that and got back to whatever they were talking about.

Before long, Mona was back at the door with a small tray in her hands and a smile on her face. She bent down and showed them what she had. In the middle of the tray was the plum without the seed divided into 17 tiny pieces, and around that were a bunch of plastic forks and knives for decoration. She called in all the others, and everyone got a little tiny piece of fruit or skin. They were touched, and they laughed, and their day was made a little brighter.[46]

Of course, Mona struggled, too. Many of her thoughts revolved around her father and what he must be going through. Then there was her sister and niece, other family and friends. Mostly, she kept any pain or sadness to herself. The only time she expressed any sadness to her mother was when she spoke of the children she had cared for in the orphanage. One day Mona turned to her, with tears filling her eyes and said, "Mother, I miss my children!"

She also had very few outlets for all her curiosity and creativity. She did manage to weave together some very fine threads into a little headband and belt for her sister. Mona loved to write, but they wouldn't even let prisoners have paper. She found some, however, and had written a few letters and gotten them mailed. She also poured her thoughts and feelings into poetry, which she would then have to hide so the prison guards wouldn't see it. She remembered all her fellow Bahá'í prisoners in her poems. Her collection grew until, one day, the guards began to sweep through the prison inspecting all the cells. Quickly she destroyed the poems so she and the others wouldn't be punished. All that care and creativity was lost.

They were not allowed to have their own books, so Mona would repeat to herself all that she had read and memorized beforehand. For reading, they did have some access to a prison library and to the Qur'án. At least that was the idea. Mona was so starved for reading material she herself purchased a copy of the Qur'án from the prison. She paid for it with her own money. Then the guards came and took it from her. They said since she was a Bahá'í, she would make the holy book "unclean" just by touching it. They did not return her money. The fact that she had touched that didn't seem to bother them.

A Special Meeting

"I wish I was a painter and could paint this beautiful scene"

Around mid-February, something unexpected happened. Over the loud speakers came an announcement:

"Attention! Bahá'í sisters, you will all report to the prison administration office! Bahá'í sisters … "

The women looked at each other surprised. Never before had they used the word "Bahá'í" over the prison intercom. Something was up. They all put on their chadors and, with a kind of excitement, made their way down the stairs and the halls towards the office. They were accompanied by a few guards who led them into a hall. The Bahá'í men were there too! Some of them stood up when they came in. Mona and her mother saw Amu. The hearts reached out to each other. The guards interrupted and directed the women to sit down in a specified area.

All the chairs faced a stage at the front of the hall. The prison warden and the public prosecutor sat in chairs on the stage, which was raised above the floor by a few steps. There were two guards on either side with green uniforms and long boots. The one on the left was on a two-way radio. The one on the right stood on the stairs. There were about seventy people in the audience awaiting with anticipation what was to come.

"I have gathered you here," said the prosecutor, "to complete my task and give you my last council, so that if you are to be executed, I can rest with an easy conscience."

The enthusiasm in the room dropped a notch. It was the same old speech.

"You only have two options. Either you are executed or you embrace Islam." The prosecutor then went on to make a haunting statement. "I wanted to kill Movahhed with my own hands, but Mr. Khalkhali vied with me for that task and he was rendered victorious by strangling Movahhed."

A shiver went through the room. Mr. Muhammad Movahhed (*Muvahhid*) was a well-known Bahá'í who had disappeared in May 1979 in Tehran. His body had never been found and his fate was unknown. Mr. Movahhed was famous because he himself was a Mulla in Shiraz before becoming a Bahá'í. He read the **Kitáb-i-Íqán** (**The Book of Certitude**) in a library and embraced the Bahá'í Faith. You may remember this was the same book that Amu first encountered when he was just a youth. Mr. Movahhed started teaching the Faith freely and inviting his friends to join. This alarmed the Muslim clergy, and they committed him to a mental institution. He managed to get released through the help of Mr. Vahdat, who had influence as an army colonel. After that, Mr. Movahhed served the Bahá'í community in extraordinary ways until his disappearance.

After making this and other statements, the prosecutor brought a man to the stage. Some of them recognized him. Some knew his name and that he had come from a Bahá'í family. This was what was different about today. They were saying this man was a Bahá'í who recanted his faith. This made many in the room ill at ease. It was as if a link in the chain had broken.

"Here is an example for you of how easy it is," said the prosecutor. "If you, too, become a Muslim like him, your release will be issued immediately." The prosecutor then signed the man's release papers in front of them. He was trying to be dramatic with this, like it was little play on the stage.

He then asked the man, "Do you have reason to believe that these Bahá'ís are involved in politics?"

The man stood up and said, "Yes, the President of Chile has taken a photograph with the Spiritual Assembly of the Bahá'ís of that country, and for that reason, they are political."

This was a flimsy piece of evidence and everyone shook their heads and murmured to each other. One of the Bahá'ís, Mrs. Haqiqatju (*Haqíqatjú*), raised her hand and asked permission to speak.

"If there was a photographer here to take a picture of us with you, would he be right to claim that we have converted to Islam? A photograph is not proof of anything."

The others agreed, but they had other points to make. The prosecutor ordered the man to leave, realizing that the situation was turning in a direction he didn't want. He defended the government's position and spoke about Bahá'í meetings and institutions.

"We have nothing to do with the Bahá'í individuals, we have just arrested the members of the institutions."

Again, the room of people disagreed. Mrs. Haqiqatju spoke again saying that all the Bahá'ís, even the old men and women, attend the Nineteen-Day Feasts. Their children, as early as age 5, attended Bahá'í moral education classes. They were all members of the institutions, so the government should arrest them all to consider its task accomplished.

The prosecutor and prison warden were getting frustrated. Before they dismissed the group, one of the men, Mr. Ishraqi, came forward with a letter for the Prosecutor from the men requesting a visit among the family members who were in prison. Enayat Ishraqi (*'Ináyat Ishráqí*) was a kind and honest man, whose pension had been stolen away because of his faith, but who gave freely of himself, including serving—together with his wife—as a marriage counselor for the community. The prosecutor read the letter he gave. And he agreed to the visit then and there! Perhaps he thought that the families would discuss recanting after this display of his?

Five families, with twelve individuals total, stayed. The rest were dismissed. Those made their way back to their wards and cells, but with a heaviness in their hearts. They whispered to each other so the guards couldn't hear: Was that young man who had recanted really a Bahá'í? *

The families instantly found each other: Mr. Ishraqi and his wife, Izzat, and daughter, Roya, gathered at a table in the corner of the room. Nusrat and her son, Bahram, sat in the middle of the room. Zarrin and her father stood together, occasionally walking and talking side by side. Likewise, Tahirih and her husband, Jamshid, walked around the room together. Of course, Mona and her mother and father came together, as well, and sat in a corner of the room and held hands. They felt so much love and so much longing, after so much suffering in the months since they had last seen each other.

It had been a few weeks since husband and wife had seen each other, but it was four months since Mona had seen her father. How could words contain what they were all feeling? Mona kissed her father's eyes. How could she help take away some of the torment he had been through? How could she show her gratitude for the example he had been all her life? She kissed his eyes again and sat down. What a beautiful and heartbreaking scene it was.

Amu had a piece of blue cloth tied around his neck, but he offered no explanation for it.

---

* The man was one of a very small number of Baha'is who recanted in this period. One other case involved a wife and husband, who were cruelly manipulated by the guards into converting to Islam.

The prosecutor, the prison warden and the guards were still in their places. Several female guards, who were heavily veiled, walked around the room to listen to the conversations.

Mrs. Mahmudnizhad looked at her husband and even then felt him slipping away. She knew how the authorities saw him: he was a traitor and an apostate; he had been a Muslim and become a Bahá'í, all those years ago before the return of medieval law. She couldn't contain her feelings, "They will execute you and what will become of me?"

He was holding their hands. He replied, "Are you or are you not the faithful daughter of Bahá'u'lláh?"

"Yes," she said.

"Therefore you will receive Bahá'u'lláh's inheritance and that is imprisonment." He then talked about the Tehran prison—the Siyah Chal ("The Black Pit")—where Bahá'u'lláh was sent. "Bahá'u'lláh had a 36-kilogram chain on his neck and fetters on his feet. He was imprisoned in that foul-smelling bathhouse, a dark and filthy place. So compared to that, it seems we are residing in a hotel. And yet, I am glad that our family has received a very small portion of that inheritance."

This was the kind of perspective that could keep you going through the most difficult times. It was also hard to keep in mind when things were so difficult.

He then asked her, "Are you or are you not a faithful daughter of the Blessed Báb?"

"I would want to be," she said.

"And we should not deprive ourselves of that divine treasure, which is none other than martyrdom."

Mona and her father looked into each other's eyes, but didn't speak. They hadn't spoken the whole time. They communicated through their eyes. Mrs. Mahmudnizhad marveled at how beautiful those eyes were. They radiated love and compassion. Mona got up and kissed her father's eyes again. She was sitting on the floor beside her parents, holding their hands, and, every once in a while, she would raise herself on her knees to reach her father's eyes and then lower back to the floor.

Amu looked at his wife with compassion and said, "These days of separation will pass in no time. Do you remember how every time we wanted to move to a new home, I would go clean the house, send you to a friend's home, move our furniture into the house, and then I would shower, wear my best clothes and bring you into our new and furnished home like a queen? I want to do the same for you now. I will go to the Realm on High and make the necessary preparations, and I will then come to take you there." *

They sat a moment. Amu was suddenly filled with deep and spiritual emotions. "Look! What a wonderful scene!" He said with a gesture.

Mrs. Mahmudnizhad looked behind her to see Bahram Yalda'i sitting crossed legged while his mother, Nusrat, who weighed about 48 kilograms, was sitting on his lap with her arms around his neck. Her chin was resting on his shoulders and she was shedding tears, beautiful and moving tears.

Bahram was in his late 20s and possessed many of his mother's great qualities. He was a calming presence to his fellow prisoners and would share with them his deep understanding of the Qur'án and its ties to the Bahá'í teachings. Both mother and son had suffered greatly, and both had for months been greatly concerned for the other's safety.

---

* Decades letters, Mrs. Mahmundizhad would remember that moment: "These words created a great feeling in me, and today I am still surviving on his promise and am counting the days for the appointed day to arrive."

"I wish I was a painter," Amu continued, "and could paint this beautiful scene. This is the most beautiful mother and son picture I have ever seen."

Tahirih walked past with her husband, Jamshid, holding tight his fragile frame. How much that poor soul had suffered. Since he was the Treasurer of the Shiraz Assembly, the prison authorities had tortured him to the limits of human endurance to find the Bahá'í community's money and to get names of all those who contributed. He assured her he had remained steadfast, and she assured him the same. And these two hearts longed to stretch out each moment, each breath here together.

The Mahmudnizhads spoke some about family and friends. The end of their visit had come. Mona rose up and kissed her father's eyes again. Perhaps this was the tenth time. Father turned to daughter and for the first time he spoke with words:

"Are you heavenly or earthly?"

"Heavenly," she said.

Amu stood as if with a burst of divine energy, snapping his fingers as if dancing with joy. "Then let's go!" he said. And as he said it, it was as if the journey to the next world had begun.

This was their last meeting on earth.

Amu's Martyrdom

*"We have to suffer separately now
and go through our tests alone"*

Four weeks passed and no change. Amu was still alive. You couldn't rely on the prison to provide information, but Taraneh would share weekly reports about her Wednesday visit with her dad. The other prisoners worried about Mona and how she would take it if he were killed. A sense of dread hung over any discussion of him. When his name was mentioned Mona would say "Fadash besham"— "May my life be sacrificed for him," and a light would shine in her green eyes.

Day by day, the dread grew. And day by day, the pointlessness of prison affected Mona and the others. You don't just make a choice once to approach difficulty in a spiritual way. Day by day, moment by moment, you must keep making the choice. You must choose hope in the face of despair each time. And Despair, who may be God's saddest messenger, was looking right in their faces. He peered into their eyes and looked about, checking to see the strength of their faith.

It was now March, the time of the Bahá'í Fast. From sunrise to sunset, Bahá'ís do not eat or drink, and the purpose is to purify one's spirit. It was Saturday evening, and the Bahá'í women were in a fairly good mood. They had just returned from visits with their loved ones. Mona and her mother had met with Taraneh and heard news of her recent visit with Amu. Naw Rúz, the New Year, was only nine days away. Naw Rúz was about life and rebirth. Perhaps the coming year would hold better things for them. It had been more than two months since the last Bahá'í had been executed in Shiraz. Maybe the authorities were changing their minds.

The Bahá'í women had spread out a tablecloth on the floor of one of the cells, so they all could break their fast together. They placed food saved from earlier meals onto the cloth. There was enough for everyone. The women prayed quietly and began to eat. Perhaps one of the prison guards noticed this but decided not to say anything;

The P.A. system came on: "Attention! Mrs. Qaraqozlú, report to the gate." The women all looked over at Mrs. Tuba Za'irpur. Qaraqozlú was her maiden name. She got up gracefully and quietly and made her way out. The women watched. There were no hugs or kisses although everyone loved her, no goodbyes in case this was the big moment. They had all had months to prepare for whatever was to come. Like Bahá'u'lláh, each was living "like a slave beneath a sword not knowing from one moment to the next when it would fall." They listened as she walked down the stairs and out the door.

Part of them expected her to come back in twenty minutes. Part of them felt she might be gone forever. None of them knew that when Mrs. Za'irpur walked out the door, she was put into a vehicle with Amu and another Bahá'í friend, Rahmat Vafa'i (*Rahmat Vafá'í*). Mr. Vafa'i was a member of the Spiritual Assembly of Marvdasht and a businessman admired by Bahá'ís and Muslims for his trustworthiness.

The three were driven to a place that was once a polo field, but the Revolution had no room for such games. It was now a killing field, and these three wonderful human beings were hanged one-by-one with a single noose until they were dead. Three goals were scored in quick succession. Heaven cheered and earth sighed, as if it were a world-class sporting match and three champions had just been born: Yadu'llah Mahmudnizhad. Tuba Za'irpur. Rahmatu'llah Vafa'i. The day was Saturday, 12 March 1983.

Within a short time, rumors started spreading among the female prisoners that Mrs. Za'irpur had been executed along with two men. They didn't know who the men were, but Mona and her mother and all the other women suspected one of them might be Amu. But they couldn't be sure. The guards wouldn't talk about it. They would have to wait until visits with their families the following Saturday. It was going to be a long week.

That Wednesday was the Iranian Festival of Fire, called "Chaharshanbe Suri." It happens on the last Wednesday before the New Year. Iranians celebrate by building little fires to jump over. Jumping over the fire symbolizes their lives being purified from all the problems and cares of the past, and they go into the new year clean and free. This is a very old ritual that most people in Iran celebrate, everyone except the extremely religious Muslims. Another thing people do on this holiday is read the poetry of the National Poet of Iran, Hafez. He was from Shiraz and lived during the 1300s, and people often read his poetry to tell their fortunes.

So starting on Tuesday evening, many of the prisoners in the ward were asking the guards to allow them to go outside. They said they wanted fresh air, but the guards knew they wanted to perform the fire-jumping ritual and said no. The guards did let them have the book of Hafez's poetry, however.

Hengameh (*Hingamih*) was one of the non-Bahá'í prisoners that Mona had painted the word "Allah" for, and she was very attached to Mona and the other Bahá'ís. She saw how anxious Mrs. Mahmudnizhad was at this time, so she tried to make her laugh and relax a little. She took a pair of her trousers and wrapped them around her head like a turban. She had a string of prayer beads in her hand and put the Hafez book under her arm. She walked around, acting like a Mulla, to make the women laugh.

She came up to Mrs. Mahmudnizhad and said, "Come, open the book. Hafez will tell you the truth!" The way they tell someone's fortune is to have the person open a page at random, then they read and interpret what it means for the person.

Mrs. Mahmudnizhad told Hengameh she did not believe in that sort of thing.

"Come on, see what Hafez has to say about that."

Hengameh was acting very funny, and she had Mrs. Mahmudnizhad and some of the other women laughing. She was also acting very sweet, so Mrs. Mahmudnizhad took the book and opened it. She opened to a line of poetry that said:

"Goft án yár kaz ú gasht sar-e dár boland, jormash ín búd keh asrár hoveydá míkard." [47]

    or

"He [the wise man] said: The friend for whom the gallows were raised, his crime was in revealing the divine secrets."

Mrs. Mahmudnizhad felt a shiver race through her. She turned to Mrs. Haqiqatju who was standing next to her and said, "Look, it speaks about the hanging noose here!"

Someone tried to change the subject, but Hafez had opened the heart's wound again. She sighed and talked about her anxieties. Mona was off in another cell, perhaps praying, perhaps serving. Each had their way of coping. No one could be certain. They hoped Taraneh would have news at their visit on Saturday.

Taraneh was their connection to the outside world. She was trying so hard, and not just to find out information about her family, but to arrange for their release. She was going to Sepah several days a week, but also making trips to faraway cities such as Tehran and Qum. She visited any office and followed any lead searching for a fair-minded person to whom she could appeal her family's innocence. She did all this despite the challenges of being a woman, a Bahá'í, and the mother of a toddler.

Her life had become so empty so suddenly. She kept reminding herself of the terrible sufferings of Bahá'u'lláh and how He responded with beautiful deeds and writings. She begged Him for steadfastness so she could endure the separation from her loved ones.

Each Wednesday and each Saturday had been a gift, to see her loved ones still alive. Taraneh did not know that second Wednesday in March would be her last meeting with her father. Looking back, however, she understood how he had prepared her and her mother.

"Tell your mother I love her very much," he had said, "and that although we've always shared our happiness and our grief, we have to suffer separately now and go through our tests alone. This is our chance to prove our true love for one another and for Bahá'u'lláh. This is our destiny."

She saw his face light up. Her eyes filled with tears, but tears of happiness. Still, they kept her from seeing him clearly. Something was weighing heavily on her heart, and it had been building for some time.

"Father, how come from a family of four, three of you were Bahá'u'lláh's chosen servants and I was deprived of this great bounty? What have I done that I wasn't worthy of being in prison for my Faith?"

He looked at her with compassion. "Do you think you are free? You on the outside are in the harsher prison. With all the oppression, you are prisoners, too. Besides, a lover is never free, but is always a prisoner of love. Taraneh, think of the outcome! Think of the outcome and the actions you take."

Still, he understood what she was saying, and she was cheered by his encouragement.

"Are you saying I should be happy and sure?"

"Be confident and happy," he said with great feeling.

Taraneh wished she could have hugged and kissed him, but instead she put her fingers to the glass. He did the same, smiled and was gone. Of that moment, Taraneh later wrote:

> "I knew I would never have the chance to embrace him in this world again, to rest my head on his chest. But, as he advised, I concentrated on what would result from their imprisonment and execution, and I resigned myself to God's will."

The Mahmudnizhad Family
(L. to R.) Mona, Farkhundih, Taraneh, Yadu'llah

Breaking the News

"I swear to God, at that moment
my whole being became calm"

We were not in Shiraz, but the effect of Amu's death on my family was profound. All of us loved him and each of us received the news in our own way.

The night of Amu's martyrdom and before anyone knew, my sister, Shahin, had a dream of him. In the dream, she and Amu were walking hand-in-hand together on a beach on the Caspian Sea. They were talking when, suddenly, Amu lay down on the sand still holding her hand. Shahin saw that his body had changed to light, and she could just see his face. She started to scream and beg him, "Please don't leave me. Please don't leave me alone." He squeezed her hand tightly and three times he repeated, "I swear to Bahá'u'lláh, I will never leave you alone!" When he finished saying this, his body of light had started to rise up into the sky, and she watched him as he went.*

At the very hour of his execution, my sister Nahid's 4-year-old son, Farjam, was watching cartoons on television. Suddenly, he turned to his mother and out of nowhere said, "Amu and his two friends got hurt and left."

The next day the news arrived. I heard on my way to school, but by the time I got home, everyone knew. Everyone was upset and

---

* Shahin has suffered enormously in the past number of years since her dear husband Saeid was imprisoned in 2008. She says whenever she feels down, she finds comfort in Amu's words.

crying. No one, however, responded quite like my mother. That day, her legs stopped working. She had become paralyzed. Doctors could not explain what happened, but they prescribed muscle injections. These didn't help, and her paralysis went on for several weeks. At Naw Rúz time, two weeks later, a samovar full of hot water fell right onto my mother's legs. She screamed in pain but still could not move. Then one day in April, we were all sleeping when the whole household was awakened by a giant cracking sound— "TAAAHHH!!" The next thing we heard was my mother saying "Yá Bahá'u'l-Abhá!" We all rushed into her room. She had just woken from a dream. In the dream, Bahá'u'lláh had reached out His hand and touched her knees, and that's where the cracking sound had come from! The next day, she started to walk again.

The news of the execution reached Taraneh on Sunday too. Her husband, Sírús, brought the news at about 10 o'clock in the morning. He only made it to the stairway when he began to sob. Taraneh remembers:

> I knew my father's spirit of sacrifice, and after his arrest I always knew he would be killed, but when I heard the news my whole body trembled with the shock and I screamed. I couldn't control myself. My one-year-old daughter, Nura, woke up because of the noise we were making, and she, too, began to cry.
>
> At length, I got a grip on myself. I said, "Father, you told me yourself the spirit of the martyrs will make this tolerable for the ones left behind. And that they will send us strength. So where is it?" I swear to God, at that moment my whole being became calm. I felt peace within me as never before in my life. [48]

Taraneh decided she should go to the morgue and try to see the body of her father and those of the others. The officials at the morgue did not want to let her in, but she kept pushing trying to persuade them. Finally, she was allowed in, but the officials insisted she keep at a distance.

There was her father's body, lifeless. She looked at the form and shivered. She could see he was not there. It was as if this was just a house he had lived in for some time, and now he had moved on to another one in another realm. Still, what a precious house this was to her. She wanted to kiss the mark on his neck that had been left by the rope. But no, she had to stay back.

She saw the dryness around his lips. He had not broken his fast that day. She later asked some of the men who were with him in prison, and they said he had been called before sunset. They had offered him bread before he left, but he refused it saying it was better this way.

The other two bodies were there, too. The woman and two men were placed together by the guards, as if this were an insult. These bodies were three mistreated shells, and their occupants were finally free. In these past months, they had been abused, kept alone and isolated for endless days. Now the officials would not release their bodies to the families, but would dump them together in a grave with no marker. Perhaps there was a beauty in their being buried together, after suffering so much isolation. And that patch of unmarked earth would be remembered as holy ground in the long memories of angels.

Saturday came. Mona and her mother made their way down the familiar halls to the visitation area. Taraneh sat with a great burden on her shoulders. One look at her face and Mona knew it was true. And yet, they were all somehow elevated at that moment. Taraneh described this later:

I had already recognized the wonderful spiritual state they were both in, but I was not expecting the gift of strength that came to me when I needed it. When it came to delivering the news to them, I was filled with an indescribable joy and happiness. I congratulated both of them, and they did the same in return.

"Dad is gone to the next world," she told Mona.

"I know," she said. "Good for him. Lucky him."

Back in the prison ward, Mrs. Mahmudnizhad shared the news. The other prisoners—it didn't matter their religion—came to comfort them. Mona walked into her friends' cell, and she asked them to congratulate her: Her father had been martyred for his faith in Bahá'u'lláh. He had persevered and stood tall before all the swords of hatred and all calamities, and she was immensely proud of him.

All were brokenhearted, and many were in tears. Mona, in her fashion, sought to comfort them.

'Please don't cry for me," she said, "I don't feel alone. I know you are all sharing my grief." She told the older women they were like her aunts and the younger women they were like her sisters. "But we must stay strong. We haven't passed our own test yet. Now we have to pray that those who have been martyred will intercede for us with Him to enable us to pass our tests." Mona turned her face to the Holy Land, sat, and began to chant a prayer.

That night was tough for her mother. When all the comfort of friends is quieted and after the sense of shock that cushioned the blow of bad news fades, the reality begins to sink in. Mrs. Mahmudnizhad was starting to struggle. She longed for some tangible proof of her husband's death, but she was stuck behind bars with only other's words to rely on. She went from prayer to needing to talk about her feelings and back to prayer.

Their cellmate, Tahirih, got up and began to unstitch the hem of her dress. From inside the hem, she pulled out a pill. She broke it in half and offered one piece to Mona and the other to her mother.

"It's a sleeping pill. I've been saving them for when I might need them." Tahirih was a nurse by trade, and had been hiding a number of sleeping pills in the hem of her dress for a long time. When she took a bath, she would move the pills from one dress to the next. She did this in secret, knowing the guards would punish her if they caught her.

Mrs. Mahmudnizhad got upset. "My husband has been martyred and I want to lay awake and pray for him. Besides, suppose that I sleep well this one night; what about the other nights to come!" She refused to take the pill.

Mona reached out her hand and said, "Please let me have the pill. Thank you for thinking about us."

Tahirih walked out of the cell. Mona asked her mother to join her in the bathroom. When they got there, Mona threw the pill in the sink and washed it down with water.

"Mother," she said, "Tahirih has been saving these pills for a day like today. How can we break her heart and not take it from her?" Mona said she already had her sleeping pill. Her prayers would help her sleep. "Father achieved his station and passed his test with excellence. It is now our turn to pass our tests. I will sleep well tonight. I suggest you also try to get some sleep."

Her mother was not able to sleep at all that night. She was pacing around the cell anxiously. This woke up Tahirih at one point.

"Look at Mona," she said, "She took the pill and was able to sleep soundly. If you had taken the pill, you, too, would have been able to rest!"

Tahirih didn't know that it was Mona's faith that had given her calm and peace of mind.

The coming days were filled with tears and laughter, as waves of joy and grief washed over them. It is true that Mona meant the words of encouragement and hope she shared with the others. It is also true that her heart was broken. From that time onward, her disposition changed. Her mother later recalled:

> "I frequently saw Mona crying and asking to be executed so that she could be in the presence of Bahá'u'lláh and her father. She was crying and asking that her blue cape be changed to the red cape."

Out of Obscurity

*"America and the world are increasingly
alarmed and dismayed"*

The Bahá'ís had been suffering in Iran a long time with little
evidence that the rest of the world noticed or cared. Of course, they
did it because of their Faith and not to be noticed. It is still
encouraging, sometimes, to have an outside acknowledgment of the
injustice one is facing.

All along, there had been a network of devoted Bahá'ís outside of
Iran working tirelessly to get the situation of the Iranian Bahá'ís
noticed. The Universal House of Justice was directing efforts in
dozens of countries to get the press and government officials to pay
attention and to make statements on behalf of the Iranian Bahá'ís.
Ultimately, the goal was to get governments to put pressure on Iran
to change.

It started to work. As the years went by, the Bahá'í world
community was able to make this systematic persecution visible to
the whole world. Newspapers were printing articles. Government
officials were making statements. It turns out the Iranian government
did not like the attention. Although Iran claimed to be independent
of the rest of the world, and especially the West, it still cared how
other nations viewed it. This even applied to Iran's enemies and
what it called "The Great Satan," the United States of America.

On May 22, 1983, U.S. President Ronald Reagan issued the
following message:

America and the world are increasingly alarmed and dismayed at the persecution and severe repression of the Bahá'ís in Iran. Recently we have learned that the government of Iran has sentenced 22 prominent members of the Bahá'í faith to death. This is in addition to the more than 130 who have been killed since the beginning of the revolution in Iran, including one man executed January 1, 1983, and three hanged in Shiraz on March 12, 1983.

These individuals are not guilty of any political offense or crime, they have not plotted the overthrow of the regime, and they are not responsible for the deaths of anyone. They only wish to live according to the dictates of their own consciences. I strongly urge other world leaders to join me in an appeal to the Ayatollah Khomeini and the rest of the Iran's leadership not to implement the sentences that have been pronounced on these innocent people. Sparing their lives would be a step forward for Iran and the world community. [49]

A few days later, the New York Times ran an editorial saying,

Iran has killed at least 150 Bahá'ís since 1979, jailed and robbed thousands more, and snatched children from their parents … Americans are helpless to halt the killings. But they should never cease to protest and they can join with other nations in providing asylum to those who manage to escape from this state of fanaticism.[50]

This reporting brought attention not just to Iran; the Bahá'í Faith had never had this kind of international publicity. An editorial like this in one of the most respected newspapers in the world would not have happened just a few years earlier. The President of the United States is confronted with hundreds of problems large and small each day, but his office took the time to craft this message of support for a small group of people on the other side of the world.

It was a testimony to the purity of heart of those who died. President Reagan's statement indirectly refers to Amu, Mrs. Za'irpur, Mr. Vafa'i, and a man executed on the first of January. That was Hedayat Siyavushi. You remember Hedayat was the man who took me and the other young people to pick out the glass pieces from the House of the Báb. These individuals were so pure as they entered the next world, the power of their souls shook this world. They added their shares to a wave of momentum that 132 souls had started before them. By the day of the New York Times article, the number of Bahá'ís martyred since the Iranian Revolution was 139 and climbing.

It was also a testimony to the purity of the efforts of those who worked so hard to tell their stories. These were the Bahá'ís around the world who met with reporters and officials, on local and national levels, to try to get them to speak out. These souls had nothing to gain themselves. They did it out of love for Bahá'u'lláh and for their brothers and sisters in faith in the land of His birth. It was hard, at first. No one had heard of the Bahá'ís. If a newspaper printed an article, it was full of errors or misunderstandings. Gradually, however, through patience and perseverance, the Bahá'í friends were able to increase awareness of the Faith in the media and in circles of government. It is funny that patience and perseverance were just what those of us in Iran needed, too.

Something else was happening, beyond striving to help the Bahá'ís of Iran. The persecuted community inside and the free community outside were working together like two hands, or two wings. Together they were raising understanding of the Bahá'í Faith around the world. Before, it had been seen as an obscure offshoot of Islam, but more and more it was understood as a peaceful and progressive independent world religion. It was winning the sympathies of leaders in the civilized world. It was still not well-known, however, by everyday people. It was almost as though the Faith stood at a new threshold. It was about to come out of obscurity into the light of common understanding. With hindsight, we can see that the big push was just about to come.

Preparations

"I just want to tell you what I'm planning to do"

Mona had won the love of her fellow prisoners, but she also had won the fear and respect of the guards. The powerful way she spoke in her interrogations and her fearlessness made her a kind of legend in the prison. Other prisoners, both Bahá'í and Muslim, who spoke up during interrogations were several times told by the guards: "We know Mona taught you to say that!" *

On Friday the 27th of May, the prisoners woke up to the sound of a radio playing over the prison P.A. system. They jumped to their feet as they heard the announcer speak about the Bahá'í Faith and the fact that the President of the United States had defended the Bahá'ís. The announcer was saying that the U.S. President's action was proof that the Bahá'ís were political spies. The women felt both a thrill and an uncertainty. They were thrilled that their Cause and their suffering were being recognized around the world. They were uncertain how this might be used against them by the authorities.

A few days later, the women were all told to return to their cells. All doors were locked. Two prison officials entered the ward and came up the stairs to the third floor. These were interrogators. They were wearing masks to hide their faces. They walked slowly down the passage in the Bahá'ís' area, checking the names of the inmates, which were written on the doors. They came towards Mona's cell.

"Which one is Mona?"

---

* Of course, this wasn't fair to the other women, so many of whom were themselves models of courage and strength.

The hair stood up on Mrs. Mahmudnizhad's neck, and her heart began to pound. She had never seen her daughter interrogated. No, no, she couldn't watch anything happen to her.

Without hesitation, Mona introduced herself.

One of the masked men spoke, "The President of the United States has risen to your defense and has proved you are indeed spies. Do you still claim that you are not?"

"The truth," Mona said, "is always hard to bear." She tried to find the eyes behind the mask, because truth is transferred more directly through the eyes. "All the peoples of the world have risen to our defense, and not just the President of the United States."

The eyes behind that mask were not seeking truth. After some more back and forth, the interrogators moved on to another cell. Still hiding their identities, they accused others of secrecy and plotting.

Mrs. Mahmudnizhad took a deep breath. Mona sighed. It had been two and a half months since her father's death. How long was this all going to go on? Mother and daughter uttered a short phrase of prayer, almost unconsciously, for some resolution to all this. Their prayers pointed in opposite directions, to two different kinds of release.

There were a lot of injustices in prison. One of the most unfair rules in the prison was the prohibition on Bahá'ís saying prayers or observing other laws of their Faith such as fasting. The women would not follow such unjust rules, but they had to hide their actions. They said their obligatory prayers while seated so no one would notice. Mona loved to do what is called the "long obligatory prayer," which includes standing, bending and bowing. She would have to get up in the middle of the night to do this. Of course, Mona loved the nighttime. It was the time when she could best commune with God and get closer to the spiritual world. In the peace and quiet, she could pray for all the peoples of the world, for her family and friends, and for herself.

Mona somehow was not yet satisfied with her spiritual growth. She would tell her mother, "I have to attain human perfections before leaving the world of dust." To everyone around her, she was already about as perfect as a person could get, but Mona hungered for more. So she fasted. With fasting, we deny our outward hunger to feed our spirit.

One morning in early June, Mona's mother asked her if she was going to eat her breakfast.

"I don't want to eat anything anymore" was her reply.

That didn't sound good. Her mother started to ask why. Her reply made it sound like she was going on a hunger strike, but no, Mona didn't want anyone else to know. This was a personal search.

So what was Mona seeking? She already had shown such courage, faith and service. She had already sacrificed so much at such a young age for the Faith she loved. Could she not be content? Anyone who knows a 16-year-old knows they are never content when they're standing still. They need to be doing or learning, moving forward in some way—whether physically, emotionally, intellectually, spiritually … Mona had been taken out of an earthly school and placed in a heavenly school. This prison was teaching and testing her in ways some of the others couldn't understand.

What are the lessons that prison teaches? Patience and perseverance, certainly. It's one thing to be patient and to persevere and yet to hate the experience one is having. It's another to embrace that experience and to feel truly content with the Will of God. Could she feel truly content here in prison day-after-day, month-after-month with so much injustice going on all around her? Could she let go of her need to see justice done? Could she let God handle that in

His good time? Could she learn that lesson that 'Abdu'l-Bahá had challenged the Bahá'ís with—to see their enemies as their friends?

You must manifest complete love and affection toward all mankind ... You must consider your enemies as your friends, look upon your evil-wishers as your well-wishers and treat them accordingly. Act in such a way that your heart may be free from hatred. Let not your heart be offended with anyone. If someone commits an error and wrong toward you, you must instantly forgive him ... Be illumined, be spiritual, be divine, be glorious, be quickened of God, be a Bahá'í. [51]

Could she learn this lesson as well as her father had—the man who forgave and loved even those who tortured him? Let's be clear: God doesn't want innocent people to be miserable and put in prison. But God does give humans free will, and there are times in human history when evil people are in control. Those are dark times when the sun of divine justice is hidden but the stars of human greatness can shine brighter than ever.

This was a graduate-level course in spiritual development for Mona, and her exam was coming up. If she passed this exam, then her black cape would be complete and perfectly made—a graduation robe, if you will. And she could move on to the next level.

All that day, Mona fasted. She spent all the night praying and meditating. The next morning she continued to fast. Her mother of course, was worried for her. She wanted to talk to someone about it, but Mona had told her not to. At lunchtime, Mona sat down with her mother and others. She had brought some bread and cheese and a piece of watermelon.

"I am satisfied." She said with no further explanation and she began to eat for the first time in 30 hours.

When they were alone, her mother asked her what she had meant by that.

"Mom, I won't tell you what I asked from Bahá'u'lláh. Just know that Bahá'u'lláh was here in the prison." And she left it at that.

A Bahá'í holy day was coming up on the 9th of June. It was the time to commemorate the Ascension of the Báb.* Mona and the others others had now been in prison for up to 7 and a half months, and they had commemorated a number of holy days together in prison. They usually had to do this quietly, but it still attracted the attention of the other prisoners. Many of them had grown attached to the Bahá'í women, including Mona. Some would have liked to participate in this kind of event and learn more about the Faith. The Muslim prisoners would talk to their family members about the Bahá'ís in favorable ways on visiting days. They would provide information about executions and tortures to the outside world. The authorities knew these things and wanted to act to prevent them in the future.

So, a few days before the holy day, they moved all the prisoners who were near the Bahá'ís to other cells farther away. This left a number of cells empty. Mona saw an opportunity for herself here. The day before the holy day, she approached her mother:

"Mother, please allow me to commune with the Blessed Báb alone in one of these empty cells during this last anniversary of His passing."

Her mother wasn't happy about this. Mona was spending too much time alone, slipping away when the others would gather. Plus, the older women had agreed that everyone would pray in groups of three in their cells. They would do this at noon exactly, the same time

---

* This holy day is now observed in July everywhere in the Bahá'í world. In Iran at the time, holy days were celebrated according to the lunar calendar, which shifts every year.

the Báb was executed. Mona's mother didn't know what her daughter meant when she said the "last" anniversary.

"You can't do that," her mother told her. "We decided that we would all pray in groups of three. You have to respect the decision of the elder Bahá'ís."

Mona went along with this. The next day at noon, she joined the other women and observed the occasion according to plan. Afterward, they all had lunch and then went their different ways to wash dishes or clean their cells.

The prison ward was noisy. People were going here and there, talking and shouting. The P.A. was loud with someone reciting the Qur'án. The month of Ramadan, when Muslims fast, was coming up. Mona found a slight sense of frustration rising inside her.

She walked back to her call, where her mother was alone. Her frustration came out: "Mama, why didn't you let me be alone with the Báb on this last anniversary?"

Mrs. Mahmudnizhad was surprised by this. She thought Mona had been okay with the arrangement. She forgot some of the heat she had felt the previous day: again, there was that "last" anniversary reference.

"Were you that serious about that?"

"Yes."

"I'm sorry. Well, you should have told me. Why didn't you insist more, if it was so important to you?"

Mona backpedaled a bit. "I knew you were right, too. That's why I didn't insist." She realized the matter was over, and there was no use in pursuing it.

She walked away and down the corridor for a few minutes. Why didn't her mother understand her better? She never had this problem with her father. She could often read his thoughts like she read her own. Then Mona felt an impulse. Now was the time. She needed to open herself up completely to her mother.

She headed back to her cell. She felt her heart opening up to her mother in a new way. "Come for a walk with me," she said.

This came as a surprise to her mother. From the time that Mrs. Mahmudnizhad had arrived at the prison, Mona had asked her not to walk or talk with her much, nor to kiss or hug her. Mona didn't want to cause pain for the other girls with such displays. So now, Mona's mother got up slowly and started walking beside her.

Mona put her arms around her mother and said, "Mama, I want to tell you something."

The walkway was narrow and not quite wide enough for two to walk side-by-side. They walked a bit until Mona stopped and looked in her mother's eyes.

"Mama, do you know that they are going to execute us?"

"You, too?"

"Yes."

Mrs. Mahmudnizhad suddenly felt her whole being was on fire. She asked her not to say these things. "No, my dear daughter, they're going to let you go. I harbor many dreams for you in my heart. Now that your father has been martyred, I would like to see us freed from this prison and for you to get married and have children. My greatest wish is to see your children. No, don't even think that way."

She was completely oblivious to Mona's spiritual state.

"Mama, I swear to God that I don't have such hopes and I don't want you to have them for me, either. I know I will be killed. I just want to tell you what I'm planning to do. Would you like to know how we are going to be martyred?

Mrs. Mahmudnizhad didn't want to hear anything on this matter.

"If you don't let me tell you," Mona said, "you will regret it later, and I don't want you to have the pain of that regret!"

Mrs. Mahmudnizhad looked at her daughter's face and how very serious she was and how concerned she was about her mother's reaction.

You could hear the chanting of the Qur'án over the prison's P.A. system, and the prisoners were crowding together, blocking the way. Mother and daughter had to stand back each time one of prisoners went past them. And each time any of the prisoners did pass, she would show her affection towards Mona either by caressing her long hair or patting her back or sending her a gentle kiss. Mona, too, would respond to the affectionate gestures of the prisoners and thank them with her smile in her beautiful way.

"OK, tell me."

"You know, Mama, the place where they are going to hang us is probably going to be higher than the ground, so they can put the rope around our necks. I will first get permission to kiss the hands of whoever puts the rope around my neck. I think they will definitely let me do that."

One of the guards was walking by, and Mona suddenly took her arm from around her mother and stood in front of her. She said, "Mother, these hands must be kissed." She was referring to the hands of the guard. "We must kiss these hands, for they are the hands that will take us to God. These are the hands that will take us to our Beloved. These are the hands that will take us to the object of our Desire. These are the hands that will take us to the Blessed Beauty."

Mona was now entering a spiritual state, and she was taking her mother with her, right there in front of the whole prison.

She continued, "Then I will say that it is forbidden in the Bahá'í Faith to kiss another's hands unless that other is the one who is taking my life for my faith."

Mona walked further ahead to where there was some more room. Her mother was clinging to the rail.

"I will then say this prayer, because mother there will be time for everything."

Mona put her hands to her chest in respect and said a prayer, "*Huvallah, Ay Khuday-i-Man Janam Fadayih …* " This is a prayer by 'Abdu'l-Bahá about sacrificing oneself in the path of the friends of God. She recited the prayer in such a beautiful manner that words could not describe it. It was as if no one was there except for her and her Beloved, and she was not at all weary of her surroundings.

She said, "Then I will kiss the rope which is about to hang me, I will pray for the world of humanity, and I will say goodbye to this mortal life." She walked through each step as if she were performing a play.

This put Mona's mother in a strange state of mind. She looked at Mona but couldn't see her. She heard her but didn't comprehend. She was deep in spiritual delight, but at the same time she did not want to lose her daughter. Inside, she was pleading with God about this test He had put before her.

"What a story!" she found herself saying out loud.

Mona turned. "Mother, do you think that I am telling you a story? As God is my witness, this is the absolute truth." Tears welled up in her eyes. Mona turned and walked down the corridor on her own.

In recalling this whole experience, Mrs. Mahmudnizhad said later:

"Oh, how I wished I could discuss what had transpired between us with the other Bahá'ís and find someone with whom I could share the pain which burdened my heart! But I knew that this was a secret that I had to keep to myself. I did not sleep at all that night, and spent all night communing with Bahá'u'lláh. I turned to Him and begged Him not to let Mona be martyred while I was still in prison in the way that it had happened with her father. I wished to be free, so that at least I could see her blessed body. I did not want to lose Mona before my eyes. It is very painful to lose a dear one in prison, in the way that I lost my kind husband, Yadu'lláh – a very painful experience."

100,000 Lives to Give

"We have become one"

Early the next morning, Mrs. Mahmudnizhad awoke with bad kidney pains. Mona was by the bed on the floor; Tahirih was gone, perhaps off for an early shower. Mrs. Mahmudnizhad needed to take a walk and there was no room in the cell. It was early, and the cell doors were now locked for cleaning until 8 a.m. She called out to one of the cleaning people. Several of the prisoners were assigned to washing the prison bars and floors every morning. She asked one of the women to allow her to go for a little walk because she was feeling sick. The woman told her she couldn't, but then she noticed her puffy eyes and realized how ill she was. The woman opened the door and told the other four women that "Mother of Mona" was taking a walk. So Mrs. Mahmudnizhad walked around the corridors a few times.

While she walked, she reflected. She had gradually reached a state of mind where she understood that true submission was possible, but at the same time she was very depressed. What is submission to God if it's not offered joyfully?

She had wandered back towards her cell, when she saw Mona sitting on the bed facing west. She had a pillow on her lap, and she had crossed her arms on her chest and fixed her eyes in the direction of the Qiblih—that is, the Point of Adoration, the Spot where the Bahá'í world turns its face at least once each day, the Shrine of Bahá'u'lláh in Akka, Israel. Recalling that moment, her mother said:

"She was beautiful, and with her long hair that fell over the bed, her green eyes, and the light that fell upon her face she looked absolutely divine. I stood still and gazed at this beautiful sight, and heard myself saying out loud, "O, my God, how radiant. She looks like the blessed Mary." Suddenly I felt that if Mona were martyred, it would be a pity. I also thought that if she were to remain in the prison for a while, she would lose this beauty. I trembled and felt that I was about to die, for I could no longer endure so much pain and suffering.

"I ran towards her to tell her of my feelings, because I always discussed my problems with her and eased my mind in that way. I went to her and shook her shoulders. She turned towards me and asked what was troubling me. I told her about my feelings and then walked away and sat on the floor, leaning on the wall. She got up from her bed, came towards me and sat in front of me. She said that she wanted to tell me something frankly. I told her to go on, but she asked if I was all right and could take what she was about to say. I assured her that I was all right and asked her to proceed or I would die! God, how beautiful she was! Her hair fell over her face like an umbrella, making her even more beautiful."

Mona began by saying, "If I knew that for every year that I am in prison a few people or even one person would embrace the Faith of God, I would wish to spend a hundred thousand years in prison, or for so long that the entire world would become Bahá'í. And now, Mother, you are worried for what? For a maximum of a 100 years of my unworthy life that may be spent in prison? Mother, could anyone live more than a hundred years?"

Mona spoke of her dreams and desires, of how she wanted the youth to acquire divine knowledge. "Mother, they will come in groups and ask us about the Faith. There will be no time for us then to go and find answers for them! We have to be prepared, and answer all their questions. We have to be loyal to our duties. The youth have to speak of the Faith on the radio and in television, and take the Cause of God to the people of the world."

"And if I knew," she said, "that because of my execution, all the youth of the world would arise, join hands in service to humanity, become selfless, teach the world about Bahá'í ideals and try to move the world, I would beg Bahá'u'lláh to give me 100,000 lives to sacrifice in His path."

Mona's mother felt small before the greatness of her daughter's soul. She now offered her daughter the approval she had been seeking. She later said:

"It was then that I submitted completely to the Will of God, in such a manner that I wished the authorities would come right at that moment and take us all to the arena of our martyrdom."

The authorities did not come right at that moment like they would have in a movie. "Cut to the chase," as they used to say. But real life doesn't often work that way. Patience and perseverance are key. Time proves the character of the hearts and separates out what is lasting and true from what is imperfect and temporary. Time also provides opportunity for imperfect hearts to become more perfect and true.

So the next day, Saturday the 11th of June, the Public Prosecutor entered the prison with a new plan. He told the Bahá'ís, "In the coming days, you have to pass through four stages of guidance, in which you will become Muslims. Otherwise you will be executed. From tomorrow, two hours of silence will be announced every day. The prison is now your university, and you all have to study."

One may well ask: why were the authorities giving this group of Bahá'ís so many chances to live? This government had no problem executing criminals and people with different political views. The Bahá'ís, in this regard, posed no threat to the regime and would not fight back, as other groups might. So why delay? Despite all the accusations that Bahá'ís were spies or devil-worshipers, did the officials recognize on some level these were decent people and not deserving of death? Maybe. Then maybe their focus was not on these individuals but on the Bahá'í community as a whole. Maybe they thought that the more effective strategy to hurt that community was not in killing its faithful believers, but in wearing down their will and seemingly killing their belief. That might explain these delays and the varying tactics.

The next day was Sunday, and the "four stages of guidance" were to begin. No one knew what that would involve. Mona woke up in the middle of that night to say prayers. It was 3 a.m. when she was saying the Long Obligatory Prayer. While she prayed, she saw 'Abdu'l-Bahá come through the wall of the prison and sit on the bed beside her mother, who was asleep. Tahirih was also still sleeping on the floor. 'Abdu'l-Bahá placed one hand on her mother's head and stretched out the other towards Mona.

"Mona, what do you want?"

Was she dreaming? The tears were coming down her face felt real. In any case, she stopped her prayer fearing He might leave. She went to Him, took His hand and put her head on His knees.

"Perseverance."

Again 'Abdu'l-Bahá asked her, "What do you want from me?"

Mona could only think of the one thing: "Perseverance for all the Bahá'ís."

A third time, He asked, "What do you want for yourself from me?"

Mona had started to sob and said, "Perseverance, perseverance, perseverance."

"It is granted," He said. "It is granted."

Later that morning, Mona told the other Bahá'í women about her vision. They went into the day more assured of themselves and the divine power behind them.

At 10 a.m., the beginning of the two hours of silence was announced over the P.A. The Bahá'ís obeyed and observed the silence. The area got very quiet.

The P.A. soon broke the silence and Mrs. Ishraqi was called down. She made her way down and out. This must be stage 1. A few minutes later, she came back. As she passed by the women's cells, she held up two fingers. She had gone through stage 2 and not just stage 1. This was moving quickly.

Right after her return, Zarrin was called. And after only a few minutes, she returned. Again, she held up two fingers as she passed. Silence.

The PA called again for Mrs. Ishraqi and Zarrin, but together this time. They were gone longer this time. Mrs. Ishraqi came back sooner and this time showed everyone the number "3", the third stage of guidance.

Then it was noon and the period of silence was over for the day. The women were gathered around Mrs. Ishraqi, none closer than her daughter Roya. She was telling them about the process she went through when Zarrin returned. She came up to the door.

"I want to take a bath," she said, "so that I will be clean at the time of my martyrdom."

The women sensed Zarrin's apprehension and lovingly called her into the cell. She didn't need to take a bath, they told that dear soul, because a martyr is baptized by God and her blood is clean. They asked her to spend the last moments of her life with them, instead. She accepted, and all 17 of the Bahá'í women came together in just one cell.

The only Bahá'í woman who had been executed since they had been there was Mrs. Za'irpur, and that had been 3 months earlier, on that same day of the month. Were they really going to execute two in one day? Everyone clustered tightly around Zarrin and Mrs. Ishraqi.

The women began to chant the Remover of Difficulties, a short prayer by the Báb said in times of trouble and hardship:

"Is there any Remover of difficulties save God? Say: Praised be God! He is God! All are His servants, and all abide by His bidding!"

Zarrin hugged Mona to herself: "O Mona, what a wonderful wish you asked from 'Abdu'l-Bahá. You know it would be a tragedy for the Bahá'ís if they executed us all, but I am sure they would be firm. You could have requested freedom for yourself and your mother, even freedom for all of us. But you asked for the most wonderful thing and He granted it."

Zarrin was a courageous and intelligent soul with a powerful presence. During her interrogations, she told the official, "In what language must I tell you, my being is Bahá'u'lláh, my love is Bahá'u'lláh, my whole heart is Bahá'u'lláh." The interrogator then threatened to tear her heart out from her chest. "Then my heart will call out and cry, 'Bahá'u'lláh, Bahá'u'lláh'," she told him, so overwhelming him with emotion that he ran out of the room.

The prayers continued. Suddenly Zarrin started to sing, "Bahá'íyan be pa konid … " It was a song that called the Bahá'ís to rise with all of their heart and soul to serve the Cause of God. All the others joined in singing, especially the young ones, who sang with all their power. Mona sang out strong for the strength of her spiritual sister, Zarrin, and aunt, Izzat.

"Baha'íyán, be pá koníd / Ze ján va del ghíyám ásheqáneh-í

Be ahd-e khísh, vafá koníd / Ke báshad az nedá-ye haqq nesháneh-í"

Or, roughly translated:

"Baha'i friends, get on your feet / Rise with resolve with all your heart and soul

Be ever loyal to your word / And shine as a sign of the True One's Call"

Singing Bahá'í songs was forbidden in prison, of course, but they continued. At that point, no one feared anything. The power of their spirit was too strong. Even the guards were compelled to pay no attention to what was happening. The other prisoners had gathered outside their cell to watch. As Mrs. Mahmudnizhad said, "One was wishing them well, and the other was congratulating them."

Soon afterward, Mrs. Ishraqi and Zarrin were summoned for their last stage of guidance. All hugged them, kissed them, and said their tearful goodbyes. Roya was the last to let her mother go.

"Congratulate my father when you see him," Mona told Zarrin. Mona loved Zarrin, and they shared a love for poetry. They would often speak to each other with poetry. It was their shared language. Now she was leaving. Mona saw her begin to go and she ran toward her.

"Rahist, rah ishq ... " Mona recited part of a verse from a classical Persian poem: 'The path you are about to tread is the path of love / A path in which you are bound to part with your life."

Zarrin turned to her friend saying, *"Tark-i-saru jan gir ... "* to complete the verse. "Give up thy head and thy life to rest in peace / For the journey of love taketh but these few steps."

The two women left, holding close to one another. The others started to pray and begged Bahá'u'lláh that these two dear souls would remain steadfast and be martyred in the path of God and become the pride of the believers and of the Cause.

After a little while, however, they both came back. They were confused and heartbroken. They had been taken to a place of execution, but then sent back.

Mrs. Ishraqi said, 'They took us to our executioners, but why did they not execute us?"

Zarrin said, "What did we do wrong that they did not execute us?"

They shared the details of what happened. The best they could figure, the new plan of the authorities was to execute all of them at the same time. The women clung together as they waited.

There was something happening here, a profound melding together that seemed the result of both human and divine action. Mrs. Mahmudnizhad later spoke of a startling incident involving Tahirih and Mona:

> Tahirih was sitting on the bed. Tahirih had been married for 10 years, but she had not gotten pregnant. She loved Mona like her own daughter. As she was sitting on the bed, she asked Mona to jump onto her lap. Mona did so, and they hugged tightly and started shedding tears and whispering to each other.

Mrs. Mahmudnizhad worried that if the guards came and found them like this, they would be punished. They would be taken to isolation or whipped!

"Mona, please let go of Tahirih." She asked her numerous times, but Mona would not let go. It was like they were in a different world.

Mrs. Mahmudnizhad turned her attention to Tahirih. She stood up and shook her shoulders. "Tahirih, I did not expect this from *you*. Why are you doing this? Let go of Mona."

Tahirih suddenly looked at her and with a rare power said: "No, we have become one. We have joined together. We have been integrated into one another."

Mrs. Mahmudnizhad was struck dumb. She later explained:

This was not Tahirih's own voice! This *voice* was not the voice of Tahirih, but it was Tahirih who was speaking it. I was overtaken by the mightiness of this voice and went aside. I sat in silence until they separated from each other.

The following day was Monday, and Mrs. Mahmudnizhad was bracing for death. Instead, and with no notice, the prison ordered her to be released. And right away.

What? she wondered. How was that possible? She had been sentenced to death like the rest.

The women gathered around her, including the Muslims. They hugged and kissed her. They were so happy for her, but sad that they might never be reunited. They each had a request that she go somewhere, do something or tell someone something else.

Mrs. Ishraqi asked her to attend her daughter Rozita's engagement party that Thursday. Rozita (*Ruzítá*) was only 18 and had been left without her parents or sister since November. "And take a red carnation on behalf of each of us here."

Mona was the last person to say goodbye. She hugged and kissed her mother, held her hand in hers, and said, "Mama, you supported everyone and warmed all the hearts here. Continue to do the same for the ones outside. Encourage them to be firm and strong." They kissed again and said goodbye.

How could she say goodbye to Mona? It was all happening so fast. Was the judge's evil statement coming true—that they would kill her husband and her daughter and that her sentence was to go home and mourn their loss? Before she knew it, she was at the door looking back. How could she leave them all here?

"Tell our story. Tell our story. Tell our story." So came the impression of their souls on her soul. This was not spoken, and Mrs. Mahmudnizhad never wrote it down as such. But she directed her life from that point onward as if that were her guiding purpose.

Final Days

"Pray that we will go to the execution ground
dancing and singing"

Outside the prison, Mona's mother was keeping her promises. She went visiting and encouraging the family members, especially the mothers of the young women inside. Her own home had been confiscated, so she was staying with Taraneh and her husband and their little daughter. They were so glad to see her, and overwhelmed with the stories she had not been able to share during their visits to the prison. Taraneh looked at her mother differently now. There was a new strength and independence about her.

That Thursday, they attended Rozita's engagement party, and Mrs. Mahmudnizhad brought 16 carnations on behalf of those who had been her fellow prisoners. She was almost as popular as the bride-to-be. Everyone wanted to hear news of the prisoners. She told them how strong the women were and she calmed their fears. Every one of them, she said, was ready for martyrdom, and they accepted whatever God willed.

Inside the prison, the women had decided to celebrate Rozita's engagement, as well. The Bahá'ís gathered together with some of the other prisoners, plus an Armenian woman who was Mona's and Tahirih's new roommate. They all had a good time. They congratulated Mrs. Ishraqi and Roya. They joked with Roya about her younger sister getting married before her. Wasn't she afraid she was going to be an old maid? She was already 22! They did their best to make mother and daughter feel less separated from Rozita.

Suddenly, Mona felt something. She said nothing and went out. The others continued with the party. Mona was gone for a while. One of the other prisoners, perhaps on her way to the bathroom, passed by her cell. She saw Mona alone, praying and crying aloud. The prisoner went back to the party where everyone was still happy, still celebrating Rozita. Poor Rozita, the bride-to-be with the worst luck.

That very night, 16 June 1983, her father and five other Bahá'í men were taken to the polo field and hanged. They were:

> Dr. Bahram Afnan
>
> Mr. Abdu'l Husayn Azadi
>
> Mr. Kúrush Haqqbín
>
> Mr. Enayat'u'llah Ishraqi
>
> Mr. Jamshid Siyavushi
>
> Mr. Bahram Yalda'i

Two of these souls I have not yet mentioned: Mr. Haqqbín was 34, with a wife and two children, and had pioneered in a Kurdish area on the Iraqi border, where fanatics had set fire to his shop. In prison, he uplifted others by chanting the many Bahá'í prayers he had memorized. Mr. Ázádí was the father of seven and also a pioneer. Despite suffering health problems following torture, he kept up his spirits and others' with his warm-hearted and cheerful nature.

When word of the executions broke the following day, the Bahá'í community in Shiraz erupted in activity. Hundreds, even thousands, came out to visit the families of those men. They brought them huge bouquets of flowers. They consoled and congratulated them. They shared their tears and their smiles. The death of a loved one is always painful, but the blessing of martyrdom somewhat soothes the hearts of those with faith. Many chose therefore to dress in colorful clothes rather than the blacks of mourning. The community was uniting like never before through the outpouring of love from above.

The next day was Saturday, the women's visiting day. Mrs. Mahmudnizhad had made a headscarf for Mona and bought her a new towel. She and Taraneh bought a watermelon for her, too, wrote her name on it, and made their way to Adelabad prison. Before going in for visit time, the families of the prisoners gathered in the prison yard. Most of the families were there, and that was good. It was good to see Tahirih had visitors today: her father from Tehran, and her grandparents.

The families had gathered to consult. What were they going to tell the women about the men's execution? The prisoners relied on these visits to get their information.

Telling them the truth might be a terrible blow to them. Tahirih had lost her husband. Mrs. Yalda'i had lost her son. Mrs. Ishraqi had lost her husband and Roya her father. Maybe they should wait, some of them thought. Maybe they could just share that some men had been executed but say they weren't positive about the names.

Mrs. Mahmudnizhad could not accept this. "Please tell them," she pleaded. "I know what is going on in there. We have to be honest with them. I know if we don't tell them, the guards will. And they will do it in a very harsh manner just to hurt them. It is much better if we tell them ourselves."

It was a hard choice for the group to accept. They wanted to bring only joy to the hearts of the prisoners. Some worried that Mrs. Yalda'i would have a heart attack if told directly. Rozita wondered about sharing news about both her engagement and her father's death. Tahirih's father just didn't know how to tell his daughter that her kind, young husband was gone.

In the end, they decided on a compromise. They would make sure to tell the other prisoners who were not directly affected. So just in case they didn't have the heart to tell the family members, the others would share the news in a wise way inside the prison. Taraneh would tell Mona, the Sabet family would tell Akhtar, Mrs. Haqiqatju would tell her daughter, and someone else would tell Mrs. Avaregan. Rozita decided to go ahead and tell her mother and sister directly.

With this decision, they entered the prison. Some family members had to stay back. A maximum of 4 were allowed per immediate family. Tahirih's grandmother was held at the gate for not having appropriately modest clothing. The old woman did not have a chador, only a shawl around her head and an overcoat. This was the middle of summer.

They walked into the visitation room. It resembled a long hallway divided in the middle by a barrier: one side had cubicles, the other had handset receivers, and a glass wall between. Today was a little different: the prisoners weren't there when they entered. The visitors had to stand back and wait until the handsets were connected. The late afternoon sun poured through the windows from the prisoners' side.

When the women entered and saw Mrs. Mahmudnizhad, they gathered behind the glass and waved. They were all so happy, as if they were already pure spirit. Mrs. Ishraqi seemed not even to be touching the ground but walking on air. Mrs. Mahmudnizhad waved back lovingly. Everyone moved to their places. And there was Mona. She sat with a big smile on her face, blew kisses to Taraneh and her mother, and reached to touch them through the glass.

The phones were then turned on, and the timer set for 10 minutes. Mrs Mahmudnizhad was first to speak. They greeted each other.

"Mother, they have brought an Armenian lady to our cell in your place. Of course, she will never be you, but she is, after all, a mother." Mona was very happy and was laughing as she spoke.

Taraneh felt hurried, however, worrying about them disconnecting phones early. She took the phone from her mother.

"Hello, Taraneh!" Mona said. She always said this full of feeling and happiness. "Oh, I wish I could squeeze you! Welcome, welcome. You must be very happy that Mom is with you?" she asked.

"Yes, I am." Taraneh answered quickly. "Mona, dear, I have news for you."

"What news?" Mona recalled the feeling she'd had two nights earlier.

Taraneh began to share the news of the men's execution. Later, recalling that moment, she said:

I wish I could describe Mona's look. It's a pity that pen can't do it justice. Pity. Pity. Her green eyes were full of tears. She put her hand on her heart and a soft voice asked who. I quickly, without noticing her tears, started to say their names.

In the booth beside Mona was Tahirih, who was talking to her father. "Her husband, Jamshid," Taraneh said, pointing.

"Good for him," Mona said.

The sunlight was shining right at eye level, right in Taraneh's eyes. Mona's scarf was slipping down, and Taraneh indicated she should fix it before the guards saw. But this was a different kind of visit: the atmosphere, the movement, the light. People were moving around, switching places, and the guards were looking the other way, as if they knew something.

Taraneh went through each name, and each name moved Mona to say, "Good for him." By the time Taraneh got to Mr. Ishraqi, the tears were pouring down Mona's cheeks.

Mona pressed her hand harder to her heart and with a soft voice said, "Good for them. Good for them. They are the guests of Bahá'u'lláh. Lucky them. Lucky them. They are the guests of the Ancient Beauty."

Mona looked at her sister and saw her concern. Her voice got stronger, "Taraneh, I swear to Bahá'u'lláh that these are not tears of sadness. These are tears of happiness. Don't think I am crying because I am sad. It is because I am happy."

With Mona speaking like that, Taraneh could see that Mona was ready for martyrdom, too, and that her time was very close. Her spirit just couldn't live here anymore.

"Mona, dear, you are going too?"

"I know. I know," she said. "Taraneh, I want to ask you a favor. I want you to pray that we will go to the execution ground dancing and singing."

"Whatever He wants, we are happy with His decision." What else could Taraneh say to such a request?

The sunlight was shining so strong it seemed she should be blinded, but no, Taraneh saw the faces on the other side so clearly. It was as if the light was shining from the women's faces. Taraneh saw the flashing eyes of Akhtar Sabet peeking at her—she didn't even know her, but what beautiful brown eyes she had! They shone like the constant light of an immoveable star.[*]

Mona kept pressing, "I need another favor. I want you to pray and ask the Ancient Beauty to forgive all of my sins before my execution. Then they can take me."

Taraneh could barely believe what she was hearing. Afterwards, she described her feelings in that moment:

---

[*] The name "Akhtar Sabet (Thábit)" literally means "immoveable star."

O my God, what a hard favor for me, full of sin, to pray for that angel! And with a look, I asked her what sins do you have that I should ask Bahá'u'lláh to forgive you? She read my look and laughed. Dear friend, I swear to God that this is not made-up. This is not my imagining. Mona was crying, laughing and talking to me like that ... She knew well that she was going. With all my strength and power, I tried not to cry so that I could see her beautiful face. I wanted to talk less so that she could talk and I could hear her voice.

Their mother had been watching all of this. She could not hear much of what Mona was saying, but had been caught up in looking at her beautiful daughter. She later remembered the following detail:

> It was as if she was lost in another world, and the veil that covered her was slowly slipping down her head ... Taraneh kept pointing to Mona to fix her veil, but Mona was in a different realm and oblivious to our worries. [Afterwards], I told Taraneh, "Why were you insisting that Mona fix her veil? I was hoping to see her beautiful neck once again."

Now, as Mona was speaking of dancing at her execution, the mood had shifted. Beautiful and deep laughter mixed with tears came from both sisters. They sent a kiss to each other and put their hands together on the glass. For the last time in her life Mrs. Mahmudnizhad saw her two daughters laughing together, and she was filled with joy.

Overcome with emotion, Taraneh told Mona to talk to their mother and handed over the phone. She moved back from the booth a bit. Next to their booth was Tahirih's father. He was kind and let Taraneh talk to his daughter.

"Tell your mother not to worry about Mona," Tahirih said. She is strong as ever, and we're looking after her."

It was obvious she had not yet heard the news. Maybe her father was hoping Taraneh would tell her now. He just couldn't do it.

Mona had her own news to deliver to her mother. "Mother, tomorrow we will be the guests of Bahá'u'lláh."

Her mother felt her legs go numb. Mona said this with such certainty, as if there was no doubt. Mona kept speaking but her mother couldn't hear her. She did manage to say something.

"Have you gone through the four stages of guidance?"

"No," she said. "I will complete all four stages tomorrow."

Her mother stopped talking and just stared. She looked as if she was about to faint.

Taraneh saw this. She thanked Tahirih and quickly switched places and grabbed the phone from her mother. "You were together for five months, now it's my turn to talk to her." The clock was ticking and she didn't want to waste a moment.

Her mother tried her best to make her way to speak to Tahirih. She had told her father she would try to share the news with her. Now, she could barely speak herself. Besides, Tahirih had so much to report about Mona, she didn't let her talk. She told her how Mona was fine. They had all bathed and were ready to go. Then there was the Armenian lady that had replaced her in the cell. Oh, and Mrs. Yalda'i and Mona had not yet passed the four stages of guidance, but that they were all waiting to be martyred.

After grabbing the phone, Taraneh repeated what she had said to her mother.

Mona laughed and said, "Do you know why I am so happy?"

"No, tell me."

"I am happy that we are the chosen ones of Bahá'u'lláh."

Taraneh just looked at her. What could she add to that?

"Taraneh, dear," she added, "send my love to all the relatives and friends, and kiss them. Everybody's face is right in front of my eyes, but I can't mention their names." She pointed to Nura and said, "I want you to raise her to be like our father."

Taraneh didn't say anything to this. She just wanted to hear Mona talk. But in her heart, she thought, "No, I want to raise her to be like you."

The phones were then turned off. The sisters kissed their fingers and touched the glass and the warmth slipped through their fingertips straight into their hearts.

Their mother had been unable to tell Tahirih the news. She got up, as Tahirih waved goodbye. She tried to make her way to see Mona once more before she left. But when she got around the corner, Mona had gone.

Tahirih's father had been sitting back and he had seen Mona run and put her arms around his daughter. No doubt Mona would be the one to share the news with her. The women were filing out, waving their beautiful hands, with tears in their eyes and smiles on their faces. Roya grabbed Mona's hand and pointed to something high up, near the ceiling. They held hands and stared at the spot. Roya's sister, Rozita, saw this and looked up, but what they were seeing was hidden from her eyes.

One by One

"The youngest was last"

The visit with the family was in the late afternoon on Saturday, 18 June 1983. The women went back to their ward where the news was spread around. They clung together out of love and support. They cheered one another, cried and laughed, and lifted each other's spirits. Those who had lost loved ones, they realized, might just be reunited with them shortly in a heavenly setting.

When it got dark, the officials started calling names of the Bahá'í women over the P.A. One by one, as the names were announced, the individual's blood started pumping and her adrenaline racing. The moment had come. But the natural reactions of the body were tempered by the profound spiritual strength of each individual and the group as a whole.

The names suddenly stopped coming after the tenth was called. Mona, the youngest of all, was among the 10. There were six not called. They, in particular, were surprised. Why had they not all been chosen?

All of them started to gather around the 10 whose names had been called. First the Bahá'ís, then the rest of the Ward: from the addicts and prostitutes to the socialists and royalists, from the husband-murderers to at least one Armenian Christian—they all came out to bid these dear ones farewell:

"Blessed are you!

"Pray for me that I will be strong!"

"Take me with you!"

Such phrases as these poured out of their hearts for the ones being taken away. Such phrases would normally go in the opposite direction as the condemned cry out for their lives. But now all things had been turned upside-down. Divisions of class and religion and politics were erased. The living wept, while the soon-to-die rejoiced.

The 10 were loaded into a bus. They chanted prayers and sang songs all the way. How could the bus driver keep from weeping? He had thought that they were to be released. It was only when he drove up to the gate at the security check that he had heard they were to be executed. How could he participate in this? And yet he feared the guards. Again, the women were cheerful, even proud of what was to come. The bus driver would later tell the Bahá'ís: "I've never seen people in such high spirits." [52]

The handful of Bahá'í women left behind in prison packed the belongings of their sisters. They wept for them and for their separation from them.

The 10 women were taken to the same polo field where their loved ones had breathed their last. One by one, they went. One by one, their souls took flight. Ten such pure, angelic throats had never so eagerly slipped into the hangman's noose.

The executioner who put the rope around those precious necks himself told of what happened:

> We gave the opportunity to recant up to the last minute. First we hanged the older women, and then it was the turn of the young girls, one by one in front of the rest. The youngest was last. We thought they would be so frightened that they would recant. We said to them, "Just say once that you are not a Bahá'í and we will let you go." But none of them did. They all preferred to die.[53]

Mona asked to be last so she could pray for the others. She witnessed the death of nine of her fellows. When it was her turn to go, Mona lightly kissed the executioner's hand, and then she kissed the rope before it was wrapped around her throat. She said a prayer for this world of ours. And then she stepped out of it and into the Greater World, the World of Light, with nine newly-born sister souls by her side.

One by one, the ten women martyrs of Shiraz were:

> Mrs. Nusrat Yalda'i
>
> Mrs. Izzat Janami Ishraqi
>
> Mrs. Tahirih Siyavushi
>
> Miss Zarrin Muqimi
>
> Miss Akhtar Sabet
>
> Miss Simin Sabiri
>
> Miss Mahshid Nirumand
>
> Miss Shirin Dalvand
>
> Miss Roya Ishraqi
>
> Miss Mona Mahmudnizhad

The Face of Martyrdom

*"That dear and innocent child proved
the innocence of all of you"*

By 10 p.m., the executions were over and the bodies of the women were brought to the morgue. The bodies were left on the floor like luggage, like sacks of potatoes. They still had their clothes on, and they leaned against each other as they had in life. As fate would have it, the first thing one saw upon entering the room was Mona's face.

The prison officials did not inform the families. But the following morning, the family members of the six men came once again looking to claim their bodies. Rozita was there. She and the others appealed to the guard at the gate. She knew he had a heart. He had been punished just yesterday for letting this same group into the morgue on Friday to see the six men. He let them by again.

The families of the men came into the morgue and the scene hit them like a shock wave. One young man described the first faces he saw in that scene:

[T]he first sight was of Mona's innocent face, lying with her head resting on Mahshid's shoulder. Mahshid looked as if she were in a deep, peaceful sleep. To Mona's right was Shirin, so beautiful, a witness to injustice ... Roya, her eyes wide open, seemed to be gazing at the crippled human beings wandering about her ... [54]

The six bodies that the families were expecting had been replaced with ten new ones. Someone found a phone, and from that time, the news spread rapidly. It was a second wave of shock as the families of the women learned what had happened.

After the previous day's visit, Mrs. Mahmudnizhad was in bed by midnight and sleeping soundly. At 7:30 a.m., Taraneh woke her. She wanted her mother to watch Nura while she took a bath. She wanted to be prepared, in case the women had been martyred.

Mrs. Mahmudnizhad took her grandchild into her arms and onto her lap. Nura was now one and a half, and she listened attentively to her grandmother's words. For Mrs. Mahmudnizhad, it felt as if two long-lost lovers had reunited with one another.

She then heard the door to the apartment building open, and she rushed to see who was there. A Bahá'í friend, Mrs. Salmanzadeh, was slowly, slowly making her way up the stairs with tears rolling down her face.

Mrs. Mahmudnizhad asked, "Has something happened?"

"Yes, they have martyred ten of our dear ones."

"Was Mona among the ten?"

Mrs. Salmanzadeh swore to God that she didn't know.

Taraneh heard the exchange and stuck her head out of the bathroom door: "Mrs. Salmanzadeh, please have pity on us. If Mona has been martyred, please let us know, so we can go and receive her body, and so we don't go through the same thing as we did with Dad."

Mrs. Salmanzadeh said she really didn't know. Then a young woman arrived with news that Mona was indeed among the martyrs.

From that moment, Mrs. Mahmudnizhad didn't feel or comprehend anything. She didn't know if she was awake. She couldn't feel her own weight. She couldn't stand, she couldn't move. She didn't know if she existed.

Taraneh emerged from her bath barely taking time to dry herself. In a moment, she had her clothes on and she and Mrs. Salmanzadeh were trying to get her mother to stand. Just then Mrs. Mahmudnizhad screamed, and it seemed to jolt her back to life. She regained control of her body, got dressed and left for the morgue with Taraneh.

Outside the morgue, Bahá'ís were gathering. They were coming and going, swirling with energy and emotion. The guards blocked the door to the morgue and stood watch on both sides of the street.

Taraneh and her mother approached the guard at the door, but were kept from entering. They were told the Public Prosecutor was inside at the moment and they should go to the side of the street and wait to be called.

They went, but soon they were back and were again refused entry.

"Do you have a mother?" Mrs Mahmudnizhad asked the guard.

"Yes."

"Listen, I am a mother. Let me go in and see my child, please!"

The guard's manner grew softer, but he said the Prosecutor had forbidden it. He moved his fingers across his throat, as if to say he would be killed himself if he let them go in.

"If you only knew who these people are," she told him, "and for what reason they are laying in that morgue, you would sweep up the dust beneath their bodies and make it an ointment for your eyes."

He still refused and asked them to stand by the side of the street until they were called.

Among the Bahá'ís gathered outside was the mother of Hedayat Siyavushi, who had been martyred in January. She was also the aunt by marriage to Jamshid and Tahirih. Mrs. Siyavushi came to Mrs.

Mahmudnizhad, hugged her and said, "Mrs. Mahmudnizhad, our women have surpassed our men in their victories."

She then turned towards the Muslims there and in a loud voice said, "O people of ignorance, how much do we have to endure? How long do we need to sacrifice because of your ignorance?"

Mrs. Siyavushi kept on speaking like this, and Mrs. Mahmudnizhad was worried she would be arrested. So she took her aside, and they stood waiting on the side of the street. The guard then told them they could go inside.

They braced themselves. The mother wondered to God how she could bear this. Entering the morgue, they saw all those dear ones, lying like angels fallen upon the ground. At that moment, Mrs. Mahmudnizhad faith was rekindled. She later said,

I was so overwhelmed by the greatness of the Cause and of the greatness of those who had been martyred in its path, that I felt weightless again. I don't know how it was. It was as if I didn't exist myself; I could only see *them!*

These had been her everyday companions for the past five months. Now she looked at them and kept repeating, "Yes, you dear ones fell at the feet of the Lord."

Her eye immediately fell on her daughter's body. Although Mona was five bodies away, the eye sees what is ahead of it, not what is directly in front of one. The mother was moved to go towards her daughter, when suddenly she heard the voice of Tahirih ringing in her ear: "*We have become one. We have joined together. We have been integrated into one another.*"

The statement sunk in. Mrs. Mahmudnizhad later recalled:

They had all become one ... Mona, Shirin, Zarrin, Simin ... There was no difference between them. So I returned to where I had started. The first body was that of Roya Ishraqi. I stood by her head and said to myself: "Bahá'u'lláh, I know not what these eyes have seen, but I know that I will never see what they have seen, so let me kiss these eyes and the mark left on their necks from the noose."

She moved from Roya to Shirin Dalvand, then Simin Sabiri, Mahshid Nirumand, and then to Mona. She kissed the eyes of each as well as the marks on their necks. She then noticed two bodies on the other side.

Mrs. Muqimi, who had been in prison herself, was sitting by her daughter, Zarrin. Zarrin had been blindfolded. "Mrs. Mahmudnizhad," she asked tenderly, "can I open the blindfold?" How does a mother know what to do?

Mrs. Mahmudnizhad told her yes and went to help. She loosened the blindfold around Zarrin's eyes. She kissed her eyes and the marks on her neck, and returned her to her mother's arms.

Beside Zarrin was Mrs. Yalda'i. She moved to her and kissed her in the same manner. She then moved to where Mrs. Ishraqi was, and she bowed down before her and kissed her as the others. One could see the bloody, inner layer of skin on her neck where the noose had cut through.

Nearby was the body of dear Akhtar Sabet, but her head was beneath a stretcher. Mrs. Mahmudnizhad kissed her feet, her hands, and her chest. Then she moved under the stretcher, pushed it up with her body, and was then able to kiss her eyes and the marks on her neck.

That was nine, but where was the tenth? She then saw a door that opened to another room. There she found Tahirih, whose height filled the length of the small room. She kissed Tahirih as she had the others.

She walked over to Mona once again. Mona's grandmother* was there with her, caressing her hair. Mona had a hair pin in her hair, but neither grandmother, nor mother, nor sister had the heart to take it. It was the only ornament Mona had worn when she had attained the presence of her Lord.

Now mother lifted daughter's head to place it against her own face. Just then she remembered no one was there to visit Shirin Dalvand. Her family had moved to England when Shirin was still attending university. Afterward, she had decided to remain in Iran.

Mrs. Mahmudnizhad approached Shirin and said, "Shirin, I will give you two kisses: one from your mother and one from your father. Please accept them from me."

Afterward, she returned once more to Mona's body. She later recalled, "I kissed her beautiful, cold cheeks and returned that treasure to its original owner." She felt someone lifting her up. It was the guard who was in charge of the morgue. At first, Mrs. Mahmudnizhad thought he was going to give her trouble for kissing all the bodies.

"Which one of these is your child?" he asked.

She showed him Mona, and he started to sob.

"I beg you by the Holy Qur'án to forgive us. This is our job. Please forgive us. We have always witnessed these executions, but nothing has ever affected us to this degree. Please forgive me. I beg you by the Qur'án to forgive me."

She felt as if she were mute. She pulled the guard into her arms and kissed him on the cheek. She consoled him like a small child, until he once again felt at peace.

"If you only knew," she told him again, "for what reason these bodies, these children, have fallen here on this dust, you would

---

* Mrs. Mahmudnizhad's step-mother

sweep up that dust beneath their bodies and make it a remedy for your eyes."

As word spread, more family and more friends crowded the area outside. The guard had a heart, but he could not allow all of these people through. The officials now had a problem on their hands. Word of these executions was now spreading beyond the Bahá'í community. Another wave of shock as all of Shiraz was hearing the news. They needed to act quickly.

By noon, all sixteen bodies—the men and the women—were placed into ambulances. They were then taken to the Bahá'í cemetery. The Bahá'ís followed them in their cars, but they were not allowed in. From the time of the martyrdoms of Mr. Vahdat and the others, this cemetery had been under the control of the government. Rozita Ishraqi explained what happened away from their view:

> They buried all the bodies with their clothes on and without coffins, in previously prepared graves. They covered them with dirt and then destroyed the boundaries between the graves so we wouldn't be able to tell who was buried where. But that didn't make any difference. They were all pure love, they were all light and they all returned to the same source.[55]

Poor Rozita had suffered the loss of mother, father and sister in three days. She was still able to find beauty and dignity in the tragedy. In remembering that day, Taraneh also was able to see through the pain and find both beauty and meaning:

> The pain I felt that day was the same as when I heard the news of my father's martyrdom. Knowing Mona, I had been certain that she would never give in. Besides, I had never even asked Bahá'u'lláh for her freedom, because I did not want anything other than His will. But several times I had thought to myself, if

they kill Mona, how am I going to endure the sight of her dead body? I thought I would go mad. The prospect was so painful that psychologically I refused to accept it. Instead, I imagined the day when she would return home; her footsteps, her laughter, her lovely voice; I imagined embracing and kissing my beautiful sister. I wanted to share the pain of my father's martyrdom with her, and I needed to talk to her about the painful days when they were all in prison. I wanted her to share with me the suffering she had gone through. I had plans for us to be together and support our mother.

But the divine plan was different from what I had hoped for, and there can be no other way but resignation. So many thoughts rushed through my head in the moments when I heard the tragic news of the martyrdoms. I hoped that someone would come in and say it wasn't true. But when my mother and I managed to get into the morgue, with great difficulty, and saw their motionless bodies, I stopped hoping. As my mother said after kissing each and every one of them on the cheek, "I wish I had the eyes of all the world, to show them how the love for Bahá'u'lláh and the truth has blossomed in these beloved souls."

I was still kneeling before Mona … I kissed her cold cheek and said goodbye to her. With all my heart, I wished she would open her eyes and let me see her smile one last time. But I knew she was observing us from above with an eternal smile, and one teardrop would break her heart.

Thus, my beautiful Mona, I smile for the love you had for Bahá'u'lláh and humankind. May the world discover why you sacrificed your life. [56]

The whole city of Shiraz was soon talking and lamenting about the deaths. They labeled them the "Brides of the City." A Bahá'í from Shiraz shared the strange mood of those days:

Shiraz smelled of blood, of love and devotion ... The families were all in astonishment and awe. They were all expectantly waiting to hear of more executions every day. A memorial service was held for the women who were martyred two or three days later. People would come in groups with bouquets of flowers. They had no thought of any personal danger to themselves. You cannot imagine the commotion in Shiraz. We could not find flowers anywhere in the whole city. Wherever we went to buy them, people would ask if we wanted them for the "Brides of the City"! Their families were strong and told us stories of the devotion of those who had died. Their high spirits truly bewildered those who came in contact with them. [57]

One friend of Mona's was a neighbor who was not a Bahá'í, but she spoke about her with tears rolling down her face:

"I loved Mona with all of my heart, and I was always worried that I may one day lose her. One evening, I spoke to her about my concerns. She suggested that we choose something by which to remember each other when we are no longer together. I agreed. She then looked up into the sky and pointed to a bright star near the moon. She told me that that brilliant star was her and that I could look at the star whenever I missed her and think about her. She also asked me to choose a star, and I chose the one at the bottom of the big bear. As God is my witness, at the beginning of each month, I start looking at the sky at night, in search of the brilliant star. On the evening that it finally appears, I gaze at it for hours and shed tears and burn with the fire that blazes in my heart with my love for Mona. My husband and children also love to look at that star. Yes, that brilliant star is my radiant Mona who comes to us and then again hides herself from us. "

Another neighbor of the family's was Mrs. K-----, whom Mona used to often visit. She was a devout Muslim, but she loved Mona very much. Soon after Mona's martyrdom, Mrs. K----- came to Mona's mother heartbroken:

> [I]t shatters my nerves to see that [your apartment] is occupied by the revolutionary Guards. Every time, I open the door, I see Mona's kind face smiling at me. Sometimes, I think that I am losing my sanity. Of course, I don't let my children find out what I am going through, because they would become concerned. However, I always feel Mona's presence, and I always see her next to me. I loved her dearly and I am burning with the pain of her loss, for I know who she was! Perhaps, even you didn't know her as I did. She was an angel who lived amongst us for a short while. She was not meant to share this earth with us. She was raised in my arms like one of my own children ... My dear Mona, that pure and innocent child, proved the innocence of all of you [Bahá'ís.]"

Shockwaves spread beyond Iran as the greater world found out the tragic news. The first to pay attention were the Bahá'ís. On Saturday, the 18th, the Universal House of Justice had sent out a cable message* listing the names of the six men saying:

> WITH GREAT SORROW IMPART NEWS EXECUTION BY HANGING LATE HOURS 16 JUNE IN SHIRAZ ANOTHER SIX VALIANT SERVANTS CAUSE: [...]

---

* Before the widespread use of the Internet, international messages were often sent by telegraph cable. Protocol for writing such messages included leaving out small words, such as pronouns, prepositions and articles.

GRAVELY CONCERNED LIVES OTHER PRISONERS THREATENED BE SUBJECTED SIMILAR FATE IF REFUSE RECANT FAITH AND EMBRACE ISLAM. THIS RUTHLESS TREATMENT BY FANATICS NOW TAKING REINS JUSTICE THEIR HANDS IN DEFIANCE WORLD PUBLIC OPINION, DEMANDS SPECIAL CONSIDERATION BY GOVERNMENTS AND PEOPLE OF PROMINENCE TO EXERT UTMOST EFFORTS PREVENT CONTINUATION SUCH ACTS WHICH VIOLATE PRINCIPLES JUSTICE AND HUMAN RIGHTS....

Then on Sunday, another cable arrived from the House of Justice giving the names of the women:

FOLLOWING OUTRAGEOUS EXECUTION SIX BAHÁ'ÍS IN SHIRAZ ON 16 JUNE, FURTHER HIDEOUS CRIME HAS BEEN PERPETRATED BY AUTHORITIES THAT CITY BY HANGING TEN INNOCENT WOMEN NIGHT OF 18 JUNE. [...]

THE EXECUTION OF THESE GUILTLESS WOMEN IN THE NAME OF RELIGION MUST SHOCK CONSCIENCE HUMANITY THEY WERE ARRESTED FOR ACTIVITIES IN BAHÁ'Í COMMUNITY INCLUDING EDUCATION OF YOUTH.

FOLLOWING LONG INTERROGATION IN PRISON THEY WERE WARNED THEY WOULD BE SUBJECTED TO FOUR SESSIONS PRESSURING THEM RECANT THEIR FAITH ACCEPT ISLAM AND IF BY FOURTH TIME THEY HAD NOT SIGNED PREPARED STATEMENT RECANTING FAITH THEY WOULD BE KILLED. ALL PREFERRED DIE RATHER THAN DENY THEIR FAITH.

FEW HOURS PRIOR EXECUTION WOMEN MET WITH FAMILIES, NONE OF WHOM KNEW IMPENDING EXECUTION. NEWS THIS DASTARDLY CRIME NOT PUBLICLY ANNOUNCED OR FORMALLY GIVEN TO FAMILIES. AUTHORITIES REFUSED ALLOW FAMILIES RECEIVE BODIES FOR BURIAL OR EVEN TO SEE THEM.

IT SHOULD BE RECALLED THAT BETWEEN OCTOBER AND NOVEMBER 1982 OVER 80 BAHÁ'ÍS WERE ARRESTED IN SHIRAZ. AUTHORITIES LATER REVEALED THAT 22 PERSONS AMONG THE 80 WERE CONDEMNED TO DEATH IF WOULD NOT RECANT NAMES OF

THESE 22 HOWEVER WERE NEVER REVEALED, INTENSIFYING PSYCHOLOGICAL STRESS AMONG BAHÁ'Í PRISONERS.

IN DEFIANCE APPEALS WORLD LEADERS AND WORLD PUBLIC OPINION, 21 OF THESE BAHÁ'ÍS HAVE THUS FAR BEEN EXECUTED, CASTING SHADOW ON FATE REMAINING BELIEVERS LANGUISHING IN PRISON....

UNIVERSAL HOUSE OF JUSTICE

Beyond the Bahá'í community, news of the executions began to spread. It was a burst of media coverage that the 139-year-old Faith had never experienced. The martyrdom of these 10, following so closely on the heels of the 6 men, was on television and radio and in newspapers for everyone to see.* The headlines said things such as: "Now They're Killing Women." Governments around the world responded by condemning Iran's behavior. The United Nations held hearings and made resolutions in support of the Bahá'ís.

Many people were just now hearing about the Bahá'í Faith. The feeling they had towards it was not suspicion, but sympathy. The impression they had of the Bahá'ís was that of pure innocence. The face that came to define that event was Mona's face. Her picture was shared in newspapers and on television around the world. One editor wrote that Mona "became, in a sense, a symbol of the group" "as a result of her extreme youthfulness and conspicuous innocence."[58]

---

* There were 22 Baha'is martyred in Shiraz between 1 January and 30 June, 1983. They include these 16, plus Mr. Mahmudnizhad, Mrs Za'irpur, and Mr. Vafa'i (on 12 March), plus Hedayat Siyavushi (on 1 January) and Suhayl Hushmand (on 28 June). One other gentleman, named Ahmad-'Alí Thábit-Sarvistání, died in prison on 30 June. He was a former pioneer, a father of nine and a healer, and he died from injuries and ill-treatment he received in prison. The Iran Human Rights Documentation Center has called them "The Shiraz Twenty-Two."

Only God can know the value and full impact of the sacrifice of any soul. We do know, however, that the execution of the 10 "Brides of Shiraz" caused such a strong reaction from the world community that it had an effect on Iran. The persecution of Bahá'ís did not stop, and it continues to this day. At the same time, the number of killings has significantly dropped. We can see now that this was a time of transition for the Bahá'í community. Hundreds died, thousands suffered, but not for nothing. The Faith they loved so much, which they willingly sacrificed for, had, according to a 1985 letter of the Universal House of Justice, emerged from obscurity, and into the light of the world's view.

Epilogue

Life was hard during those times, but it was also a precious time. It was a time when our conversations were important, when the decisions we made might decide life or death for us or our families. We wanted to make the right decisions, the decisions that were based on our spiritual values and not just our physical well-being. We felt responsible for helping Iran and the larger world.

It was a time of confirmations, of people doing great, almost superhuman things and of others doing terrible and painful things. It was a time when dreams were vivid, as if the spiritual world was eager to take part in our conversations. It was a time of midnight prayers and then dawn prayers, when we prayed not just because we had to, but because we needed to.

About nine months after Mona's martyrdom, I had a special dream. I was then sixteen and living with my family in the North of Iran in Mazindaran. I was in the habit of praying between midnight and 1 a.m. It was during the Naw-Rúz holiday, which you remember is celebrated over a period of 13 days in Iran. So on the fifth night of Naw-Rúz and after my midnight prayers, I had this dream. A gentleman wearing a suit came to me and said, "Do you know who I am?"

I said, "No."

He said, "My name is Muhammad Movahhed, and I've been told to introduce to you all the martyrs that we have in the Faith."

When he said his name, I knew who he was. You may remember Mr. Movahhed was the Mulla from Shiraz who had become a Bahá'í after reading *The Book of Certitude* in a library.* He was kidnapped kidnapped in May 1979 and never heard from again. As you may remember, the following year, the nine members of the National Spiritual Assembly of the Bahá'ís of Iran also were kidnapped and never heard from again.

So here is this prominent Bahá'í telling me that he is going to introduce all the martyrs to me! I was very surprised and didn't know what to say. He asked me to follow him. We passed through a curtain into a very big hall. For a moment, we stopped and I looked. The room was very bright but there weren't any lights. I didn't see any decorations or even a ceiling, and I couldn't see the end of the hall. As far as I could see there were just people—all seated in circles, in groups of nine. They all had long white gowns on and were sitting on their knees with their eyes closed and their hands lifted up in prayer. All of them were deeply immersed in meditation and prayer. My words cannot describe how spiritual the environment was.

As I walked beside Mr. Movahhed, we went around to each circle. Without interrupting them, he would tell me their names one by one and then we would go to the next circle. Every so often, I would turn and look out over all the people we had passed and just be amazed at how beautiful it all was.

Soon it was morning and time for me to get up. I said my morning prayers and was still thinking about my dream. I had always read in the Bahá'í writings that we should call on the Concourse on High for assistance, and now I could fully picture what that looked like. I still didn't know what the dream meant, and I knew I hadn't had a chance to meet all of the martyrs. After all, there are twenty-thousand or so of them in our Faith. I went to my parents and told them about my dream and I told them who I saw. There was Mulla Husayn, Quddus, Alí Bastamí, and many others.

---

* His story is briefly told on page 191.

My mother told me then that when I was two or three years old, Mr. Movahhed was the chairperson of our local Nineteen-Day Feast. He had introduced his future wife, Núríyyih Ansárí, to our family the day before they formalized their engagement at the House of the Báb. I had certainly heard of him but didn't realize the personal connection. All day I kept going over the dream.

Then night came, and I said my prayers again from midnight to 1 a.m. and went to sleep. And there was Mr. Movahhed again and, without saying a word, we continued what we had been doing the night before.

This dream took seven nights! After the second night, I knew that he would be there when I went to sleep. All day, I would look forward to it being night again so I could go to sleep. As we got closer to the end, I started to recognize the faces, especially the martyrs of Shiraz. Up to this point, I had been introduced to those that I heard or read about. Now, I started to see those martyrs that I had known, such as Mr. Vahdat, Dr. Afnan, and Suhayl Hushmand, and so many others. It was so great to see them again.

But of all the martyrs, it was only Mona who broke from her prayer when I came. She looked at me and gave me a wink.

That was the seventh and final night of my dream. Mr. Movahhed had finished all the names. It was then that I asked him, "What about you? And the members of the National Spiritual Assembly who disappeared?"

"We are all here," he told me.

I awoke and it was all over. Afterwards, I thought a lot about this dream and tried to make sense of it all. I shared it with a few people, but no one was able to tell me what it really meant. I didn't feel worthy of this great honor, and I felt that I should do something about it. Reading *The Dawn Breakers* again and the history of the early heroes and martyrs felt very special after I had had this dream.

I paid much more attention to the names, since I felt so close to these souls and wanted to know each of them better. And yet reading wasn't enough. How was I supposed to serve after being given this rare gift?

In June 2000, I went on Bahá'í pilgrimage to Haifa, Israel. That is where Mark and I met. He told me he had written a play about Mona, and I surprised him by telling him that I knew her. From that point, a central feature of our marriage has been sharing with others the stories of Mona and other martyrs. I think this is the simple answer to my dream. I have to remember those wonderful souls and to share stories about them with the people of the world.

Mona would do the same. She was born into a pioneering family and she wished to be a pioneer herself. With the energy and detachment of youth, she would say,

> "It makes no difference where I go. I just want to put on my backpack full of Bahá'í books and travel barefoot to the remotest villages of Iran and speak of the Faith to whoever wishes to listen … My greatest desire is to be able to go to the Amazon, Africa or India and teach the Faith."

How similar was her wish to 'Abdu'l-Bahá's wish:

> "O that I could travel, even though on foot and in the utmost poverty, to these regions, and, raising the call of 'Yá Bahá'u'l-Abhá' in cities, villages, mountains, deserts and oceans, promote the divine teachings!"[59]

One of Mona's "crimes" was teaching her children's class. She had so much love for humanity and for the children of the world. This is one way I've tried to be like Mona. When I became a youth, I decided to follow her example and I became a children's class teacher. Since then I've been teaching classes for children, junior youth and youth. It brings so much joy to my heart because I know she's really happy about it. In my job, also, I work with children every day, and every day I feel that joy.

We have a prayer room in our home. In it, we have pictures of many of the important people in our lives. We have a picture of Mona with her father. Every day when I say my prayers, I turn my face to Mona's picture and ask her to help me and pray for me. Every week, when I'm planning classes for the children, I want her to be a part of it, as well. When I hug the kids and kiss them, I hug and kiss them for her, as well. And I know how happy she is. Through me and others like me, Mona is teaching every day.

I am happy for my life now, for the work I am able to do with children and youth, in planting and nurturing seeds of virtue and understanding in their hearts. But I miss that time, the dear people I lost, and the feeling I had during that time that everything I did really mattered, the closeness of the divine world.

It was as if our lives were moving along in a state of prayer, and the divine world was only half a step away. We still had fear and anger, at times, but we could be rescued from those lower feelings in a moment just by saying "Alláh-u-abhá" or "Yá Bahá'u'l-Abhá" or "Is there any Remover of difficulties save God?"

God's hand was always there to steady us along that rocky path. We just needed to trust Him in that moment and to reach up in faith.

In my heart, I know life is always like that. The divine world is steady, ever present. It is we in this life that create distance and put up veils. I know I have a friend that I can call to just on the other side of that threshold. And she will help me. Now that you know her story, you can call on her too. She is not just my friend Mona. She is our friend Mona.

Appendix A

Samples of Mona's Writing

6 Day 1358 [27 December 1979]

O Iran, O Land of Many Jewels

Iran is my birthplace, the place where I and my ancestors were born and raised. They went and we came, they are not and we are, and all have one thing in common and that is living in Iran.

Iran has seen difficulties. The people of Iran have gone through difficulties. The blood of many people poured into the dust and they wallowed in it, and through that blood, the earth was watered and we came into existence. We should continue on the path of their deeds, those who preceded us, but it hasn't been completed yet. Still we have many things to do to reach our divine purpose. Still Iran has not been calmed. Still Iran's people are not at ease. They're full of energy, enthusiasm and love. If they would let them move, if they allow them to perform the work, with much diligence, they will soon achieve their purpose, their modern and magnificent purpose.

Iran has witnessed many attacks and wars, and has had the stamina to withstand all of them; it has not been destroyed and has remained.   After all these sufferings and difficulties, Iran was poisoned by past events but the truth-seeking and fair-minded people restored Iran again to its original state.   The soil of Iran is pure and precious.

Iran itself is pleasant in appearance, in fragrance. We must take it in. Iran is full of glory, magnificence, defeats and victories.

The people of Iran have the capacity to transform themselves because of the difficulties and commiseration they have witnessed. They have not always lived a life of comfort and ease. Iran has always been full of agitation, motion, like a roaring torrent that has never been calm. Iran is firmly established, and posterity will never forget its memories, bitter and sweet.

7 Mehr 1359 [29 September 1980]

"What was your main responsibility over the summer?"

Summer is a good season for students because the time for studying is over to and it allows a relative kind of freedom.

I, personally, had lots of plans and projects in mind before the summer arrived, things I was definitely going to finish on schedule. Soon, summer arrived and I had to put those plans and projects into action.

I remember well that when I finished my last test, which was on Sunday the 4th of Khordad (May 25th), the plan was that all the students that were friends together would gather at one of our classmates' home that evening. Then the next day, it was decided the same group would come to my house, and the next day it was someone else's house, and so on until the end of the week. This was our routine, to go to each other's homes. In short, it was an unforgettable week, and the day after all these comings and goings were over, I tell you, was the first day after exams had finished that I had a few hours of complete relaxation at home without worrying about homework or exams.

From that day on, it was my responsibility each day, before anything else, to do the housework, and this would take me from morning to noon to do. After cleaning the house, I would eat lunch at 12 or 12:30 and then I was able to do things of interest to me.

Two times a week, on Sundays and Thursdays, I would go swimming with a few of my friends from 2:30 to 4:30 in the afternoon. Coming home, we would walk some of the way and then catch a taxi the rest of the way, so by the time we got home, we would be very tired.

Once I got home, if we had visitors I would visit with them, or if we had somewhere to go, I would go out. Otherwise, I would go to the home of my friend, who lived across from us, or I'd call her to come to my home.

One of my other projects was to go to Arabic class, which was Wednesday afternoons from 6 to 8, but I didn't get out of the class what I was hoping for, however I did learn many things, which, of course, would bring me happiness later on.

Also, I read a series of books that had been suggested to me. Mostly these were history books—the history of the lives of the early martyrs, and for each book I would write out questions and answers or copy out some beautiful sentences in a separate notebook. Those were the things I did each week, plus, well, a bunch of other things, and in this fashion the day would become night.

One of my projects was to change my major at school, and for this I had to take exams on a series of courses related to my new major. So from the 24th of Mordad (August 15th), I had to put aside all my other plans and I began studying the subjects and, on the specific days of the 2nd through the 6th of Shahrivar (August 24th-28th), I took the exams. After the exams, my projects were no longer scheduled and I did things whenever I wanted.

On the 18th of Shahrivar (September 9th), I went to Tehran with my mother. In Tehran, my mother and I went separate ways; I went to my cousin's house and we spent time together. I had such a good time that the days just flew by for me, and on Friday the 28th of Shahrivar (September 19th), I joined my mother at my other cousin's home and back to Shiraz we went. After arriving in Shiraz, I started to get ready to go back to school. On the last day of summer, I looked back on the projects that I had done over that time period and I realized the number of projects that I had cultivated in my mind and didn't accomplish.

"How many days, how many moments, how many hours … have come and gone" *

---

* This final line resembles one of Baha'u'llah's statements about the swiftness of this passing life: "*Night hath succeeded day, and day hath succeeded night, and the hours and moments of your lives have come and gone …*"

28 Bahman 1359 [17 February 1981]

Meditation of a caged bird

The place for me and some of my friends is in a cage in the corner of an empty room, which has a little opening to the outside where sometimes our friends will come in and bring us news about the outside world.

They would tell us: The sky is blue, the sun is golden, and the wild flowers are red and beautiful. The trees are green, the birds are flying in the blue sky, and there are springs bursting and waterfalls flowing. People are moving about and everyone is trying to achieve their goal.

And I would recount to them: Here it is narrow. It is dark. The sun here is blacked out. The sky here is dim and dusty. The winged birds are caged.

In here, there are no springs bursting, rather it is our tears. Nature here is gloomy. In here silence prevails and this silence is occasionally broken by one of us groaning. Here we are all asleep. What can we do? We have goals, but how can we achieve them? We want to fly, but how? We want to set out for the mountain, and the field, and the wilderness. We want to learn about love and kindness. We want to see that blue sky, that golden sun, those green and beautiful trees, the seas, the waterfalls, the springs, but how?

11 Farvardin 1360 [31 March 31 1981]

If time stops

If I speak based on my feelings, how good …

The time of pleasure drinking a glass of water after having such deep thirst

The time of eating a meal after being so utterly hungry

The time of a flower blooming

The time of the sun rising and setting

The time of enjoying dreams and wishes

The time of happiness and laughter

Then, at those moments, time should stop.

Now, if I replace my feelings with reason and fairness, all my thinking will be different, because if time stops …

Maybe a flower while blooming might die!

Maybe the pain of sorrow would devastate someone

Maybe separation from a loved one would desolate someone

And maybe someone's conscience forever would be stuck in regret.

So, in this regard, thinking just of yourself would be wrong. Period!

Why would I want to stop time to enjoy a sunrise when this stopping might harm someone suffering with pain and sorrow?

Following the sunrise there may be a magnificent brightness that I had never discovered before.

And following the sunset there may be a gleaming Star whose light would conquer the world and its truth might stay hidden.

Or perhaps behind the flower blooming is a Flower whose perfume would intoxicate everyone.

Good and bad can reveal themselves with time in motion, and with the passing of time people can recognize their own reality. With the passing of time, the results of spiritual tests will be revealed. It is absurd that a person should stay forever in ignorance. Therefore in this world, the passing of time is necessary.

[Date unknown]

Journey of Tears

Why do people cry? One day I asked a tear this while it was rolling down my cheek.

It stopped, and with a meaningful look, said, "You, too, ask me this question? It is a journey that I have just begun and I am far from my abode. I have suffered in separation and remoteness. I am a wandering tear that has lost my home and dwelling." [The tear continued,] "A heart separated from a person had also started its journey. When I got close to it, I asked, 'Where are you going?' It looked at me, gave a deep sigh, and said, 'I am separated from a person. Much I have suffered. I was a celestial throne, a site of divine reflection and a dawning place of inspiration, but the person who carried me in his chest was always thinking about worldly things. He* had abandoned his lofty station and left me to my own devices, so I also left him alone. Now he is a person with no heart and no feelings." [The tear continued further,] "I empathized with the lonely heart and flowed down your cheek. And it's odd that you don't understand my condition and ask me this kind of question! And that heart will answer your question with its sighs—one cannot speak in such a heartrending manner until one's heart has caught fire. If you want to know my condition, search the things I have said."

While it was talking to me, other tears came and surrounded it and told it, "We are happy tears. We came to take you back."

But it answered, "Come, all gather together, and from all our tears, make a sea of happiness as a gift for humanity. Raise the Peace Flag and invite all together under the Tabernacle of unity. God is

---

* He or she. The Persian pronoun is used for both female and male.

kind, why should we be unkind? He is the Provider, why should we cut it off?"

In the sea of love, they became one, scattered the petals of love under the people's feet, and left. Is everything really forgotten?

That tear sometimes visits me and leaves again, but each time with a new tale. Sometimes its stories repeat, but those happy tears come again and take it away with them. But we promised each other never to lose our friendship and never to forget each other.

Appendix B

Further Reading and Sources

Further Reading

<u>Release the Sun</u>, by William Sears. [Wilmette, IL: Baha'i Publishing Trust, 2003]

This book tells the amazing stories of the "dawn breakers," the early heroes and heroines of the Baha'i Faith, such as Mulla Husayn, Quddus and Tahirih. The faith and courage that they showed in the most violent circumstances is almost beyond belief. These stories inspired Mona and those other great souls who gave their lives to spread the Cause of oneness.

<u>Olya's Story</u>, by Olya Roohizadegan. [Oxford: Oneworld Publications, 1994.]

Olya was imprisoned along with Mona and the others, before being released on bond. She eventually escaped with her family to England. This book not only tells her story but also goes into detail about the lives of many of the Baha'is who were imprisoned and executed in that time.

<u>A New Dress for Mona</u>, a play by Mark Perry. [Chapel Hill, NC: Drama Circle, 2016.]

This is Mona's story adapted for the stage and written by my husband Mark. This play integrates many of the stories included in this book but in a 2-hour drama. Having a play reading or performance is a wonderful way to spread Mona's story and the message of faith, love and unity.

<u>Community Under Siege: The Ordeal of the Baha'is of Shiraz</u>, a report by the Iran Human Rights Documentation Center. [New Haven: IHRDC, 2007.]

Here is a well-documented report about "The Shiraz 22" from a non-partisan group of human rights lawyers and scholars. It presents this case against Iran's government methodically to shine a light on its human rights record and call for accountability. The report is available as a PDF online. Their website is www.iranhrdc.org

The Bahá'í World, Vol. XIX: 1983-1986, prepared under the supervision of The Universal House of Justice. [Haifa: Bahá'í World Centre, 1994.]

"The Bahá'í World" is the official record of the worldwide Bahá'í community. This volume contains biographical material on Baha'is executed between April 1983 and April 1986. It also contains lists and photos of all Baha'is known to have been executed in the wake of the Iranian Revolution.

Visit www.ANewDressForMona.org
for more resources, including many photographs.

Sources (Published)

'Abdu'l-Bahá, Promulgation of Universal Peace. (Comp. by Howard MacNutt). Wilmette, IL: Bahá'í Publishing Trust, 1982.

'Abdu'l-Bahá, Selections from the Writings of 'Abdu'l-Bahá. (Trans. by Marzieh Gail and committee). Wilmette, IL: Bahá'í Publishing Trust, 1997.

'Abdu'l-Bahá, Tablets of the Divine Plan. Wilmette, IL: Bahá'í Publishing Trust, 1993.

Bahá'í National Youth Committee, Unrestrained as the Wind. Wilmette, IL: Bahá'í Publishing Trust, 1985.

Bahá'u'lláh, The Hidden Words. Wilmette, IL: Bahá'í Publishing Trust, 1985.

Bahá'u'lláh, The Kitáb-i-Aqdas (The Most Holy Book). Haifa: Bahá'í World Centre, 1992.

Bahá'u'lláh, The Kitáb-i-Íqán (The Book of Certitude). (Trans. by Shoghi Effendi). Wilmette, IL: Bahá'í Publishing Trust, 1931.

Bahá'u'lláh, The Seven Valleys and the Four Valleys. (Trans. by Marzieh Gail). Wilmette, IL: Bahá'í Publishing Trust, 1991.

Bahá'u'lláh, The Summons of the Lord of Hosts. Haifa: Bahá'í World Centre, 2002.

Bahá'u'lláh (et al), Bahá'í Prayers. Wilmette, IL: Bahá'í Publishing Trust, 1954.

Furútan, 'Alí-Akbar, Stories of Baha'u'llah. Oxford: Oneworld Publications, 1986.

Háfez-e Shírází, Díván-e Háfez (Persian). Kerman, Iran: Kerman Cultural Services, 2002.

Iran Human Rights Documentation Center, Community Under Siege: The Ordeal of the Baha'is of Shiraz. New Haven: IHRDC, 2007.

National Spiritual Assembly of the Bahá'ís of Canada, The Story of Mona: 1965-1983. Thornhill, ON: Bahá'í Canada Publications, 1985.

Roohizadegan, Olya, Olya's Story. Oxford: Oneworld Publications, 1993.

Shoghi Effendi, The Advent of Divine Justice. Wilmette, IL: Bahá'í Publishing Trust, 1990.

Shoghi Effendi, Messages to the Bahá'í World: 1950–1957. Wilmette, IL: Bahá'í Publishing Trust, 1971.

The Bahá'í World, Vol. XIX: 1983-1986. Prepared under the supervision of The Universal House of Justice. Haifa: Bahá'í World Centre, 1994.

Zarandi, Nabíl ('Azam), The Dawn-Breakers: Nabil's Narrative of the Early Days of the Bahá'í Revelation. (Trans. and ed. by Shoghi Effendi). Wilmette, IL: Bahá'í Publishing Trust, 1932.

Sources (Unpublished)

[Name withheld for safety], "Memories of the Martyrs" (Persian, pp. 127-193)

[Name withheld for safety], "Mona's Life." (Persian. English Trans. by Azadeh and Mark Perry, 11 pages)

Mahmúdnizhád, Farkhundih, "Notes for a Film." (Trans. by Gloria Shahzadeh). Unpublished account of correspondence with Jack Lenz and Alexei Berteig, 2001. 62 pages.

Mahmúdnizhád, Farkhundih and Taraneh, "Notes for a Film: Dubai Interview." (Trans. by Gloria Shahzadeh). Interview recorded by Jack Lenz, 2006. 30 pages.

Mahmúdnizhád, Taraneh, "Phone Interview, April 2016" Interview recorded by Azadeh Rohanian Perry, 17 April 2016.

Sources by Chapter & End Notes

INTRODUCTION

General: "Notes for a Film", 18; "Phone Interview, April 2016".

[1] Bahá'u'lláh, The Hidden Words Persian #44, p. 37

1. AMU'S STORY

General: "Memories of the Martyrs", 128-132; "Mona's Life", 1; "Phone Interview, April 2016".

[2] Bahá'u'lláh, The Kitab-i-Aqdas, 85

2. PIONEERING

General: "Memories of the Martyrs", 132-138; "Notes for a Film", 60, 62; "Mona's Life", 1; "Phone Interview, April 2016".

[3] Shoghi Effendi, Cablegram "to the Baha'is of the World" dated 4 May 1953, Messages to the Bahá'í World: 1950–1957, 152-153.

[4] 'Abdu'l-Bahá, Selections from the Writings of 'Abdu'l-Bahá, 199

[5] Selections from the Writings of 'Abdu'l-Bahá, 201

3. MONA'S EARLY CHILDHOOD

General: "Memories of the Martyrs", 138-143; "Notes for a Film", 9, 58-59, 62; "Mona's Life", 1; The Story of Mona, 1-2, 5-6; Olya's Story, 126; "Phone Interview, April 2016".

[6] NSA of the Baha'is of Canada, The Story of Mona, 1

[7] The Story of Mona, 5-6

4. SCHOOL

General: "Notes for a Film", 17, 58-62; The Story of Mona, 2; "Which Teacher, Which Method" essay.

[8] The Story of Mona, 2

5. ADOLESCENCE

General: "Notes for a Film", 7, 11, 13-14, 17-20; "Mona's Life", 2; The Story of Mona, 2, 5; Olya's Story, 127.

6. REVOLUTION

General: "Notes for a Film", 6--7; The Story of Mona, 6; Olya's Story, 28-29, 128; Community Under Siege, 3-10.

[9] Community Under Siege, 3

[10] Olya Roohizadegan, Olya's Story, 28

7. MONA'S RESPONSE TO REVOLUTION

General: "Notes for a Film", 3-5, 13-15, 32-33, 61-62; "Mona's Life", 2; The Story of Mona, 2, 6; "What was your main responsibility" essay.

8. DREAMS AND VISIONS

General: "Notes for a Film", 9, 14-18, 24-25.

[11] Ali-Akbar Furutan, Stories of Bahá'u'lláh, 69-70

[12] Matthew 7:7

9. MATURITY

General: "Notes for a Film", 2, 3, 12-13, 17-20, 32-33; "Mona's Life", 2; The Story of Mona, 5-8; Olya's Story, 126-128; The Baha'i World, 601; "Which Teacher, Which Method" essay.

[13] The Story of Mona, 6

[14] The Story of Mona, 6-7

[15] Bahá'u'lláh, quoted in Shoghi Effendi, The Advent of Divine Justice, 78

10. STEPS OF COURAGE

General: "Notes for a Film", 9-10, 15-16, 31; The Story of Mona, 8, 11-12; The Baha'i World, 183, 602; Community Under Siege, 24.

[16] The Story of Mona, 8

[17] The Story of Mona, 11-12

11. WAITING

General: "Notes for a Film", 2, 3, 7, 33; "Mona's Life", 2; Olya's Story, 126-128.

[18] Olya's Story, 126-127

[19] Olya's Story, 128

12. THE ARREST

General: "Notes for a Film", 33-36; "Mona's Life", 4-5; The Story of Mona, 12-13; Olya's Story, 128-130.

[20] Olya's Story, 129

[21] Olya's Story, 129-130

13. ARRIVAL AT PRISON

General: "Notes for a Film", 36-37; The Story of Mona, 13-14; Olya's Story, 130-131; Community Under Siege, 11-15.

[22] Olya's Story, 130 & Community Under Siege, 14

[23] Olya's Story, 130

[24] Olya's Story, 130

[25] Olya's Story, 130

[26] Olya's Story, 130-131

[27] Olya's Story, 131

14. LIFE IN SEPAH

General: "Notes for a Film", 37-39, 53, 56-57; "Mona's Life", 5-6; The Story of Mona, 14; Olya's Story, 70-72, 131; The Baha'i World, 183; Community Under Siege, 33-34.

[28] Olya's Story, 70-71

[29] Matthew 5:10

[30] The Bahá'í World: 1983-1986 is one source that makes this claim directly. (p. 183)

15. THE FIRST STAGE OF INTERROGATION

General: "Notes for a Film", 3, 39-40; The Story of Mona, 14-16, 19; Olya's Story, 133-134.

[31] The Story of Mona, 15

[32] The Story of Mona, 16

[33] The Story of Mona, 16

[34] The Story of Mona, 19

[35] Olya's Story, 133-134

[36] The Story of Mona, 15

16. THE BLACK CAPE

General: The Story of Mona, 19-20; Olya's Story, 105-109, 134-135; Community Under Siege, 16-20.

[37] Bahá'u'lláh, The Summons of the Lord of Hosts, 273

[38] Olya's Story, 134-135

[39] Olya's Story, 135

[40] The Story of Mona, 20

[41] Olya's Story, 106

[42] Olya's Story, 106

[43] 'Abdu'l-Bahá, Selections From the Writings of 'Abdu'l-Bahá, 147

17. HER TRIAL

General: "Notes for a Film", 43-44; The Story of Mona, 19-20; Olya's Story, 131-133; Unrestrained As The Wind, 52.

18. THE MOTHER'S ARREST

General: "Notes for a Film", 44-47; The Story of Mona, 22; Olya's Story, 174-175, 193; "Dubai Interview", 1-2.

[44] Olya's Story, 193

19. THE MOTHER'S TRIAL

General: "Notes for a Film", 44, 47-51; Olya's Story, 162; "Dubai Interview", 2-7.

20. THE MOTHER'S ARRIVAL

General: "Notes for a Film", 51-52; "Mona's Life", 6; The Story of Mona, 22-23; Olya's Story, 135-137, 143; "Dubai Interview", 7-8.

21. TIME IN ADELABAD

General: "Notes for a Film", 5, 21-22; The Story of Mona, 23, 27-28; Olya's Story, 134-135, 137-138, 155; "Dubai Interview", 8-9, 25-27; Community Under Siege, 30.

[45] Olya's Story, 155

[46] Olya's Story, 137-138

22. A SPECIAL MEETING

General: "Notes for a Film", 53-56; The Story of Mona, 23; Olya's Story, 138-139, 172; Community Under Siege, 25-26, 34.

23. AMU'S MARTYRDOM

General: "Notes for a Film", 22-23; "Mona's Life", 6; The Story of Mona, 24, 27; Olya's Story, 139-140; "Dubai Interview", 22-23; Community Under Siege, 35-36; "Phone Interview, April 2016".

[47] Hafez, Divan, Ghazal 143, which begins "Sálhá del talabe jám…"

24. BREAKING THE NEWS

General: "Notes for a Film", 6, 23-25; "Mona's Life", 6; The Story of Mona, 23-24; Olya's Story, 139-140; "Dubai Interview", 24-25.

[48] Olya's Story, 140

25. OUT OF OBSCURITY

General: "Notes for a Film", 23; The Baha'i World, 130-143, 268-282.

[49] White House, "Message on the Persecutions and Repression in Iran", 22 May 1983.

[50] NY Times Editorial Board, "Satanism in Iran," 26 May 1983

26. PREPARATIONS

General: "Notes for a Film", 8, 25-28, 52; "Mona's Life", 6; Olya's Story, 219; "Dubai Interview", 9-12; Community Under Siege, 36-37.

[51] 'Abdu'l-Bahá, The Promulgation of Universal Peace, 452-453

27. 100,000 LIVES TO GIVE

General: "Notes for a Film", 28-30, 44; "Mona's Life", 6; The Story of Mona, 28-30; Olya's Story, 152, 221-222; "Dubai Interview", 12-13, 19.

28. FINAL DAYS

General: "Notes for a Film", 40-43; "Mona's Life", 7-11; The Story of Mona, 30, 33, 43, 45; Olya's Story, 222-225; "Dubai Interview", 14-16, 23, 28-30; The Baha'i World, 179.

29. ONE BY ONE

General: The Story of Mona, 33; Olya's Story, 225; "Dubai Interview", 26; The Baha'i World, 183, 602.

[52] The Story of Mona, 33

[53] Olya's Story, 225

30. THE FACE OF MARTYRDOM

General: "Notes for a Film", 21; The Story of Mona, 43-45; Olya's Story, 222, 225-230; "Dubai Interview", 16-22; The Baha'i World, 182; Community Under Siege, 39-42; "Phone Interview, April 2016".

[54] The Story of Mona, 43-44

[55] Olya's Story, 226, 227

[56] Olya's Story, 225, 228-230

[57] The Story of Mona, 43

[58] The Bahá'í World: 1983-1986, 182

EPILOGUE

General: "Notes for a Film", 15.

[59] 'Abdu'l-Bahá, Tablets of the Divine Plan, 41

Azadeh Rohanian Perry works at the UNC School of Dentistry as a clinic manager. Her husband, Mark Perry, teaches in UNC's Department of Dramatic Art. They live together in the Triangle area of North Carolina, where they love to work with children, junior youth and youth, and where they join with others in learning about community building.

4/18

Made in the USA
San Bernardino, CA
11 March 2018